LOOKING GOOD
IN PRESENTATIONS

MOLLY W. JOSS

Looking Good In Presentations, Third Edition

Copyright © 1999 by The Coriolis Group

Limits of Liability and Disclaimer of Warranty

The author and publisher of this book have used their best efforts in preparing the book and the programs contained in it. These efforts include the development, research, and testing of the theories and programs to determine their effectiveness. The author and publisher make no warranty of any kind, expressed or implied, with regard to these programs or the documentation contained in this book.

The author and publisher shall not be liable in the event of incidental or consequential damages in connection with, or arising out of, the furnishing, performance, or use of the programs, associated instructions, and/or claims of productivity gains.

Trademarks

Trademarked names appear throughout this book. Rather than list the names and entities that own the trademarks or insert a trademark symbol with each mention of the trademarked name, the publisher states that it is using the names for editorial purposes only and to the benefit of the trademark owner, with no intention of infringing upon that trademark.

The Coriolis Group, Inc.
An International Thomson Publishing Company
14455 N. Hayden Road, Suite 220
Scottsdale, Arizona 85260

602/483-0192
FAX 602/483-0193
http://www.coriolis.com

Library of Congress Cataloging-In-Publication Data
Joss, Molly, 1959-
    Looking good in presentations / by Molly Joss. -- 3rd ed.
      p. cm.
    Includes index.
    ISBN 1-56604-854-0
    1. Computer graphics. 2. Business presentations--Data processing. I. Title.
T385.J6765 1999
658.4'5--dc21   98-46581
                  CIP

Printed in the United States of America
10 9 8 7 6 5 4 3 2 1

Publisher
Keith Weiskamp

Acquisitions Editor
Stephanie Wall

Marketing Specialist
Dylan Zoller

Project Editor
Mariann Barsolo

Technical Reviewer
Craig Swanson

Production Coordinator
Jon Gabriel

Cover Design
Anthony Stock
Additional art provided by Brandon Riza

Layout Design
April Nielsen

an International Thomson Publishing company

Albany, NY • Belmont, CA • Bonn • Boston • Cincinnati • Detroit • Johannesburg
London • Madrid • Melbourne • Mexico City • New York • Paris • Singapore
Tokyo • Toronto • Washington

AUG 2 1 2000

Looking Good In Presentations

This book is dedicated to the men and women who, in whole or in part, make their living by creating and delivering presentations. And to my mother, for her efforts to make me one of the best presentations she ever delivered.

෨

Looking Good
In
Presentations

ABOUT THE AUTHOR

Molly W. Joss is a freelance writer and graphic artist who has been writing and working in the graphic arts and computing industries for almost 20 years. She spends most of her time in her office writing or creating designs (multimedia and otherwise) or on the telephone talking to people about their work in these industries. When she's out and about, she enjoys traveling to companies and trade shows to find out more about computers and design.

In addition to this book, Molly has written two other books (*Clip Art Smart* and *Graphic Design Tips & Techniques*, which she co-authored). She has also written hundreds of magazine articles for graphic arts trade and general interest computer magazines. When her friends wonder aloud why she gets paid to play with interesting "toys" and then write about them, she smiles and says, "Somebody's got to do it."

LOOKING GOOD
IN
PRESENTATIONS

Acknowledgments

My sincere gratitude to the staff of Coriolis for giving me this book to write and for being so wonderful to work with during the entire process. Thanks, too, to my friends for being so patient with my work schedule. Finally, I must thank the Dale Carnegie organization for its help (many years ago) in turning me into a professional presenter.

Special thanks to those who contributed artwork to the book, including: photographer Chris Potter of Chapel Hill, N.C.; Marcia Erickson with the North Carolina Museum of Art; and Jen Petrin with KRUPS North America, Inc.

I must also acknowledge the following companies for the presentation artwork used in the examples: Digital Graphics, Broderbund, Microsoft, and Little Men Studio (please see the Resources list at the end of the book for contact information).

LOOKING GOOD
IN
PRESENTATIONS

LOOKING GOOD
IN
PRESENTATIONS

FOREWORD

If you're one of those people who has avoided presentations to date, you'll find *Looking Good In Presentations, Third Edition* offers an invaluable guide to presentation success. *Looking Good In Presentations, Third Edition* provides a concise guide to the entire presentation process, from developing presentation objectives through translating them into meaningful visuals. It ends with tips for confidently delivering your presentation.

Presentations For Everyone

Looking Good In Presentations is for you, whether you're facing your first, or your one-hundred-and-first, presentation. Newcomers will benefit from the step-by-step guidance it provides and its introduction to the tools used to plan and create presentation visuals. Experienced presenters will appreciate the straightforward, solid emphasis on the fundamentals of presentation communications. *Looking Good In Presentations* also offers experienced presenters a welcome opportunity to review the numerous details involved in creating and delivering successful presentations.

In either case, just one of the ideas in this book can make the difference between failure or success in your next presentation.

The Inevitability Of Presentations

The appearance of *Looking Good In Presentations* is good news for those who have been informed that presentations are now a part of their job description—and this includes just about everyone! In just about every field, at businesses large and small, success and career advancement is difficult, if not impossible, without the ability to efficiently create and confidently deliver presentations to audiences of varying sizes.

Yet, although presentations are increasingly a part of everyone's job description, paradoxically, fear of public speaking is our Number One fear. More than death, more than job loss, people fear getting up in front of others and conducting a presentation.

By taking the fear out of presentations, by replacing uncertainty and insecurity with confidence, *Looking Good In Presentations* can make a major contribution to its readers' careers.

Message Over Glitz

In contrast to all-too-many presentation books, *Looking Good In Presentations* consistently emphasizes a down-to-earth, message-oriented approach. I'm particularly fond of Chapter 2, "The Message." As the author writes: "Your audience needs to hear it—to hear, understand, internalize, and retain it." All too often, presentation books emphasize visuals that dazzle, but—unfortunately—often don't inform. You won't find that here.

The importance of making every word, every illustration, and every animation work to communicate and strengthen your message is emphasized throughout *Looking Good In Presentations*.

Looking Good In Presentations is a balanced book. It emphasizes the details as well as your presentation's "big picture." The tiniest nuances of onscreen typography and fine-tuning of business graphics is balanced by an emphasis of how the details affect the message you are communicating and the impact your words and your visuals will have on the audience.

Chapter 12, "Design Crimes And How To Prevent Them," is one of the most enjoyable chapters. It discusses and shows typical pitfalls and describes how they can be avoided. The numerous before and after illustrations and discussions of the changes made effectively drive home the lessons illustrated and help you avoid similar problems in the future.

Up-To-Date Information

Looking Good In Presentations does not sidestep hardware and software issues. Although many readers will be preparing simple presentations for delivery using overhead transparencies or from the screen of a computer, the latter chapters describe how and when "presenter-less" multimedia makes sense and the special opportunities—and constraints—that presenters face on the World Wide Web.

Looking Good In Presentations includes several appendixes and resource lists. You can photocopy and use the storyboard sheets and grid sketch sheets for use as "hands on" partners when planning the development of your message and design of your visuals. The comprehensive Resource List will help you locate the right tools to do the job. The Glossary will help you quickly master the language of presentations.

Roger C. Parker
Author of Looking Good In Print, Fourth Edition

Looking Good
in
Presentations

CONTENTS AT A GLANCE

Chapter 1   For Starters

Chapter 2   The Message

Chapter 3   Presentation Media

Chapter 4   Design And Layout

Chapter 5   Understanding Type

Chapter 6   Exploring Color

Chapter 7   Text Frames And More

Chapter 8   Using Graphs

Chapter 9   Using Diagrams

Chapter 10   Moving Into Multimedia

Chapter 11   Moving Onto The World Wide Web

Chapter 12   Design Crimes And How To Prevent Them

Chapter 13   Sample Scenarios

Chapter 14   A Final Glance

Appendix A   Storyboard Sheets

Appendix B   Grid Sketch Sheets

Appendix C   Creating 3D Objects

LOOKING GOOD
IN
PRESENTATIONS

TABLE OF CONTENTS

Introduction   **xxv**

Chapter 1
For Starters   **1**

How To Not Be Boring   2

Creating Effective Designs   4

Defining Your Audience   7

How Much Time Do You Have?   8

Who Does What?   9

Moving On   11

Chapter 2
The Message   **13**

The Plan   14

Expressing Information   15

Information Sources   23

Concentrating The Message   25

Having Your Cake...In Layers   29

Moving On   29

Chapter 3
Presentation Media   **31**

Environment Considerations   32

Equipment   33

Electronic Presentations   34

Overhead Transparencies   37

35mm Slides   40

Web-Based Presentations   43

Posters And Flip Charts   46

Handouts   47

Moving On   48

Chapter 4
Design And Layout   49

A Principled Vision   50

Focus And Contrast   51

The Idea Stage   53

Layout Decisions   57

Graphic Design Devices   65

Motion And Animation   69

Ground Relationships   70

Restraint: Say It Again!   73

Moving On   74

Chapter 5
Understanding Type   75

Carriers Of Content And Style   76

Setting Type Is Not Typing   77

Type Terminology   77

What's In A Font?   83

Type Distortion   91

Type Sizing   93

Sizing Type For Projection And Display Media   96

Copy Fitting   98

Spacing   98

Moving On   100

Chapter 6
Exploring Color   101

Go For Color   102

Coding With Color   106

The Language Of Color   108

Making A Palette   110

Some Winning Combinations   113

Graduated Color   116

Black, White, And Gray   117

Moving On   118

Chapter 7
Text Frames And More   119

Terrific Text   120

Opening Titles   122

Section And Conquer   124

List Winners   125

Setting The Table   132

Illustrated Text Frames   136

Question Frames   137

Blank Frames   138

Moving On   138

Chapter 8
Using Graphs   139

Focus On The Data   140

Graphing Terminology   140

Define Your Purpose   142

Types Of Graphs   142

Anatomy Of A Graph   145

Time-Related Graphing   150

Comparing Component Parts   155

Comparing Places Or Things   158

Distribution And Correlation   161

Moving On   164

Chapter 9
Using Diagrams   165

Links And Nodes: Modular Thinking   166

Process Diagrams: Visual Stories   170

Organizational Diagrams: Relative
Positioning   176

Time Lines: Clocking To History   177

Exploded Diagrams: Disassembling Reality   179

Floor Plans, Maps, And Other Scale Drawings:
Demonstrating Relationships   181

Moving On   185

Chapter 10
Moving Into Multimedia   187

Love At First Sight—And Sound   188

Multiwhich?   191

Animation And Pseudo-Animation   196

Moving On   200

Chapter 11
Moving Onto The World Wide Web   201

Visual Punch For Web Sites   202

Wanting It All   205

Weaving The Web   209

Moving On   214

Chapter 12
Design Crimes And How To
Prevent Them   215

Type   217

Layout   220

Background Design   221

Color   222

Multimedia   223

Web Pages   224

Alignment   225

Emphasis   226

Clichés   227

Moving On   228

Chapter 13
Sample Scenarios   229

Delivering The Goods   230

Peer Group Meetings   230

Web Crawling   232

**Scientific And Professional Conference
    Presentations   234**

Sales Shows   236

Traveling Shows   237

Courtroom Exhibits   238

Financial Reports   240

Boardroom Graphics   241

Instruction And Training Materials   242

Moving On   244

Chapter 14
A Final Glance   245

Rhythm, Pace, And Depth   246

Proofreading   248

Back To The Drawing Board   249

Parting Thoughts   249

Appendix A
Storyboard Sheets 251

Slides 253

Screen And Web Site 255

Transparencies 257

Handouts 259

Appendix B
Grid Sketch Sheets 261

4×3 Grid 263

4×4 Grid 265

5×5 Grid 267

Page Grid 269

Appendix C
Creating 3D Objects 271

The Classic Concept 272

Casting Shadows 274

Examples Of 3D Effects 276

Premade 3D 276

Glossary 279

Further Reading 291

Books 292

Periodicals 293

Seminars And Trade Shows 293

Resources 295

Presentation Software 297

Multimedia/Animation Software 297

Image Creation And Editing Software 298

Image Management And Image Database Software 298

Computer Hardware And Peripherals 299

Digital Cameras 300

Presentation Equipment 301

Stock Image Sources 302

Clip Art Sources 304

Font Sources 305

Free Stuff Web Sites 305

Index 307

Looking Good
In
Presentations

INTRODUCTION

Most of the time people like to think of themselves as individuals with their own unique tastes, likes, and dislikes. One of the exceptions to this preferred self-concept is when people don't like to do something or are afraid of doing something. Then misery loves company.

If your hands get clammy and your heart starts to pound at the very thought of creating or giving a presentation, you're not alone. Stop a minute and let that idea come slowly into focus in your brain. You are not alone—everyone except the most extreme extrovert experiences some degree of panic when they have to create and deliver a presentation. Think about that the next time you're on a panel and everyone else seems so self-assured and confident.

Tools For Presenting

Now that you know everyone else is just as uncomfortable as you are up on that raised stage, you can get beyond the feelings and start wondering how to make this task easier for yourself. There are presenters who didn't spend four years in acting school who do a wonderful job with their presentations. How do they do it?

One of the ways they do it is by reading a book like this one. This book is a systematic examination of the whys, how-tos, and how-not-tos of all kinds of presentations, including live presentations, multimedia presentations, and even Web-based presentations. Every chapter has information you can use, along with practical, immediately effective tips on making your next presentation more of a dream than a nightmare.

Another way they do it, frankly, is by doing it. Once you've read this book, I hope you will have enough confidence to start volunteering for presentations. That's right, I mean actually asking to get up in front of people and talk. With the basics firmly in hand and with this book as a ready reference, the more presentations you make, the better you will be, and your discomfort will lessen steadily. I promise.

Presentation Types

This book covers three major kinds of presentations: live presentations; standalone presentations; and electronic, self-running presentations. A live presentation is one where you or someone else is the main component, while a standalone presentation is designed to run without a live presenter on hand to help convey the message. Several people can simultaneously access standalone presentations, such as those you see on large screen displays at public events.

Electronic presentations sent out on CD-ROM or available on Web sites have around-the-clock access and can pack a lot of information into a small amount of time. They can also be as long or as short as the person viewing the presentation wants them to be.

What Are Presentation Graphics?

Presentation graphics are the visual elements that help convey your message, your information, and your ideas. They are the meat on the bones of your presentation. You need content and ideas to make any presentation come alive, but you also need to flesh out the presentation with presentation graphics.

For example, say you have a binder full of information about the buying preferences of your customer base. It's your task to present the most important part of this information to your sales representatives at the annual company meeting. Presentation graphics help you provide this information visually in a variety of ways, such as in the form of a pie chart, a few stock photo images, or even a multimedia show.

Who Makes Presentation Graphics?

If you have a computer, you can make presentation graphics. Even students in junior high school routinely whip up a few graphics to add spice (and take up space) in their reports. If your twelve-year-old son or daughter can do it, so can you—if you want to.

Unless you were hired to create presentations, you may not like the idea of having to create your own presentation graphics. After all, you were hired to do a job that may have little or nothing to do with graphic design. You may feel that the illustrations are best done by a graphic artist or designer. Like it or not, unless you're running a Fortune 1000 company, creating presentations and presentation graphics are a de facto part of your job description.

If you're a graphic designer, you may want to expand your design services by taking on the creation of different kinds of presentations. Today, more than ever, these new kinds of presentations are likely to include multimedia and Web elements. You may also find yourself having to work with a design team or even making a presentation about your design work itself!

In either case, this book will be helpful to you. It is filled with up-to-date information about the latest technology for creating your own presentation graphics, as well as information on how to get them onto slides, posters, film, and paper. It also contains current information on multimedia and Web presentation technologies, with particular emphasis on design and color.

Who Needs This Book?

If you need to deliver a detailed message, this book is for you. The venue might be a sales seminar, corporate meeting, sales presentation, or symposium. Whatever the topic, however it is presented, you can learn from this book how to make your presentations more effective and how to take less time to create them.

In particular, if you need to create clear, effective visual graphics that bring text together with graphic elements such as charts, diagrams, photographs, and multimedia elements, *Looking Good In Presentations* is for you. You'll learn new information about type, color, and presentation design that will help you make the most of the time you invest in creating presentations.

What this book doesn't have is something only you, the reader, can contribute—your own stamp of individuality. As with any creative endeavor, a presentation is always more than the sum of its elements. It reflects the imagination and intelligence of the creator and presenter. All I can do in this book is help you learn the skills of creating and delivering better presentations. The real magic comes from you.

How To Use This Book

Looking Good In Presentations makes some assumptions. For example, it takes for granted that you have some experience with a computer and feel comfortable using one. It does not assume that you have experience creating presentations or creating computer graphics. Although I mention specific software programs in the text, this is a software-independent design guide. You don't have to use, or own, any particular software to benefit from reading this book.

I hope you will take the time to read all of the chapters, although you don't have to read them in the order presented. Before you tuck in and start reading, take a few minutes to study the chapters in the table of contents. Depending on your computer experience and presentation experience, you may want to skim some chapters or turn immediately to others. If you are familiar with planning presentations, you may find the chapters on design more interesting. If you need to put together a multimedia presentation, you may want to start with that chapter first.

No matter where you start reading, put aside time to read the entire book. No matter what your level of experience is, you'll find something that makes you glad you took the time. If you don't know where to start, the beginning is always a good spot.

FOR STARTERS

So, you need to prepare a presentation. Here's where you begin.

If you've ever watched television, attended school, or worked for a living, you've sat through some kind of presentation. In first grade (or kindergarten) we sat around in circles and watched the teacher wave flash cards around to teach us the alphabet. In college we tried to stay awake and watch slides in art history class. In the office we tried even harder not to nod off during the latest human resources multimedia presentation.

It's sad but true that most of the presentations we've watched could compete with the leading sleep aid in inducing REM sleep. Consequently, we expect to be bored and restless when we sit down for a presentation. It's a rare treat when we feel energized and excited after a presentation. Fortunately, we all get those rare treats from time to time.

How To Not Be Boring

No one wants his or her presentation to be boring. Presenters want their audience to sit up and pay attention, enjoy themselves, learn something, and leave happy. They just don't know how to make this happen. You don't have to be one of the boring presenters of the world. You can become one of those providers of rare treats if you put the lessons in this book into practice.

The first lesson has nothing to do with your presentations. Rather, it has to do with other people's presentations. You can learn from every presentation you sit through, and you can learn more than the presenter intended. You can learn about the right and the wrong ways to create and deliver a presentation. All it takes is for you to use another set of eyes and ears, along with an attentive mind, while observing the presentation. In other words, use a separate channel in your mind to monitor how the presentation looks and how the presenter behaves during the presentation.

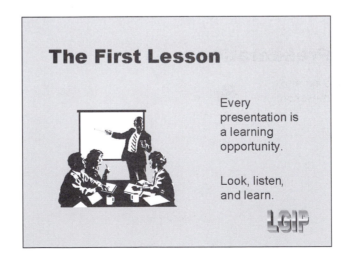

While part of you is focusing on the message, let another part of you pay attention to the design and delivery. Here are a few key areas to focus on:

- *How the screens are laid out.* Is the design clear, consistent, and easy to understand?

- *How color has been used.* Does it strengthen the message or hamper it?

- *How the text looks.* Can you read it easily? If not, what would have made it easier?

- *How the graphics are used.* Do they help you understand the main message better or do they hinder it?

- *How the graphics look.* Can you understand them readily?

- *How the presenter does his or her job.* Does the presenter help or hinder? Does he or she pace the presentation well? What did the presenter do well? What could he or she have done better?

Another question you may want to ask yourself after the presentation is over is whether the material really needed to be in a presentation. Not all material is suitable for a presentation. Some, such as highly complex and detailed material, is more powerful and useful if it's written up in a book. Other material is too shallow and would be best served up in a short memo or email.

The best material for a presentation lies somewhere between these two extremes. It has enough depth to be interesting, but not so much as to be impenetrably dense. Information that can be easily illustrated and is best conveyed with graphics is also a good source for presentations. If you have to do a presentation, choose the most appropriate information for this medium and put the rest on paper.

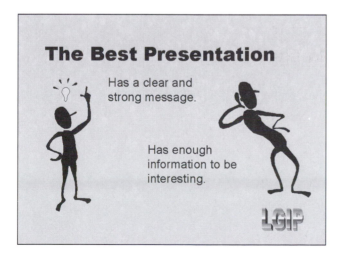

Creating Effective Designs

Once you've done that, you can move on to creating an effective design for the presentation. Good presentation design isn't a mystery—it's a learned skill. As is the case with any skill, the first few times you practice it, you'll feel clumsy and stiff. Take the process one step at a time, though, as outlined in this book, and you'll be a pro in no time.

The second lesson you need to keep in mind is something all professionals take to heart: Effective presentation design isn't about the prettiest pictures or the coolest special effects. It's about creating designs that help meet the daily communication challenges found in the office, in the classroom, on the road, or in the meeting hall. Effectively designed presentations convince real people and move them to action. They help people understand and remember your message.

Begin With A Plan

Planning prevents problems and helps you spot them early enough to avoid them. That's only two of the reasons why planning is the first step in the design process. It also gives your mind time to mull over your message. Sometimes if you take a little time to ponder what you thought was the most important point, you'll find it gives way later to a clearer, more central concept, which makes for a stronger presentation. Planning also gives you time to think about what resources you'll need and when you'll need them.

Objectives And An Outline

Start the planning process by listing the objectives you'd like to achieve by giving your presentation. Clarify your expectations, both for yourself and for the others you may be working with on the project. Take the time to write these objectives and expectations down on paper. Writing them down forces you to focus and will help you catch unrealistic or conflicting desires. The lists will also help you evaluate your efforts after you've finished creating and delivering the presentation.

Use the objectives list to create a content outline and, later, a preliminary structure for your presentation. On the content outline, make sure you write down the major point you'd like the audience to walk away knowing. Then consider all the related points they have to know to understand the main point.

Next, you should take a step back and look at that objectives list somewhat objectively. You have constraints on your time, your budget, and your resources, and you need to match the constraints to the objectives. You may have a database of wonderful content, but it won't fit in a five-minute presentation for which you have two days to prepare. Above all, be realistic, and if these are your first few presentations, be cautious and know it will take more time, money, and resources than you expect to create your presentation.

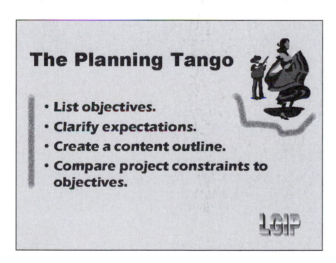

Realistic Expectations For Your Design

Once you've examined your objectives and your constraints, it's time to look at your expectations for yourself and for others. If you're creating a multimedia masterpiece, but you've got only days and a few hundred dollars to do it, you can't expect a graphic artist or designer to drop everything he or she is doing to help. You also can't expect to learn multimedia programming in two hours. Make life easier on yourself by adjusting your expectations to fit reality.

No matter how many presentations you've done, achieving good design and creating graphics to support your message will take you plenty of time and effort. A complete, successful presentation requires several steps, including the planning and execution, editing, and revision steps. Even before you sit down at a computer to start your work, you can spend a few hours sketching rough diagrams of screens and noodling the project around in your head.

When it comes time to design the presentation, keep in mind you'll have to spend a few hours picking out elements of your design. You're trying to achieve a consistency in the graphic design of the entire presentation. This consistency will help you unite disparate material into a comprehensible whole. Choose a typeface, color palette, and layout grid structure for the entire presentation. The audience will quickly learn how to "read" the screen for important information. A mix of design styles can irritate an audience and may make them stumble while looking for the message in the mess.

On the other hand, every presentation should have a few elements of controlled change built into it. If all the screens are almost identical, the audience will quickly tune out your message. Their brains will find it hard to distinguish between one screen and another. Planned change in your design, rather than haphazard change, helps keep the audience interested.

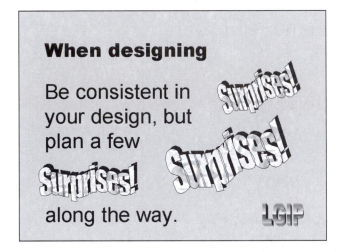

Before you go any further, take time to attend to an often overlooked, but important part of the planning process. You must find out as much as you can about your audience. Unless you do that, you could create the perfect presentation only to have it fall flat because it was the wrong approach for the audience.

After that, it's time to take a more detailed look at the production process, including the time required for each step and who's going to be responsible for getting the job done.

Defining Your Audience

Imagine that the people who will attend your presentation are filing into the room right now. Look at them closely; focus on two or three of them chosen at random. Why are they here? What do they expect to achieve by attending your presentation? How does your planned presentation match up with their expectations? If you haven't any idea how to answer these questions, don't go on to the next step in the process until you can get some of these answers. If you work without the answers, your presentation will not be the success you want it to be.

That's how important it is to evaluate your audience's background, initial attention level, and sense of engagement. If you know your audience is a highly educated and technically astute group that has already attended six seminars that day, you can be sure your presentation has to be something special to get and keep their attention.

What's In It For Them?

It is especially important for you to understand what the audience feels it could gain if it paid attention to your presentation. Is it new information that will help them make their business more profitable? Is it data to take home to impress the boss? Or is their attitude such that nothing will make them sit up and pay attention? The answers to these questions will give you what you need to know to set the proper tone for the presentation. The tone is the approach that would work best with this particular audience and give it an incentive to take part mentally. It's your job to figure that out before you get too far into the presentation preparation process.

FULL OF BOLOGNA

Everybody knows the Oscar Mayer bologna song, right? Wrong! And even if they do know it, they may not like it. Be careful to choose audio and visual materials appropriate for the audience. Taste changes as age and socio-economic groups do. Take the time to do some research if you have to, but get it right.

While you're thinking about the audience, take a few minutes to sit in their seats mentally. When you attend a presentation, are you looking to get every nitty-gritty detail about a topic? Do you expect the presenter to give you such a level of detail? Of course not—even Internal Revenue Service auditors don't expect that from a presentation. Keep it simple and concentrate on giving the audience the essential basics of information.

If you've got a lot of numbers at hand, you may be tempted to pile on the data to make yourself look more professional. Resist that impulse and the related one to cram too much into one presentation, particularly if the audience has sat through more than one presentation that day. Even if you are making a presentation to a trade audience, leave jargon and acronyms out of your presentation unless you present definitions. No one will think you're talking down to them if you keep the explanations and definitions short and to the point.

No matter what age groups may be in your audience, consider using multimedia elements such as audio and video in your presentation. You can even make references to Web sites the audience can turn to for additional information. It's a wired world, after all, and even many senior citizens know their way around a computer and the World Wide Web. You might as well take advantage of what your audience is already familiar with to help it buy into your presentation.

How Much Time Do You Have?

It's true that you never have enough time to make a presentation perfect. That's because no presentation is ever perfect; there's always something you could tweak that would make it a little better. The real question, then, is how much time do you need to design an effective presentation and one that meets your realistic objectives?

You'll face the same question when you choose the amount of time you want to have to deliver your presentation. Sometimes, particularly if you are speaking at a conference, you may be given a maximum amount of time you may speak. At other times you will be able to set your own time limit. How much time do you need to be effective?

Many professional speakers limit their presentations to less than 10 minutes. Some say any presentation longer than 20 minutes is really a lecture and refuse to go past 15 to 20 minutes. If you can set your own time limit, let your experience and gut feelings guide you. Ask yourself how long you think the audience can listen attentively to a presentation, and then shave a few minutes off that time to keep within a reasonable time limit, particularly if you want to leave time for questions.

No matter how long you want the presentation to be, you can avoid that rushed, ragged, and out-of-breath appearance by leaving yourself plenty of time to design and create the presentation. You'll need enough time to plan, create, check, and double-check the design, and then you'll need time to practice the presentation until you are totally comfortable with it.

All of these comments about time have to do with manned presentations where you (or some other human being) will be on hand to deliver part of the message, which will be accompanied by graphics of some kind. Time takes on a different flavor when the presentation is unmanned and is available on disk or on the Internet. In these kinds of presentations, you'll still need to leave yourself enough time to plan the design, but keep in mind that the audience members may come and go as they please during the presentation.

In these presentations, the audience (one or several people) controls the time and pacing. If you have a complicated message, your presentation must be compelling enough to get this audience to stick around until the final curtain. If you can't manage that, break the message down into smaller segments and make the segments compelling. Another idea is to make one short presentation that hits all the highlights and present additional material the audience can go into if it wants to take the time.

Who Does What?

Some people do solo acts for their presentations and are responsible for every aspect of the project from planning to execution; others work with writers, designers, and producers. You may even find yourself doing some of both—working solo and as part of a team.

Working independently gives you total control of the project and allows you to imprint the project with your own style and personality. It can also give you major headaches and worries as you struggle to complete the presentation. Unless you hate to work with other people, consider working with others on at least a part of the project. Even if all they do is listen sympathetically to your ideas or serve as the test audience for the presentation, you'll find their participation helpful.

Put It In Writing

When you work with other people on a presentation, it's helpful to jot down your expectations of them, including what you expect them to do and what you expect their efforts to help you do. You'll be able to spot potential problems or unrealistic expectations more easily this way. You might also want to take the time to write down what you think they want from you and to discuss expectations with them.

Once you've done a few successful presentations, expect others in your organization to drop by to ask for advice or even to ask you to create presentations for them. Congratulations, you're now officially a presentation guru! Tread carefully, though, as you don't want to start doing other people's work for them. Giving a few tips over lunch is fine, but doing a whole presentation for another person can eat up a lot of your time.

If your boss assigns you the task or asks you to create a presentation for him or her, that's another situation entirely. In that case, put on your designer hat and pick up your pen and notebook. Try to put yourself in the speaker's place before you start the project. Ask lots of questions and note the answers. Watch as the person speaks, too, to get valuable information about his or her tone of voice, gestures, natural speaking rhythm, and pacing. Use this information to help guide your design selections for the presentation.

You may be asked to create a presentation that several or more people will deliver, and you will not have an opportunity to meet any of them. That's a more difficult assignment, but here are some tips to get you through:

- Make the presentation more formal than you would if it were your own, but encourage each presenter to personalize the presentation by adding his or her own spoken introduction.

- Leave room and time in the presentation for the speaker to add information or anecdotes that relate directly to a particular audience. Tell the speaker where these breaks are before the presentation.

- Find one decision maker in your group or company that has the final say on the presentation and its message. That's the person you're trying to please most, so try to get some time to talk with him or her about the objectives of the presentation before you start creating it.

- Schedule time with the decision maker to review the presentation at set times during the creation process. Try to get his or her comments and suggestions in writing, particularly if the decision maker approves or disapproves of something.

- Find out if there are other key players in the decision-making process, and keep them involved and informed.

- Be aware of the politics and personalities involved in the project. Your design and content might be wonderful, but you may discover that corporate design rules specify the use of a certain typeface and certain colors.

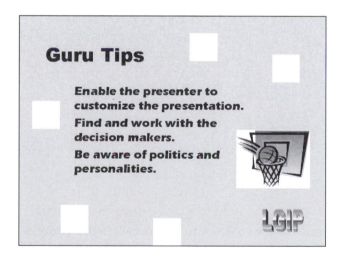

Guru Tips

Enable the presenter to customize the presentation.

Find and work with the decision makers.

Be aware of politics and personalities.

Moving On

Planning is key, and a lot of the planning takes place in your mind before you sit down at a computer. Outline your objectives and expectations, get a clear idea of your audience, and find out if you'll be working with others. Ask yourself how much time you need, and figure out how much time you really have. After you've done all that, it's time to focus on the message itself, which is the task we tackle in the next chapter.

THE MESSAGE 2

You have something important to say. Your audience needs to hear it—to hear, understand, internalize, and retain it. The message you want to deliver to your audience is the energizing force pushing any presentation forward, no matter how basic or elaborate the supporting graphics.

The message is the whole reason you're here in the first place: you have new information to convey, or you want to explain existing facts more completely and look at familiar ideas in a new light.

The Plan

The logical first step, the footing for the whole endeavor, is to determine the key points that you'd like your audience to walk away with.

Objective Reality: The Results You Want

Imagine your first audience listening to your presentation, then set out the specific communication objectives for the project. Keep the list short and the wording brief. You don't have to squander your time and creative energies on perfectly phrased objectives—just punch them out so you'll know where you're going and when you've gotten there. Share them with colleagues working on the project with you, and incorporate their feedback. These cooperatively developed objectives provide an excellent groundwork for collaboration. Refer to them frequently when selecting and organizing your material.

You might have only one *goal:* to communicate the benefits of organic coffee, for instance. But your *objectives* relate to the specific points you want your audience to grasp: coffee tastes vastly different without chemical overtones; it's much healthier to drink an infusion without herbicides and pesticides; and local agriculture benefits from renewable organic growing practices.

The more focused you are at the outset, the more effective your presentation will be. It works!

Getting Started
- Set objectives
- Outline concepts
- Visualize content

Your list of objectives will clarify your task right from the beginning. It'll allow you to learn as much as you can about the information you're going to present, while avoiding time-consuming detours into extraneous material. You'll become the resident expert on growing organic coffee and on coffee-tasting procedures. The better you understand coffee cultivation in Sumatra or the physiology of discerning flavor, and the less you diverge into historical practices or the commodities market, the easier it will be to organize and visualize concepts, ideas, facts, figures, and relationships.

Sequential Reality: The Outline You Need

Even though you're probably impatient to start creating your show, restrain yourself until you've planned the conceptual outline. Such an outline will aid you in your quest for clear thinking and an engaging presentation. Outlining need not be dull and dry if you approach it as a creative, imaginative process. Start by jotting down ideas as they occur to you, without order or priority. When you run dry, refer to your list of objectives to refresh your thinking. Allow one point to suggest others. After making one point, say to yourself, "And then..." or "Which means that...." Challenge yourself by asking "So what?"

Look over your notes and highlight three or four main topics. Cluster the other ideas around them. Ask yourself which subpoints make significant contributions to your message, and which don't. Which ones bridge two concepts? Which contribute to none of the objectives, even though they're interesting factoids? Where are the gaps in the message you're planning to convey? Then establish a flow between the main topics or groups and list a hierarchy within each cluster. There! You've already sketched out the basics of your sequential outline.

Expressing Information

...With Words

A huge number of the presentation graphics you see are text frames, with words serving as the most important visual elements. Despite their simplicity, these graphics can be quite effective. The key to elegant text frames is careful choosing and editing of the phrases that connect the basic skeletal structure of the message. When you've done this, the words really do reveal all: your reasoning and content is crystal clear—and your mistakes, gaps, and inconsistencies are likewise obvious. For this reason, they present a real challenge to the designer, who must create a flexible, dynamic, and engaging format to accommodate and pull together a range of bullet lists, key words, and narrative concepts. The building blocks of successful text frames are type style, color palette, simple graphic elements like lines and bullets used wisely and consistently, and a well-developed sense of proportion.

Keep the phrasing of your text frames crisp and to the point.

Choose your words carefully. You can be expansive and word-rich in your oral delivery, but your audience will still appreciate concise, condensed visuals.

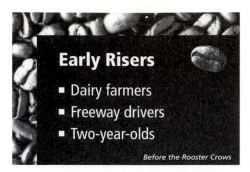

Early Risers

- Dairy farmers
- Freeway drivers
- Two-year-olds

Before the Rooster Crows

Limit yourself to the points that are most important to your viewer, and eliminate extraneous content that confuses your argument or distracts from the primary line of reasoning. When accompanying a live presentation, the graphics do not need to reproduce the whole script. They should hold the audience's attention to the salient concepts and ideas under discussion, and provide an anchor for excursions and side notes. The audience should be able to absorb them without realizing that they're actively reading. When a particular point requires more than four or five contributing lines of text, divide the concept into a couple of logical components so that each frame is easy to grasp at a glance.

...With Numbers

Because people like to count things and use the results to back up conclusions and proposals, statistics are the second most commonly presented type of information. Entire state and federal agencies have been established to count specific types of data, analyze these statistics in different combinations, and compare them over time or between categories: the Census Bureau, the Internal Revenue Service, and the Bureau of Economic Analysis, to name just a few.

Numbers can help groups as far-flung as our organic coffee growers in Sumatra, who might expect a yield of 10,000 kilos this year, based on last year's performance. When they review the crop figures from the past 20 years, however, they see that production tends to be cyclical and influenced by rainfall and market patterns outside their control. They conclude that they should be prepared for a significant drop in yield this year.

Numbers can clarify and substantiate your points—but don't overdo the use of raw figures and limit the complexity of your tables.

Figures help us predict, plan, and forecast, but they're very abstract. Written numbers can help make the concepts more concrete, since they're easier than spoken numbers for the audience to grasp and compare. But don't be a slave to exact quantities—learn to approximate, round off, and contrast.

Coffee Drinkers

	1996	1997
Instant	541	580
Perk	453	476
Drip	622	690

Coffee Consumer Reports

Decimals, especially, can be very confusing on the screen. Far from lending more credence to your points, at this level of detail they're likely to steal emphasis from the content and slow down the audience's ability to follow you. Consider the alternative of citing your most exact numbers in a handout, while presenting precise figures on screen only when they truly serve an important purpose.

...With Other Relational Information

While numerical values frequently form the basis for examining relationships and making comparisons, they're only one part of a much broader category of information. Don't limit yourself to expressing ideas that rely on quantity; sometimes important material can be expressed best through links, hierarchies, and relative size or position. Flowcharts and organizational diagrams are examples of standard treatments for such concepts.

Depict relational information with graphics that provide a context for comparisons. Pie charts, graphs, and maps can show how the parts compose the whole, change over time, or are distributed across the country.

Imagine, for instance, the flow of work on a coffee plantation as a simple diagram. It can be confusing to talk about the way an individual task relates to the operation, especially when you're tempted to add statistics for kilos picked or processed per day, without giving the audience an overview of the whole process. A diagram can convey the broad sweep of work at a glance and anchor the viewer throughout the more detailed material. The salient portion of the diagram can even be used to introduce each point in the process under discussion.

Relational data often deals with temporal and spatial relationships—events that occur over time or in different places. Maps, graphs, and diagrams illustrate these correspondences and show how time or events are linked and interrelated. The yearly cycle of the coffee tree—from flowering through bean maturation—would make an excellent timeline diagram, providing a basis for understanding why tasks are scheduled at certain intervals.

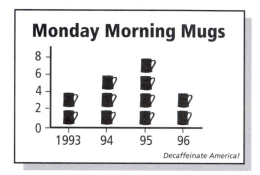

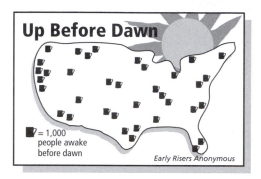

...With Sequence And Motion

Nothing shows change so well as movement. Animating a line graph, growing a piece of a pie chart, or drawing a connecting link is almost as much fun as zipping to the top of the big ladder in your old Chutes and Ladders game. Be sure that change is the concept you want to emphasize in a set of data, though; the splashy motion effect carries attention away from more subtle considerations and details. For instance, a dramatic increase in the demand for organic coffee lends itself readily to motion graphics because the point is to emphasize growth rather than precise starting or ending values. Your audience will follow the steep upward curve with ease as it arcs across the screen.

Motion emphasizes the course of change. Be sure the change itself is dramatic enough to sustain this focused attention from the audience.

When your point requires a finer brush, consider demonstrating change through sequencing. Design a series of frames connected by dissolve effects that break down motion into smaller steps. Perhaps you realize that two factors influenced your digital coffeemaker sales this year: component availability and consumer demand. How did one affect the other and how did both contribute to the bottom line? Sequence your data in a series of frames to reveal relative importance.

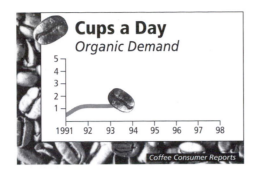

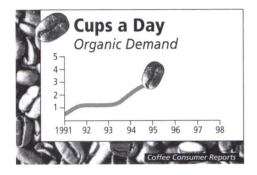
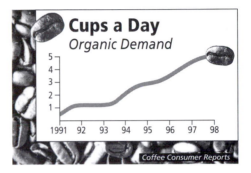

...With Artwork

Many great graphic communications give us a way to visualize actual objects in the world around us. An anatomy diagram, a cutaway view of a jet engine, and a pictorial comparison of cloud types are all examples of representational art. While most of us find this type of illustration relevant and easy to understand, it takes a good deal of time, skill, and experience with drawing programs to render a detailed, lifelike representation from scratch. Far too often, we're disappointed with our efforts to capture the images in our imaginations. Fortunately, we have alternatives that will help tremendously when faced with this dilemma.

Representational art is time-consuming to produce from scratch. Careful, considered use of specialty clip art can rescue the beleaguered technical presenter.

Images On The Web

The Web is a great source for images for your presentations. You can often get the okay from Web designers to use their work, although some do charge a fee to use their images.

Please see Resources at the end of the book for a few helpful Web sites for images.

First, make it a point to keep current with clip art CDs of images relevant to your field. Specific medical and engineering materials, for instance, need not be reinvented by each presenter. Look for images that reflect the style and level of detail you'll need; be sure you can open the images in a drawing program to adapt them for your presentation—for instance, changing colors for emphasis or removing irrelevant objects. Take time to work these images into your overall frame design, giving them the same careful consideration you'd give original drawings. Successful clip art images support the scale, color palette, and typography of the presentation. They need a carefully created context and placement in the frame. It's important to maintain consistency in artwork throughout a presentation, so avoid grabbing pictures created with different techniques for the same show: nothing looks as cobbled together as a program where the illustrations for various frames are obviously pulled from different sources.

Your presentation doesn't have to include pictures of every idea. Resist the temptation to flip through the clip art that comes with your presentation program or other generic "business" files. There's no inspiration here, and chances are people in the audience are already familiar with these images. They can actually draw attention away from the information you're trying to communicate. Moreover, they pull you toward cliché. Don't be desperately literal! Instead of pulling up a tired telephone graphic when discussing telemarketing projections, for instance, try for a visual translation of the important concepts. Everyone knows we're talking about telephony here; they're interested in costs, benefits, strategies, or projected profits for this particular project.

As an alternative to a strictly realistic representation, try creating a stylized graphic stripped of details. Flat, bold, colorful images emphasize one aspect of the subject matter and convey selected information without extraneous elements. They help you "telegraph" your message to the viewers. The following illustration was created based on an actual photograph of the product, shown on page 22.

The concept of drinking coffee, for instance, can be conveyed effectively by a cup and a face. Look through your trade journals for ideas of this type of simplified representation. If you don't feel comfortable working with computer drawing tools, try sketching in broad strokes with a wide marker and scanning your sketches. This type of artwork is fun to draw, especially since it allows you to infuse your program with some personality. You can easily apply this style of drawing to any illustrated frames of your presentation, building a consistent and memorable program. Create icons for the main sections of your program the same way: select simple shapes and colors that tie the related materials together visually.

...With Photographs And Video Clips

Photographs and video are the extreme of realistic artwork, so they're very helpful in showing specific people, places, and things. Incorporate them into your presentation when you want to represent a particular location or an exact moment. A sequence of photos or a video clip can show change or motion with clarity and precision—or with obscurity and confusion. An effective presentation photo or video shot focuses clearly on one main element in the foreground. The stages of coffee beans ripening, for instance, would make an excellent sequence—but not if the beans are just barely visible in a leafy canopy. Be sure the audience doesn't need to ask, "What am I supposed to pay attention to here?" or "Where is it?"

Because the audience will have little trouble grasping the importance of a good, clear photographic image, you can tell a story quite rapidly by showing a series of still photos or a video sequence. Experiment with combining graphics, photographs, and video: insert a photographic image into a window of a text frame, for instance, or filter a photographic image for the background of your title frames. Both techniques are excellent additions to your stylistic repertoire.

Especially when they occupy just a portion of the screen area, the best presentation photos focus clearly on an element in the foreground, avoiding extraneous objects and confusing backgrounds.

Courtesy of Krups North America.

Although stock photo and video CDs may provide just what you need, be careful to choose images that you can integrate convincingly with the rest of your presentation. Choose locations, backgrounds, and key colors carefully. Avoid generic shots—after all, the purpose of your images is to add specificity and clarity.

Keep your final format in mind when planning photographic and videographic shoots. Will you end up with a window set into a computer screen, a vertical black-and-white flip chart, or a horizontal 35mm slide? Pay close attention to the elements that can provide continuity from shot to shot: subject, camera angles, lighting, product packaging.

...With Graphic Style

Allow the content of your presentation to set the tone for the visual style. Describe for yourself and others on the project team the essential character or temperament of the presentation; use words like *friendly* or *polished, warm* or *cool, high-tech* or *low-key*. Translate these concepts into the style of artwork, background treatment, color palette, typography, and layout grid you'll design for the presentation. Make sure each visual element, right down to the lines and dots, works with you to communicate your message.

The tone and graphic style of a consumer-oriented presentation about organic coffee, for instance, might best reflect the human values of health and good taste with vibrant colors, informal type, and video clips of people in coffee bars radiating energy to set the scene. The visual approach to a presentation for investors, on the other hand, might emphasize fiscal reliability with a more subdued palette and restrained typeface selection supported by photographs depicting an efficient, ship-shape plantation. Harmonize your visual tones with the substance of your presentation. Graphic style congruent with content goes a long way toward convincing your audience that the points you make are sound.

...With Variety

The more presentations you make, the more you'll need to break out of the same old format, even if it has worked wonders in the past. Although you want to learn from your successes as well as from your less astonishing performances, it's easy to get stuck in a favorite graphic treatment and use it for show after show—regardless of the kind of information in your message or the audience you're addressing. Eventually, you'll get bored with the same thing, and that will come across in your presentation.

Although most information can be conveyed adequately in a variety of ways, you can choose the graphic form that represents it best only when you concentrate on the content, making sure you understand thoroughly both this particular set of information and its position in the whole presentation. Suppose you want to show production data for the 10 largest coffee plantations in Sumatra. You could create a map to show the spatial distribution pattern, a graph to show relative changes over time, a pie chart to show how each plantation relates to the sum, a table to show exact production numbers, or a keyword list to highlight the points you want to stress while discussing production. Before you choose an interpretive device, think about where you're leading the audience with this information—what they've already seen and will see in the presentation. Your goal is to focus on the message and to create a visual presentation that supports the whole flow of information as well as each point along the way.

Information Sources

As you work to refine your message and content, make sure you don't lose track of the information sources from which you've drawn your material. Occasionally one person is responsible for the content of a presentation from start to finish. But more often you'll be assembling data gathered by a number of people, groups, and agencies. Keep source references firmly attached to each bit of information so that you know who is accountable for its accuracy. The audience looks to you, the presenter, for reliable facts and figures. Be sure you're passing along verified data.

You're responsible for giving accurate information to your audience, so be sure you know the source of every fact and figure. Displaying these sources—discretely—on the screen can boost credibility and eliminate questions of authenticity.

PIE IN THE SKY

Some people get hooked on bullet lists; others like graphs. Pie charts have become so popular in recent years, you'd think someone was running a special on them! Do they all show parts of a whole, adding up to 100 percent? And even when they do, is that the most important aspect of the information?

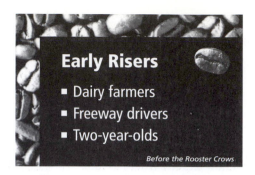

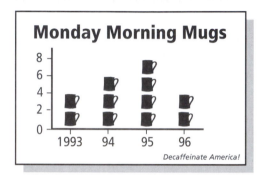

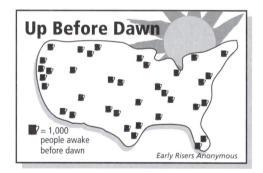

SOURCE CODE

Determine if your audience will benefit from knowing about your sources. Make it clear to them whether you're presenting opinions and speculations, or documented information derived from respected studies or carefully monitored internal assessments. Think about the enormous difference we perceive between data generated in research funded by a special-interest group and figures drawn from studies monitored by the Centers for Disease Control.

When you'll be gathering information from other people within your organization, prepare a package about the presentation to give each source person. Include a description of exactly what information you need, ask how it was derived, and state your deadline. When it's appropriate, support your request with background materials on the presentation, such as an audience analysis, a list of objectives, and a content outline.

The nature of your sources can affect your graphic treatment as well as the presentation of content. For findings from a preliminary study, for example, you might avoid precise units and instead sketch quickly with a broad brush to indicate trends and tendencies.

Certain situations call for your judgment in providing background about the information you're presenting. Let your audience members know how current the data is so they can evaluate its worth at the moment. Indicate whether your figures are forecasts or known values. And, of course, it's never a good idea to deliberately conceal relevant information. Respect your own credibility.

Because verbally crediting sources is often tedious and cumbersome, certain presentations benefit tremendously from a standard format for citing sources right on the presentation graphics. When you implement this format throughout the program, the audience will know exactly where to look for attribution and date information. Credibility is no longer an issue.

Concentrating The Message

Quite often, presentation graphics are the visual accompaniment to the spoken word, or, more precisely, to many spoken words. These visuals can't begin to cover as much territory as a presenter, speaking naturally, conveys in passing through the same material. Even when the presentation stands alone, its essential nature is punchier and more condensed than a lively, anecdotal talk. Tighten the language in the visuals to the essential words or phrases; plan to use different, more expansive language for the verbal presentation. Your audience will appreciate graphics that are easy to take in while listening. Even great material becomes tedious when the speaker reads it aloud; use this opportunity to amplify the basics on the screen.

Condense narrative information into a few key points for visual presentation.

Roasting the Bean

A skilled coffee roaster knows how to adjust temperature over time to transform the raw, green beans, which are compact and tough, into flavorful coffee beans that grind readily into coarse or fine particles.

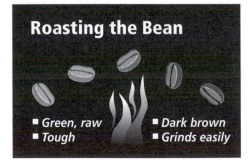

Roasting the Bean

- *Green, raw*
- *Tough*
- *Dark brown*
- *Grinds easily*

TRUTH IN PRESENTATION

How many times have you heard people complain that it's easy to fool an audience with fancy materials and a slick presentation? Don't you believe it. Chances are they're just peeved because their presentations haven't been as well received. People aren't that easily snowed; in fact, some audiences won't tolerate fancy graphics at all. They've become sensitized to hypesters who've tried to pull the wool over their eyes with expensive productions and misleading information. Just as a glossy brochure can become anathema in certain contexts, the presentation that glosses over the tough points loses credibility.

Audiences are savvy and cynical. Refresh them with the materials you'd like to see if you were on the other side of the podium. Be truthful, straightforward, and scrupulously honest.

PITHY POINTS

When writing the text for your graphics, think "tight and concise." Extract the critical points and distill them into a few key words. Aim for titles and headings that can be read easily without losing the thread of the speaker's words. Complete sentences or (worse!) entire paragraphs interrupt the listener's concentration, demanding a different kind of visual attention—and frequently straining the eyes as well.

Once you've extracted the key elements, assign them a particular function. These visual- and content-oriented distinctions are most important to maintain throughout the presentation. In a bullet list, for instance, the title is clearly differentiated from the bulleted items by position, size, typeface, color, or other design choices. Subheads, quotations, attribution lines, explanatory notes, labels, reference values, and other identifiers all work best when managed as separate graphic entities with particular style attributes that remain constant throughout the show.

Consistency in the application of your design to each frame or sequence will maximize the overall power and pizzazz of the presentation.

Titles

Remember the strength of well-stated, well-placed titles when you write the text for your presentation. You can think of the title as the linchpin of the graphic: it's the key to understanding the material. Your viewers won't be as familiar with your subject or organizational approach as you are, so help them out by stating the point of each frame as clearly as you can. Try to capture it in two to five words, leaving out such unnecessary stock phrases as "Graph of" (people see that it's a graph) and "Percentage of" (that information will appear on the graph scale). A presentation is a temporal event, moving through time under the control of either the presenter or the viewer, so it's unnecessary and distracting to include a figure number or other reference in the title.

Titles and subtitles unlock the meaning of a screen for the audience.

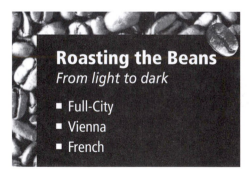

Subtitles

When you find you need more than a few words to describe the import of a frame, employ a subtitle. This handy division of labor allows your viewers to absorb the idea in two stages, organizing the message for them. Try to include something in the subtitle that will intrigue your viewers and make them listen or look more closely.

Reread your titles and subtitles from the audience's point of view. Do they sketch out a story with a beginning, middle, and end? Say them aloud. Think of the poor presenter who didn't realize until she was in front of her audience the full implications of titling a chart showing statistics on male and female demographics with "Population Broken Down by Age and Sex."

Punctuation

On a printed page, punctuation marks signal the reader to prepare for a break in the flow of ideas. Because the ideas in presentation graphics are already grouped and arranged visually, the punctuation requirements are quite different. We rarely need a period or colon at the end of a title or bullet line. Your formatting—size, type style and weight, position, and color—reveals the organization of the material.

Parentheses can be particularly annoying in presentation graphics. Keep them to a minimum, especially in titles—otherwise, you'll give your audience the impression that you're whispering to someone off-stage, over your shoulder. If an idea is so subordinate to the main title that you're tempted to enclose it in parentheses, drop it to the subtitle or eliminate it altogether. Keep your titles strong and clear.

Avoid using punctuation marks whenever possible; instead, rely on the visual treatment to group and relate ideas.

"Limit" punctuation, (please)!

If you find yourself peppering your text with quotation marks, break the habit. Presentations aren't the place for "so-called" phrases. In the same way that lots of air quotes can make a speaker seem arch or sarcastic, graphic quotes cast doubt on the force of your message. If you're citing someone directly, be sure you know whom you're quoting and whether it's a verbatim citation or a paraphrase before you reach for the quote key. Consider using alternative graphic treatments for these passages—italics or contrasting color in conjunction with the name of the quoted person, for instance, usually carries it off quite clearly. Make punctuation work in your favor by using it very sparingly and only for clarity.

Abbreviations

For some audiences, a presentation that relies heavily on abbreviations and acronyms will look like gibberish; for others, a presentation must include such phrases for it to appear professional. Indeed, many of us are more familiar with certain acronyms than with the phrases they replace, and use of the actual phrase will seem stilted and lack credibility. In introductory-level programs, however, you can't go wrong spelling things out, even if that makes your material slightly more bulky. Take this opportunity to introduce the acronym, if it's common usage in the field. Audiences already acquainted with the subject are used to familiar acronyms and abbreviations, so key in to this common lingo. When you're not sure, spell it out, at least once. Practice reading the phrases on the graphic out loud, using both the abbreviation and the full phrase. Do both make sense and sound right to you?

Use long phrases sparingly, but resort to acronyms only if your audience is familiar with the subject, or you've introduced it thoroughly.

If abbreviations and acronyms are new, viewers will have a hard time remembering those explained in the first slide and used sporadically thereafter. Offer a few reminders to be sure everyone's with you. Viewers must find these terms meaningful enough to stand alone through the show. Consider that you'll have at least one latecomer or daydreamer, and ask yourself whether those people will understand the presentation even if they don't remember what the acronym stands for. As an alternative to abbreviations, replace wordy phrases with simple graphics or icons.

Sometimes a simple graphic treatment packs more punch than a wordy phrase.

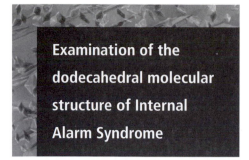

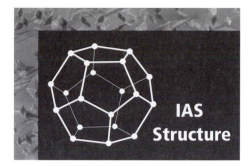

Your goal is to keep the character count in each image to a minimum, but don't try to accomplish this merely by abbreviating into a kind of code. There's a big difference between distilling a message to its essence in a few words and cramming a lot of words into a few letters. Go for simplicity.

Having Your Cake...In Layers

Some presentation media allow you to offer inquisitive viewers excursions outside a linear organization of the material. On a Web site or touch screen, the viewer can click a button, bar, or area of the screen to investigate a more detailed screen, to see where this topic fits into an overview of the material, or to leave the current line of discussion entirely. By making these supplementary screens available, you concentrate the essential message and keep it consistent throughout the primary presentation path. In the same way that these multi-layered standalone presentations engage the viewer interactively, live presenters can design backup screens to answer audience questions and respond to specific requests in more detail. Make sure that you provide easy access back to the main flow from these other levels, and keep your signposts positioned consistently.

Moving On

Put yourself in your viewer's shoes. Can you follow the message? Is it concise or rambling? Does it flow smoothly and logically? Is it interesting to you?

Once you've developed some concrete ideas about your message, you'll want to decide which medium will suit your presentation situation and audience best. In Chapter 3, we'll examine these options and their relevant characteristics.

PRESENTATION
MEDIA
3

Combine the right media and a carefully crafted message, and you can increase the effectiveness of your presentation tenfold. Use the wrong media and you can deflate even the best presentation. Fortunately, choosing the right media is easy if you understand some basics.

The basics of presentation media include an understanding of the presentation environment and the presentation methods (slides, overheads, and so on) available to you. An understanding of the choices and related decisions will make creating any presentation a faster, more productive, and more enjoyable task.

Environment Considerations

If you are preparing a presentation for a specific event, try to visit the room where you will be making the presentation before you start creating it. If that's not possible, get as complete a description of the environment as you can.

Major considerations affecting your design include the size and setup of the room, the amount of light available during the presentation, and how the presentation area is set up. For example, the presentation area could be on a raised area at the front of a brightly lit large room with high ceilings. Making a simple scale drawing of the room will help you remember all these factors.

Use the considerations to guide your media and design choices. For large crowds, the type in illustrations and visuals must be large enough for people in the last row to read clearly, yet not so large as to overwhelm those sitting in front. A good rule of thumb to keep in mind is that the distance between the screen and the last row of the audience should be no more than eight times the height of the screen. The distance between the monitor or screen and the first row should be no more than two times the height of the screen.

Most visuals can be seen more easily in a dimly lit room than in a room filled with light. If sufficient light control isn't possible, you can boost the color hues in the graphics to help people see the full detail of the illustrations. Turning off the lights around the screen and leaving the rest of the lights on in the room can also help.

Make your display choices with these considerations in mind, as well:

- For small groups (less than 12), the audience will be able to see overhead transparencies on a small screen or even a computer display.

- For large groups (more than 12), you will need to project your presentation onto some kind of screen or large, wall-size monitor.

Remember, too, that when images are projected, low-resolution images look grainy and blurry enlarged several times their original size. To prevent this problem, use images that are at least 600 dpi for large-screen presentations.

Equipment

One of the most important decisions you can make during the planning of your presentation is the choice of your equipment. If you will be making the presentation at a trade show or conference, ask the event's organizers what kinds of equipment will be available. If you are making the presentation outside your office, either bring all the equipment you will need with you or make sure the facility already has the equipment and it will be available when needed.

Choose the media for the presentation after you know what kind of equipment will be available. There is nothing worse than preparing a presentation on your computer only to find upon your arrival that a slide projector is the only equipment at hand.

Be prepared for the unexpected and plan for problems. If your presentation is designed for a high-technology medium, such as direct projection from a computer, bring a low-tech version of the presentation with you. That way if the computer or projection equipment isn't working, all you need to make your presentation is an overhead or slide projector. In a pinch, handouts can be converted into overheads by photocopying the handouts onto overhead transparency paper.

Practice your presentation on-site with all the equipment. Try to do this several times and well in advance of the presentation so you can uncover any problems and gain firsthand experience with the setup. If you are traveling to make the presentation, you can often meet the technicians who will operate the equipment before the event. Look for them in the room you will be speaking in and ask them if they can accommodate your request. Chances are, they will make time—they know if you don't look good, they don't look good!

Practice makes perfect—and for less wear and tear on the nerves. Make trial runs of your presentations using all of the equipment several times before the big event.

During the practice runs, take the opportunity to walk yourself, and any technicians, through every step of the presentation. Even the small details count, such as where you will put your notes and if a microphone is needed. If you will be walking around on a raised platform during your presentations, memorize where the outer edges of the platform are so you don't accidentally fall off.

In the rest of this chapter, I will discuss several presentation media in detail so you can decide which media are the best choices for your content, audience, and presentation environment. I will also point out ways you can use each specific media type to its full advantage.

Electronic Presentations

Thanks to the widespread availability of presentation software and computers, particularly laptop computers, many business professionals now prepare electronic presentations. These presentations can be created in a few hours, and making last minute changes is quick and easy. If you intend to deliver the presentation on screen, you don't have to take the time to produce slides or overhead transparencies.

You can incorporate into your presentations some of the latest and greatest special effects, such as digital audio and video clips and animation, as well as motion and transition effects. You can even create self-running presentations that fit on a floppy or CD-ROM.

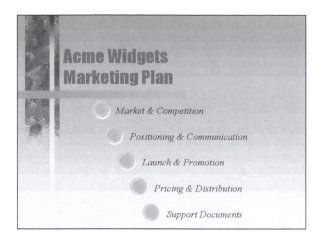

Characteristics And Qualities

The only major problem with electronic presentations—beyond the fact that making them is so simple and quick that it's easy to put the task off until the last minute—is tied to the nature of the medium itself. When your presentations are created on a computer and reside on a computer, they are susceptible to computer glitches. If the battery on the laptop or the hard disk on the desktop computer is dead, so is your presentation.

If you are making the presentation to a small group, you can seat the audience around the computer screen. For large groups, you must make sure the computer can be connected to a large display so everyone can see the presentation. Computer-capable, large-screen displays are expensive, and many conference organizers don't want to pay for the equipment rental and technicians. Before you create a computer presentation for a large group, make sure the necessary equipment and assistance will be on hand.

Your computer must also be capable of releasing the electronic presentation to the projection equipment. Some projection systems can be hooked directly to the computer and act as a giant monitor. Others require the digital information on your computer to be converted to television format. First, determine what type of large-screen equipment will be used, and then make sure your computer has the necessary adapter card or hardware to transfer data to the equipment.

Production

Unless they are the latest state-of-the art digital displays, most projection screens and computer displays offer, at best, viewing quality comparable to that of a large-screen television. Keep this in mind when you create your graphics. Here are a few guidelines to observe when creating electronic presentations:

- Use only simple graphics without a lot of intricate detail.

- Use sans serif typefaces and generous letter and word spacing.

- Use a muted background color if you want graphics to stand out. Use a solid dark-color background if you want brightly colored text to stand out.

- Use only a few colors.

If you use one computer to create the presentation and another to deliver it, run the presentation on the delivery computer several times during the creation process. That way you can make sure the presentation runs at the same speed as it does on the creation computer and catch any differences in how the presentation looks on screen.

To make colored text stand out, use a sans serif typeface against a dark background; doing so will make your presentations instantly comprehensible—or, at least, instantly readable.

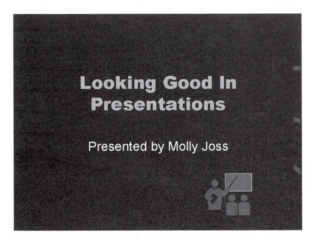

Presentation Environment

All electronic presentations are viewed on a display of some kind—a computer monitor or large-screen display. This means the presentation environment should be somewhat dark, but not so dark that it prevents note taking. A too-dark room can also lull an audience to sleep. In addition, you should arrange the screen or the lighting so no light falls directly onto the display; otherwise, part, or all, of the screen will look washed out.

If you can control the color and contrast on the display, experiment with these two settings before the presentation. Lower the lights to the level they will be during the presentation, then adjust the display to get the best balance of contrast and color. Make sure to step through the entire presentation with the new settings before making your final changes to the monitor.

If the presentation contains audio, the presentation environment should be equipped to deliver the sound from the presentation. Check the volume levels of the audio equipment before the presentation to make sure the sound is audible and the sound level is comfortable everywhere in the room.

Using The Medium

Go ahead and have some fun with electronic presentations. Find some good presentation software, learn how to use it, and then start incorporating multimedia, digital video, and audio. Be careful, though, not to overload any one presentation with special effects and thus drown out the central messages. A little whizbang is a good attention-getting device, but too much and the audience will remember little more than the bells and whistles.

You must be prepared for technological problems when using electronic presentations. Brainstorm all possible disasters and be prepared to cope with each. Take an extra battery or power cord (with extension) for your laptop. Take along a backup copy of the entire presentation (graphic and multimedia elements included), plus a copy of the software needed to run the presentation. Always take along a low-tech version of the presentation just in case all your high-tech solutions fail.

Overhead Transparencies

Overhead transparencies have long been the standard presentation medium for business and academic presentations and still have a lot to offer any presenter. They are less expensive and easier than ever to create and aren't susceptible to the technological glitches that can occur with electronic presentations.

Characteristics And Qualities

Overhead transparency presentations proceed step-by-step, with each portion of the presentation appearing on a single sheet of overhead transparency film. They can be used in a dimly lit room or in a room filled with a normal amount of light. Because each step stays on until you physically remove it, you can pace the presentation to fit each audience and can easily make eye contact with the audience during the entire presentation rather than having to fight the urge to look at the computer screen.

Although a static medium, overhead transparencies do not have to be dull. If you have access to a color laser or inkjet printer, you can make overhead transparencies with glorious color in them as easily as you can make simple black-and-white ones. Use good quality, high-resolution clip art and professional-looking charts, graphs, and text and your presentations will be anything but boring. Use color throughout the presentation unless you absolutely must use black-and-white only.

Production

If you can create a page on a computer and print it on a letter-size sheet of paper, you can output it on a sheet of transparency film. When creating overheads, remember that the background of the sheet remains clear unless you apply a color background in the presentation or page-layout software. Unless you have a high-quality (600 dpi or higher) color output device, leave the background of each sheet clear to avoid streaks appearing in the large areas of solid color.

With a clear background, you can use color and large images. Avoid filling a transparency with lines of small point size text (such as text smaller than 10 points). No matter how many times you twist the focus knob on the projector, the text will still be too small to read even for someone sitting in the front row. To check, hold the sheet at arm's length and don't squint. If you can read the text comfortably, it should be readable in all but the largest of rooms. When in doubt, use less text per sheet and larger type sizes.

The easiest way to produce a presentation on overhead transparencies is to create it on your computer and print it using either an inkjet or laser printer. Large office-supply stores and mail-order supply houses sell the overhead transparency film you need. If you don't have access to a printer, you can take the files to a local service bureau and it will print them for you. Check to make sure it can take files directly from your software. If it can't, ask what format the files must be in.

If you have a good scanner and high-quality printer, you can create a transparency using a photograph or piece of line art. Scan the image and then print it on the film. You can have a service bureau do the whole job if you don't have the equipment or expertise. Be wary of using a photograph to fill the whole sheet, as the end result may look overwhelming when projected on a large screen.

Presentation Environment

Overhead transparencies can be viewed in a wide variety of lighting conditions. Unless the room is overly bright or light is shining directly on the screen, the whole audience will be able to see the presentation easily. That makes this medium a good choice for presentations where you are not able to control the lighting.

Make sure the projector is working properly and that the screen is not twisted or wrinkled. Also, make sure the screen is large enough to be seen from the back of the room. View each transparency on the screen to make sure every element is visible. Have room near the projector for two piles of transparencies—the ones you've used during the presentation and the ones you haven't.

If you are using a microphone, try to get one that clips on your lapel rather than one you have to hold while talking. That leaves both hands free to move the transparencies around. No matter what kind of microphone you use, make sure the cord is long enough to let you stand near the projector. If not, enlist the aid of another person to flip the transparencies on your command. Finally, have an extra projector bulb on hand in case you need it before or during the presentation.

Using The Medium

If you want to include several bits of information on a single transparency, such as a question and its answer, you can cover a portion of the transparency with an opaque sheet of paper. A piece of cardboard or a file folder makes a good shield. You can also create a progressive layered effect by printing portions of a complete page on each of several transparencies. Experiment with this technique to add a dramatic or comic flare to the presentation.

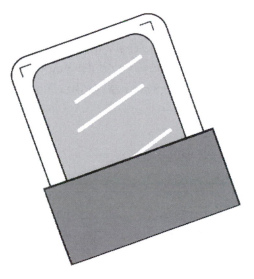

You can create companion handouts from any overhead transparency presentation by printing the presentation on plain white paper. You can add additional information to the handouts before printing and save the annotated version as a separate file. You can also omit information from the printed version and ask the audience to copy it from the overhead display to boost their attention and retention.

After you've printed the overheads, it's always a good idea to mount each sheet in cardboard or plastic mounts similar to the ones that surround slides. Office-supply or mail-order companies usually sell the mounts and some other interesting accessories such as boxes for storage. It's also a good idea to number each transparency in case an assistant will be changing the sheets during a presentation or if someone accidentally reshuffles the pages.

Before you deliver the presentation and afterward, separate each transparency with a sheet of tissue or paper to prevent them from sticking together or becoming scratched. Keep the presentation in a storage box to protect them further and to keep them in one place.

35mm Slides

Like overhead projectors, 35mm slides have been around a long time. Slides are a good way to present almost any material but are especially good for presenting high-quality color images. They are also one of the easiest kinds of presentations to create, if you leave yourself enough time to create the presentation and produce the slides. You'll need at least a few days for the slide production stage alone.

Characteristics And Qualities

Well-designed slides always look professional. They are wonderful for presenting vivid color and crisp detail, especially if you use high-quality photographic images. They are small and compact—the slides for an hour-long presentation can fit in one small box. Most companies have a slide projector handy, and slides are almost always welcome at conventions and conferences.

Slides are usually presented in a horizontal format with an aspect ratio of 3:2. To make full use of the slide image area, prepare your images in that same proportion. This is easy to do if you are using presentation software or are taking photographs using slide film.

You can also create vertical slides with the opposite aspect ratio (2:3). This is a good format to use if most of your images are tall or long and slender, such as a presentation about skyscrapers or moon rockets.

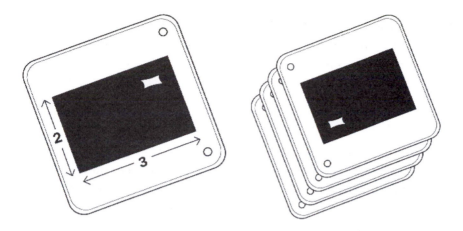

You can create slides using computer software or from photographic film. Use slide film if you know you will be creating slides directly from photographs to get the best-looking slides. You can also import scanned images and add text using your computer if you want to overlay text on an original photograph. You can create the same kind of effect using digital files of stock photography images.

Once the design of each slide is completed, the slides are imaged on film using a slide recorder. This film must be developed, and the slides must be cut apart and mounted before you can use them. Because slide recorders are expensive, only service bureaus have them. Check around for a local company that can take your digital files and turn them into slides *before* you create the first slide in your software. Ask the company what settings you need to set in your software and what kinds of digital files it needs for imaging. If you've never done a slide production before, allow a month for design and production.

If you plan to use the slides more than once, ask the production house to use glass mounts instead of paper ones. The glass mounts will protect the slides themselves from scratches and fingerprints, plus the slides won't warp over time. Store the slides in either a slide storage box or in ring binders fitted with special slide collection sheets. These sheets are made of clear plastic and have individual pockets to hold slides in place.

Presentation Environment

No doubt about it, slides are best suited for dark environments. The darker the room, the better the slides will look and the easier it will be to read the text. In a small room, try to position the projector close to the screen. In a large room that holds several hundred people, the slides may be projected from the rear of the room onto a very large screen behind the presentation area.

Because slides are best viewed in the dark and people tend to nod off in warm, dark environments, your best bet is to use only a few slides as needed and combine them with media that can be used in brighter conditions, such as overhead projections. Group the slides together in a mixed-media presentation so you don't have to alter the light levels too many times.

Your audience will quickly lose interest if your slide presentation is too long. They may also nod off if the presentation is immediately after lunch and they are in a dark room for too long.

Using The Medium

Most slide projectors use a standard tray, which means you can (and should) carry an extra tray along with you to the presentation site. Load your slides in your tray before the presentation and hand the tray with the slides in proper order to the slide projector operator. Do a few dry runs with the operator so he or she knows how to read your cues as to when to change the slides. If you can control the slides yourself using a remote control, do so. A presentation interspersed with numerous "next slide please" phrases will distract even the most interested audience member.

If you are going to operate the slide projector yourself, make sure there is a remote slide changer available and run the whole slide show through several times before the presentation. Practice moving ahead and moving back several slides in case you want to refer back to an earlier slide during the presentation.

Use the time between slides as a new slide is being loaded to your advantage. You can use it to set up the next slide or underscore a point on the previous slide. You can even make the pauses longer while you elaborate on a point. Think of the slides as a backdrop to your verbal presentation rather than as the focal point. You'll make a better presentation that way.

Carry a duplicate set of slides with you if traveling via airplane or train. Keep each set in a separate piece of luggage or send the duplicate set along with a colleague. You may never need the backup, but if your briefcase is lost, the backup will seem heaven-sent.

Web-Based Presentations

The Internet in general, and the World Wide Web in particular, have made such a profound impression upon the world over the past few years, no discussion of presentation media would be complete without information on this invaluable medium. You can create your own Web-based presentation or pay someone to do it for you. Either way, you've got a readily accessible and memorable way to get your point across.

Characteristics And Qualities

Web-based presentations can either be seen live on the Web or offline using software designed to let you view Web materials you've downloaded. Similar in kind and scope to electronic presentations, Web-based presentations can combine text, data, multimedia, audio, video, and still images.

Unlike electronic presentations, Web-based presentations can be linked to other Web sites, online databases, and other storehouses of information. They are also normally self-guided tours and can even be interactive, whereas electronic presentations are normally presented by an individual leading the way.

A Web-based presentation is usually divided into segments that can appear in several windows on screen. The viewer uses scroll bars and buttons to view text and images further. There are also buttons and "hot" areas (images with buttons hidden beneath) that allow the viewer to navigate through the site.

Web-based presentations often contain several scrollable windows of information that appear on screen simultaneously, giving the viewer several options for touring the site.

Make sure the various segments are small enough to be viewed in a few moments. Time speeds up when you're navigating the Web, and you can get bored easily. Cut the presentation up into short, yet meaty, chunks and make sure everything meshes well. In other words, when designing keep in mind that the viewer will poke around the site rather than move in a linear manner as in a guided electronic presentation.

Production

Several computer software programs are available that allow novice Web designers to create their own sites. These programs work well for modest and simple projects. For more ambitious ones, particularly those with multimedia elements, databases, and searches, it is best to turn to a seasoned professional.

As mentioned, to view a Web presentation, you have to have software (usually called browser software) that allows you to see the presentation and move around in it. Different browsers interpret text and color data differently, so one presentation may look dramatically different in various browsers. If you're making your own Web presentation, look at it in a few different browsers to spot potential problems. Better yet, make sure the company or person you hire to create the presentation does this for you and knows how to fix any problems.

Once you've completed a Web presentation, you must place it on a server connected to the Internet. You can rent space on communal servers or set up your own Internet server. If you expect the site to be visited frequently and for long periods of time, you're better off with your own server. Otherwise, renting space is a lower-cost option with less hassle.

Presentation Environment

Once you've ironed out any problems presented by various browsers, you can rest assured your Web presentation will be seen the same way by everyone who visits the site for as long as you make the presentation available. Viewing quality and speed depends on the kind of computer the viewer is using. In other words, your zippy presentation with lots of images may bog down considerably on a 486 computer with a slow modem.

Your best bet is to create a presentation that gets quickly to the heart of what you want to say without a lot of bells, whistles, and flashing animations. A simple, yet beautifully crafted Web site will communicate your points better than one that has a lot of flash and little substance.

Using The Medium

For round-the-clock, around-the-world availability nothing beats a Web-based presentation—your message is available instantly whenever someone wants to see it. That's the good news. The bad news is you aren't there with them to guide, inform, and observe. To help counter this reality, include in your Web site a way the viewer can send you a quick email note, and check that email account frequently.

That's not all you should include—put in your Web site every possible way of getting in touch with you, including your email address, mailing address, and telephone number. Although the person is using the Web to view the presentation, he or she may prefer to write or telephone you afterward rather than sending email.

The Web may be hot, but people still use the mail and the telephone. Include all contact information in your Web site. It doesn't add to your cost, and it increases your chances of hearing from the viewer.

You will want to change the content and look of your Web-based presentation frequently to attract Web surfers to stop again. If the look of the page remains the same for long, these surfers will slide right by looking for fresh material.

Posters And Flip Charts

Ordinary paper is still a wonderful and inexpensive way to communicate. Some presentations don't lend themselves to electronic wizardry or projected images, yet still require large, high-impact graphics. Posters and flip charts are great for all of these kinds of presentations.

Characteristics And Qualities

Posters, of course, are large sheets of paper that can be mounted on rigid backing materials so they can stand on their own. Flip charts are smaller individual sheets of paper held together in a binder with rings at the side or top. The larger kind usually rests on an easel, whereas tabletop flip books come with a built-in stand.

Audiences show a remarkable tolerance for viewing posters and flip charts, and are often content to sit for much longer periods of time viewing these materials than other presentation media. Posters and large flip chart sheets allow you to pack a lot of material into a single sheet, as long as you keep the image and text legible.

Production

Full-color posters can be created in less than an hour using wide-format inkjet printers. Such equipment makes it possible to create the file on your computer and output the poster in your own office. You can also take the file to a service bureau for output.

These printers turn out full-color images in a rainbow of rich, deep colors on a variety of materials, including glossy, translucent, transparent, and even canvas. There are other kinds of printers, such as electrostatic and dye-sublimation printers, that can be used to create posters.

If you want more than a few copies of a poster, check out the cost of printing the posters on a regular printing press. Even if you need only 50 or so, compare the cost with the price of running them out on an inkjet printer. You may be pleasantly surprised at the cost of offset printing in lower quantities.

Flip charts can be created from individual posters or large-format prints that you have not added a backing to. You can mix black-and-white pages with full-color pages for variety and to keep production costs as low as possible. Not every page requires full color to be effective.

To get the most professional look for your work, output the pages on a wide-format printer. Although this will add to the cost of the presentation, it looks much better than printing the large image on a series of smaller pages and taping or gluing them together into one large sheet.

Tabletop flip charts are very easy to create if you have a color printer. Buy a ready-to-use display kit from an office supply store, print your pages on letter-size paper, slide them into the slots, and you're ready to go.

Using The Medium

Use posters and flip charts in environments where other presentation media are impossible or unavailable. Depending on what your aim is and the environment, flip charts can be effective. For example, if you're visiting someone's home to make a sales pitch for a sunroom addition, a nice table-top flip chart presentation is great. They can also be a good idea if you want an understated means of delivering your message. Courtrooms, boardrooms, and even trade shows can be good places to use posters and flip charts. Intimate presentations given to two or three people are good times to use tabletop flip charts. You can add color to the inexpensive black-and-white poster or flip chart sheets yourself and add punch to your presentation at the same time by using colored markers to annotate the pages during the presentation. You can even add photographs or on-the-spot drawings to liven up the presentation.

Posters and flip-top presentations are the least technology-intensive media available for presentations. Keep that in mind if you are venturing into lands unknown and want to make sure you can always get your point across no matter what—unless you lose or damage the papers, that is.

Handouts

Some presenters make it a rule never to hand out copies of their presentations on paper. They want the audience to pay attention during the presentation and not daydream, thinking they can pick up the major points later from the handout. Others feel a presentation isn't complete without handouts. Conference attendees have been known to complain bitterly if there are no handouts—thinking they need to walk away with something tangible.

Handouts are expected at some kinds of conferences and presentations. Ask the event organizers what the standard practice is, and when in doubt, bring along some material to hand out.

To decide the matter for yourself, think about whether a set of handouts will complement your message or take away from it. A good rule of thumb is to use handouts when you want to convey a lot of information and you want the audience to have some reference material for later use. If the amount of information or data is limited, as in some sales presentations, you may not want to make the handouts available before or during the presentation, as people may pay more attention to the handouts than you. Encourage people to come to you with questions. Not using handouts allows you to move the sales process along or even close the deal more quickly.

If you do use handouts, make sure they are a complete paper-based presentation and can be used as a standalone reference. If you don't have time to create this "extra" presentation, take the time to print out your slides or overheads and hand the packet out at the beginning of your presentation so the audience can take notes on it.

Moving On

Now that you've had a good look at the equipment and various presentation media, it's time to concentrate on creating the presentation itself. In the next chapter, I will examine in detail some of the core design and layout concepts you'll need to create a winning presentation.

DESIGN AND LAYOUT 4

Design makes all the difference. It affects perception, understanding, and retention.

Design rules in the visual realms of computer monitors and projection screens. Over the past 10 years, style and content have merged into a single communications force; it's increasingly difficult for an audience to tease meaning apart from its concrete, visual realization. We rarely find ourselves approving of one while maintaining reservations about the other. Rather, we see presentations as a unit and respond to the impact of the integrated message.

In essence, design is simply a visual plan to achieve a desired goal or effect. That means everyone is a designer in one way or another. When you're putting together your presentation, you're the design director for every frame you create.

A Principled Vision

Don't be daunted by the visual world—you participate in it every day. Effective presentation layout relies on an understanding of quite simple design principles you can learn and articulate for specific projects. These skills will help you to compose attractive, informative frames and to sequence the individual units into an integrated and compelling program.

Fundamental Choices

As you arrange the basic elements on the screen, you'll make a rather terrifying number of design decisions on position, size, color, shape, and texture—all the while knitting them together with decisions about interaction of elements and their relative importance. Fortunately, understanding just a few fundamental design concepts will help you make the right choices, and give an energetic direction to the material at hand.

Something Old, Something New

Examine closely the design of an object you find especially outstanding, whether it's an espresso bar or a Miata, a poster for a jazz session or brochure for The Gap. Chances are good that an appealing place or object combines the old with the new, generating a lively interplay between them. Often, just combining familiar elements in an unexpected way can make them look fresh and memorable again. The tension created by blending traditional and innovative aspects keeps us involved and tells us something interesting about the way we perceive the world. It gives us a ground for understanding but wakes up our aesthetic sensibilities. By avoiding both the cliché and the bizarre, good design strikes exactly the right note for the audience and subject matter.

In all its varied applications, excellent design enhances our lives, combining familiar elements with an innovative eye.

Chris Potter.

The Louvre with Pei pyramids.

The Basics

Although you can organize graphic elements into an infinite number of combinations, the actual marks you can put on paper or computer displays are limited to points, lines, shapes, and letter forms. Each of these elements is associated with attributes or properties of color, size, texture, and position. Elements and their properties, specified during the design process, are the building blocks of presentation graphics.

The finished frame is nothing more than a record of many small choices, selected to sustain the overall composition. Your design's success reflects the attention you gave each decision along the way.

Focus And Contrast

We've all experienced indifferent presentation graphics—ho-hum frames that aren't ridiculously bad but leave us cold. The presenter clearly labored long and hard over them. What was missing?

Usually, dull graphics lack focus. They're missing the clarity brought with selecting one element as the most important point in the frame. When nothing is more important than anything else, or when our attention is drawn to several equally weighted elements, we're confused. We don't know where to look first.

Frames with a clear focus draw the viewer into the visual world of the information at hand. We sense that we'll be able to grasp the material, even before we begin consciously exploring it. We need direction to feel that a frame is well organized. When we look at a Rembrandt or Vermeer, we have a similar reaction: It's reassuring and Old Masterly. The elements are arranged so that they direct our eyes to a starting point, and then move us around the canvas, unfolding its story. That's a kind of narrative in itself.

Even static images can be dynamic. The artist supplies the path, and the viewers energize it, moving their attention around the canvas in a planned pattern.

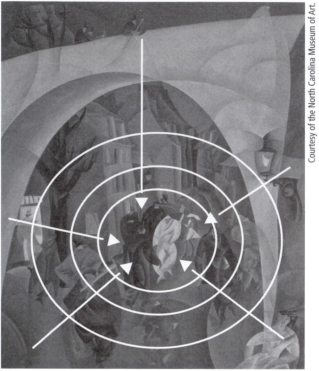

Lyonel Feininger, "The Green Bridge II," 1916.

Jan Brueghel the Elder, "Harbor Scene with St. Paul's Departure Caesarea," 1596.

Use the graphic elements at your disposal—type style, size, alignment, weight, and color, as well as design devices like rules, boxes, open space, illustrations, and photographs—to direct viewers to the single most important point. Engage the eye, moving into the rest of the frame in a smooth transition from the focal point.

Contrast is your ally in creating a focused frame. Contrast in size, color, or weight attracts the viewer's attention, but resist the urge to use all three at once! In this context, less is definitely more. Remember that contrast can be created within the context of a sequence, as well as within a single frame. Extra open space around a particular element will sharpen the contrast and heighten its importance, even without other changes. Often, the effect is obliterated when you increase size as well. Try it yourself and see.

The Idea Stage

When we see and appreciate the power of a speaker's presentation graphics, it's only natural to assume that the visual concept arrived somehow with the content, a package dropped out of the clear blue. The designer must have known exactly what to do at the outset of the project.

Too bad that's rarely the case. Well-made images look so finished, it's hard to imagine that other solutions were considered and rejected before a satisfactory constellation of elements and attributes was found. Relax. Almost no one, not even the experts, can arrive at the perfect design solution without some trial and error. In fact, it's the exploration of design ideas that will reveal much of the character of the presentation to you. Learning by doing—that's what keeps this work interesting.

As you generate ideas for your presentation, remember your objectives (Chapter 2) and consider each idea with them in mind. If you want to generate excitement about a new product, will this overall design help convey the sense of innovation? On the other hand, if your objectives require an aura of security, will the visual design enhance the calm and steady feeling of reliability? Work from your content outline, visualizing different ways to present particular points. Experiment; develop several alternative approaches. Evaluation and selection will come later. Don't try to get from start to finish in one giant step. Instead, just let the ideas flow and see where they take you.

Thumbnail Sketches

Although rendering your graphics on the computer is much easier than with traditional methods, sketching the initial designs is not. Computer images look too finished to have that experimental feeling, and you might find yourself accepting a design you don't like simply because it looks "done."

Instead, start experimenting by making thumbnail sketches. These are simple, small-scale pencil drawings set down quickly—usually on tissue paper so they can be copied and varied easily.

It's not necessary to write out all the words on your sketches. In fact, it's preferable that they remain impressionistic, showing the organization of space in the frame. With a few simple strokes, indicate where type will be placed and the approximate relative size you expect to use. Similarly, block out graph areas, artwork, and photographs in basic shapes and lines. The overall relationships between text and graphic elements are most important at this stage. Your goal is to establish a harmonious underlying framework that will work for all of the types of information in your presentation.

Begin by making thumbnail sketches to help you visualize the concepts and explore options for translating ideas into organized frames.

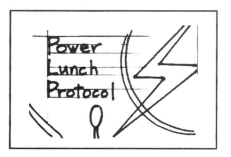

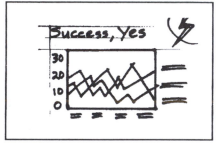

Think with your pencil. The main purpose of this step is to get a sense of how the graphics might look, translating the vision in your mind's eye onto paper so you can evaluate and revise. Sketch out several types of frames you'll want to include in your presentation to see if the overall layout will work with all your material.

It may surprise you that even the best hardware system and the most flexible software in the world can't replace pencil and paper at this beginning stage. You don't need training in studio art to jot down a few simple elements—visual notes. Don't worry if your concept sketches aren't masterpieces—they're not supposed to be! Finished art comes later in the game, when you can bring in the big computerized guns.

Storyboards

The storyboard is a visual and verbal outline of your presentation. A helpful tool for both your own use and for others who might need to evaluate your plans or offer their input, the storyboard shows the underlying structure of the presentation in frame-by-frame sequence. Titles and illustrations are consistently sized and placed; relative type size and line-length patterns can be indicated.

A storyboard will help you evaluate the structure, development, and impact of your presentation-in-the-making.

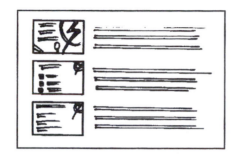

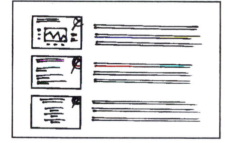

The storyboard answers many structural questions. True to its name, it asks you to provide a beginning, middle, and end—a premise, justification or denouement, and conclusion. It pinpoints the areas you will need to amplify, and the places where one frame should be split into two or more. How will you indicate major shifts in emphasis and keep your audience oriented? The storyboard lets you experiment with techniques for accomplishing these essential tasks. Is the presentation nicely balanced with the right number of frames for each point, based on its importance and complexity? If you're tempted to dwell on one small point too long, it will be revealed in the storyboard, allowing you to escape unscathed.

Use your thumbnails to sketch out the storyboard. This rough paper draft will provide a check for continuity, allowing you to adjust sequencing, insert frames, or delete repetitions.

STORYBOARDS AND SOFTWARE

If you have a storyboard option on your software system, ignore it in these early stages. Its forte is establishing continuity during the production phase. Save this feature to check your sequences as you develop them, and to revise by shifting sections or individual frames to different positions in the presentation.

Design For The Medium

Each of the presentation media discussed in Chapter 3 brings its own inherent qualities and properties to the project—that's why it's so important to identify your medium early in the conceptualization process. For example, sometimes a major project like an interactive kiosk might begin life as a computer-based presentation that can be tested with a variety of audiences; it will save a lot of time if it's planned that way from the outset. Design with your medium's particular characteristics firmly in mind and you'll realize the greatest return on your efforts. Although the basic graphic elements are the same for all media, their applications are quite different. And be sure to keep in mind a fundamental difference that separates many presentations from print media: presentations are often team players rather than standalone components; they're meant to accompany and reinforce live delivery.

The physical characteristics of each presentation medium are different. Check your orientation—horizontal or vertical—and the aspect ratio, or the relationship between the width and height of the image. Maintain the same orientation throughout a presentation, or you'll destroy design continuity and risk severe projection problems. Proportion your art to match the aspect ratio required by the medium.

When you use the same artwork for more than one presentation medium or carry it over into the print world, differences in aspect ratio can give you some headaches. On one hand, it's delightful and efficient to create a complicated drawing or diagram once and then use it in a multitude of applications, importing and incorporating it into various files. On the other hand, you must design carefully at all stages to preserve the integrity of the image. When you make artwork serve two media, plan the design primarily for the more important use.

Let's say you're planning to tour the country with both an electronic presentation and a take-home report on organic coffee. Design the time-consuming diagram of an organic coffee plantation to fit your 4:3 horizontal format for the presentation, because it's more vital to your success on tour. Then adjust the design to make the best use of the more vertical space in the $8^1/_2 \times 11$-inch report—or consider moving away from standard print sizes. A third option would be to design the graphic to fit into a window in each medium, planning to use the "extra" horizontal or vertical space for other design elements. On the other hand, it's best to design for the page layout first if you're just going to make a few overheads of illustrations from a brochure, using them to review information with a group that will refer frequently to the printed piece.

Printed pages frequently work best with black type and colorful images on a white background; projected images are more effective with light type and artwork on a dark background. When you incorporate artwork from a presentation into a printed page, try shifting the color palette while you're adjusting the aspect ration before exporting the image.

Layout Decisions

Your audience will never see your most important design tool, and probably they won't even be aware that you've used it. But they'll be very cognizant of the results: clear and organized presentation frames. This mystery ally is the grid, the layout structure on which all your decisions about sizing and placement of various elements depend.

Grounding In Gridwork

Early in the design process, establish the grid that will underlie each frame in your presentation. This pattern, like coarse graph paper superimposed on the image area, does more than any other tool to make your show a coherent whole. It establishes a coordinated use of open space to offset graphic elements, and it provides the greatest impact for contrast.

Use grid blocks to establish a consistent structure for your layout—the simpler the elements of the show, the simpler the grids.

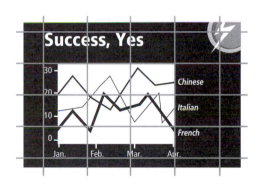

Simple shows need only a few grid marks to structure their basic elements; larger and more complicated projects call for more complex tools. Horizontal and vertical grid lines and their intersections give you spatial anchors for positioning headings, text, bullet lists, graphs, illustrations, and photographs. The more elements you plan to use, the more detailed your grid must be.

The grid establishes a frame's working area, inside the safety zone of margins. These outside border areas ensure that no important content will be lost to poorly projected edges; on the other hand, allowing nonessential artwork to bleed through the margins to the very edge of the frame can be dynamic, opening up the presentation.

Suppose you're designing a simple, brief, and informative meeting presentation, and you plan to follow a title frame with six bullet lists. Your grid will help you plan the size and placement of three kinds of elements: the main title, the heading for each bullet list, and the bullet items themselves. With the finer points of layout in mind, you will also consider the underlying grid when establishing standard spacing between lines of type and between bulleted items, as well as the distance from a bullet to the first word of each line. If you want to add a chart or diagram, or a window for a video clip, look to the grid for guidance in positioning. Although the title frame may be the only one of its kind, design it on the same grid pattern as the text to incorporate it into the structure of the show. That way, it won't look radically different, like an orphan from another presentation.

Staying with the same basic grid structure for each frame in your presentation creates an underlying visual pattern that ties everything together.

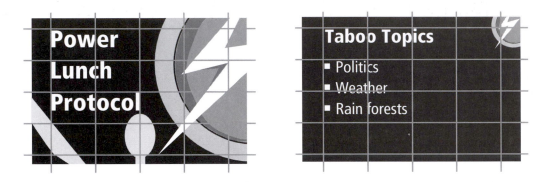

It's amazing how a grid can revise the haphazard placement of various elements into a forceful, consistent organization. It works by concentrating open space, rather than dispersing it around the frame. This creates an interesting tension between this negative space and the full space of type or artwork.

Alignment

The alignment scheme you choose for each presentation dictates whether the elements in your frames will line up along a left-hand margin or grid line, along a right-hand margin or grid line, or smack in the center. A consistent vertical alignment scheme contributes to unity and continuity. It sets up a clear pattern to help the viewer find information in each frame and so creates a sense of clarity in the graphics.

Keep your vertical alignment pattern consistent—whether it's left, centered, or right—to give your presentation continuity.

Flush-Left

Because it's the type of vertical organization with which we're most familiar, a flush-left, ragged-right alignment scheme seems natural and easy to follow. It allows our eyes to find the beginning of each line quite easily. Because type and other elements line up along the left-hand margin, or flush-left along another grid line, the elements appear crisp, blocked with a clean left edge.

The "ragged" right edge results from naturally varying line lengths. Our eyes are accustomed to following text with a consistent left-hand starting point in everything from business letters to phone books. Reading type set with this alignment requires much less effort to follow the lines back and forth. Try a flush-left style first; when moving away from this organization, be sure you have a clear reason to depart from convention.

Your grid will stand you in good stead with flush-left alignment. You need not design frames that require each text block to start at the same vertical axis. Instead, use your grid to define a series of vertical axes that you can use for the left alignment of headings, subheads, text or bullet lists, charts, tables, artwork, attribution lines, and other elements.

The strength of flush-left alignment is its establishment of a solid visual anchor for the viewer. The softer ragged-right edge keeps the frame from becoming too evenly balanced, static, and boring. It also allows you to avoid hyphenation in most cases. It's easy to lay out and to read, making it an excellent choice for most presentation graphics.

Centered

It can be tempting to center lines over one another or over other elements like illustrations and charts. The alignment style makes both the left and right edges of the type ragged, with the axis in the middle. Although this may seem likely to convey a classical balance, it must be handled with great care to avoid awkward, indecisive layouts. There is no strong vertical stroke defined by center-aligned elements. Think of the traditional wedding invitation: it's hard to create effective contrast and emphasis, because each line tends to have equal visual weight unless it's surrounded by additional open space. The cushion of white space above and below the centered type allows your eye to discern the line as a unit, and then move down the card to the next line.

The most formal and conservative alignment format for elements like headings, centering is a safe choice, but not often interesting. Without a distinct visual anchor within the frame, it can be hard to read more than a line or two of type. The left and right edges aren't well defined, and odd-shaped areas of negative space are created. Another difficulty occurs when centering headings over a bullet list or other text. Unless all the bullet points are consistent in length, the centered heading can appear oddly positioned above them. Try out a flush-left alignment alternative on one or two frames of any presentation you're considering centering, just to see the difference.

Flush-Right

The mirror image of flush-left alignment, a flush-right layout forces lines of type and other elements against a right-hand margin or grid line. Legibility is affected by the ragged-left edge, because eye-tracking from one line to the next becomes more difficult. As with centered type, increasing the space between lines can help overcome this difficulty. Still, as a general rule, align type flush-right only when you want to create a strong visual effect with relatively few lines of type. Align graphics and illustrations flush-right only when you have already established a strong right vertical stroke from which to work.

Justification

When type is justified, the lines are flush along both edges. Newspaper columns are a prime example of justification. This technique doesn't work well with presentation graphics, because presentations require larger sizes of type, shorter line lengths, and fewer words than newspapers. Because text justification divides the space left in the line after the last word into equal increments and inserts it between every word on the line, justifying text can create gaps throughout your presentation. When there are only a few words, the extra space makes very odd patterns from line to line and breaks up the even flow of text. Your copy suddenly looks like it's written in a foreign language with a lot of extremely long words.

If you've followed earlier advice and condensed your message into key words, your graphics won't have enough type to warrant a justified alignment. Flush-left, flush-right, or centered alignment will produce more attractive and readable frames.

Even on page layouts, justified columns look best when the line length and type size are carefully matched. Many print designers are moving away from justified columns because they look more mechanical and less compelling that a flush-left layout. The inconsistent word spacing from line to line may also make justified columns more difficult to read.

Organic Layout

Occasionally it's refreshing and rewarding to break out of the established grid and position type and other graphic elements according to some internal logic or pattern indicated by the elements themselves. The organic approach can be applied much more effectively to one or two graphics, rather than to an entire series of frames. Beware of first impressions, however: admirable frames that appear to be organically organized frequently turn out—on closer examination—to be based on an underlying grid structure.

Following the irregular edge of a particularly dramatic drawing can tie type and illustration together. Diagonals represent another strong source of dynamic energy for organic alignments. If you suspect an organic layout would work with one of your frames, sketch and experiment until you find an arrangement that pleases you with its informal balance; there are few rules to follow beyond working with the natural movement of the eye from top to bottom and left to right and remembering to work off the grid you've established for the other frames in the presentation. Usually you can maintain some of the formatting you've set up in the show—heading and subhead, for example—while combining the rest of the text and artwork in a more organic manner.

Occasionally an organic layout can be striking, but it's tricky to find the right informal balance in each frame.

As you watch other presentations and analyze their fundamental layouts, you may notice some that mix alignment styles. Sometimes headings are centered in the frame, whereas labels for graphs or tables are placed flush-left. This can work when the graphs, text, or tables define a space for the centering; otherwise, they will leave the centered heading floating, without context. Some designers even incorporate use of three axes—flush-left, centered, and flush-right—to good effect; the results depend a great deal on the content and the particular elements in the frame. Remember that you don't want to set up a format that you can't follow from frame to frame, causing wild readjustment on the screen. The only way you'll know how the more experimental types of layout will look is to go ahead and try them. But do yourself a favor by sketching them out very quickly first!

Experiment with layout variations that mix vertical axes—all tied to your grid structure, of course!

Units Of Measure

Many software programs offer a variety of measurement systems, but presentation software is often limited to its own measurement system, based roughly on screen inches but influenced by monitor resolution and zoom controls on frame size. Inches are familiar and comfortable to most of us. You've probably been using rulers with eighths and quarters of inches since grade school, so that's good for a simple layout when you'll just need to check positions quickly. On the other hand, when you're implementing a fairly complex grid, it's helpful to express your alignment columns in decimal inches so you can size and scale with a calculator.

People who work extensively with type use points and picas (Chapter 5 offers more detail on typographic terms) for all measurements, including the page width and depth, grid dimensions, and margin widths. Some programs use only their own measurement systems based on rasters or pixels, which are proportionate rather than fixed units. It takes a while to adjust to these increments, but they will become more intuitive with persistence.

Integration And Continuity

To construct a design structure that will work for your whole presentation, list all the various components that will appear in any frame, so you can give each kind of element a uniform graphic treatment. For example, almost every slide will have a heading, so that's a start. Will some frames need subtitles? How about a corporate, product, or project logo? If the images include illustrations, photographs, and video clips, can you size and position them consistently in the frame? Could you group several smaller images to fit the same space as a large one, allowing more options for flexibility? Consider quartering the illustration space for graphics that each show a detail, or building a gridwork of close-up photos.

How will the main title frame of the presentation relate to section titles throughout the show? Should they receive similar visual treatment? How can these "guidepost" graphics work as a unit to help viewers understand the structure and pacing of the show?

Will it be possible to design all the charts, graphs, photos, and video windows in your presentation so they can be sized similarly and placed into the same area of the frame? By keeping the layout treatments consistent, you'll be able to integrate all the different ideas and information into a visually coherent presentation.

As you integrate the graphic components of each frame, strive for a visually coherent presentation. The key to this endeavor is establishing an underlying organization of space.

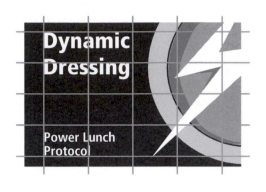

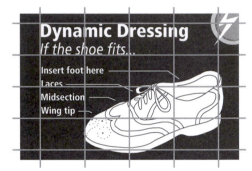

Despite all your efforts, you may be confronted with one or two oddball frames that resist your overall layout plan. If you must make exceptions in frame design, do it subtly. Carry over the most obvious visual properties of the common structure—color palette, type size and type style, heading placement, and alignment. That way, this frame will offer less of a break with continuity and slip more easily into the rest of the pack.

Suppose your show will be composed of bullet lists and bar graphs, except for one pie graph. How can you integrate that round shape with its scattering of labels into frames designed for strong verticals? See if it works to use the left-edge location of your bar graphs to align a callout list of pie labels. That visual reference will probably give you enough rope to catch the maverick frame.

If all your images start to seem like renegades, however, it's time to reevaluate your structure and devise a more graceful graphic plan that will allow for continuity between frames. You may need to go even further back and rethink the content and the points you want to convey at each step.

Use your creative ability, grid, and continuity elements to integrate a "maverick" into your frame series.

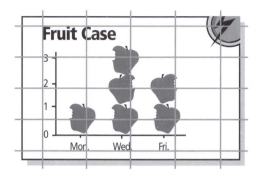
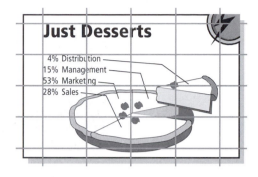

Graphic Design Devices

As you establish the overall design of your presentation, you'll find it helpful to review your arsenal of basic graphic devices: rules, borders, boxes, and open space. These big guns organize frames by separating elements and directing the viewer's attention. They become part of the layout of each frame and should be used sparingly and consistently.

Below, you see too many visual trends without reference to content (left) and a much more balanced approach (right).

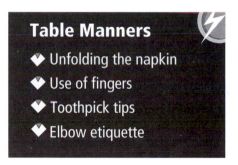

Refrain from adding merely decorative applications of these devices, which will clutter the frame and interfere with understanding—the graphic equivalent of too much icing and not enough cake. Decree your own rules for their use and follow them. If headings will always be underscored by a rule of a set width and length, placed in the same way against your grid mark and dropped a certain amount below the heading baseline, stick to your guns. Don't drop the rule in a particular frame because it interferes with a chart. Instead, adjust the chart, or shift the position of the rule on each frame. Fine-tune the whole show to make the frames work smoothly together.

Rules

We have been laying down the law, but by rules, we don't mean the guidelines that you follow here. We're talking about rules that you draw—horizontal and vertical lines. These types of rules can clarify and organize frames consistently throughout a presentation, especially when space is frequently tight. Rules are quite adaptable: draw them across the whole frame, or just between certain points in your grid; choose from a whole constellation of widths, textures, and colors to support your type, artwork, and theme.

Although rules function well in distinguishing one category of information from another, they're not as effective as you might think in creating visual emphasis. We tend to anticipate that underlining will bring a point to the viewer's attention, but sometimes the extra clutter has just the opposite result, repelling the eye. Try changing the type color or weight rather than adding a rule where it's not necessary.

Traditionally, rules are measured in printers' points (72 points to the inch). Your program may allow you to select weights from the thinnest hairline to a hefty 18-point rule that measures about a quarter-inch. Begin with rules on the lighter end of this spectrum, between .5 and 2.5 points. When rules are set in a bright accent color against a dark background, even a very fine line will "pop." Thicker rules need less contrast with the background to be effective.

When you come right down to it, rules are really a variant of the rectangle; therefore, when you want to fill the rule with a neat texture, graduated color, or other special effect, consider making it from a very thin rectangular shape.

Borders

Like rules, borders act as separators; however, because they enclose on four sides rather than simply one, their impact is even greater. Borders convey the unmistakable message that whatever is inside them doesn't belong with what's outside. Your job is to use this discriminatory quality to your advantage. Depending on the specific graphic treatment you give them, borders can create a range of effects, from delicate picket fences to thick stone walls with razor wire coiled along the top.

Presentation graphics rarely benefit from a border around the whole frame. Projected images define their own space very well without extra help, and screens are already framed and bordered by the monitor's hardware. You're eating up valuable landscape and crowding all your other elements together when you insist on a full border. Challenge yourself to find ways to open up the frame—to make it expand rather than shrink.

Borders tend to separate more than they emphasize. Check out other ways to set up a visual structure and focus.

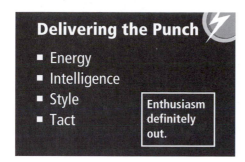

When a particular statement is boxed in by a border, it's emphasized less than we might expect. Extensive framing can decrease impact by cluttering the visual field, so use subtle contrasts and unobtrusive graphic techniques to keep the frame clean. Try using a fill color in low contrast to the background, as described below, and no box rule at all. Compare this effect with a sharply drawn bordering outline and consider which best accomplishes your purposes.

As you attend meetings and conferences, develop your awareness of presentation clichés. Make a mental list of overused effects to avoid, like radius corners on borders, ornate line patterns, and several bordered items in a single frame.

Boxes

A solid-color or subtly textured box, set against the background, offers a good alternative to a border. No outline box rule is necessary in most cases. One of your primary goals is to enhance the text—not fight with it for the viewer's attention. If the box and background colors are close in value, the low-contrast definition of the enclosed space can be pleasantly soft and subtle, yet still do a good job of setting off the content.

Low-contrast boxes enclose and set off an element of the frame without cluttering the foreground.

BOXES THAT FOCUS

Low contrast between box and background is especially good for slides and screen shows, where color is rich and definition is crisp. When projecting electronic images from a pad, or whenever your conditions may be less than ideal, test out these subtle contrasts in similar delivery situations to be sure they continue to be visible.

Be careful when setting gray boxes behind type or other delicate graphic elements when the final frame will be laser-printed. Laser printers use screened patterns of black dots to simulate gray. When you overprint black type on this dot pattern, it may be difficult for the printer to maintain the necessary contrast. Dark grays work best with type reversed to white; light grays usually are able to support black type. Color inkjet printers are also liable to create some effects you might not anticipate from the way your work looks on the computer monitor. Screened dots tend to clump raggedly at the edges of the letter forms and the type won't appear as sharp as it would with a solid black-and-white contrast.

Open Space

From the time you could first hold a crayon, you discovered that making pictures is a matter of marking on surfaces. You probably described your pictures in terms of the marks you'd applied to the surface of the paper—the positive elements. You might not have thought much about the areas of the paper that had no marks at all—the negative elements. These open or blank areas are actually integral parts of the whole image.

When we see three lines of type together, evenly spaced and consistently sized, we naturally assume that they form a single statement. If the third line is pulled down, away from the other two, the relationship changes. The only difference between the two frames is in the use of space, but the effect is profound. The amount of space that separates the elements can vary in degree and effect from a subtle addition to an exaggerated gulf; in both cases, open space emphasizes and draws attention.

Negative space can produce a profound impact.

It may seem contrary that open space will direct the viewer's attention, because we're more accustomed to *adding* marks to clarify a message. When we highlight a sentence in an article, we make it easier to find again. Presentation graphics work differently. Each frame is a canvas. Instead of loading the live area with arrows, lines, borders, and boxes, remove all extraneous elements and simply make small adjustments to the size and placement of the remaining essential elements.

On the top of the facing page, you see how extraneous elements (left) crowd the message. Clean images (right) cut to the chase.

You might take it as a warning sign if your frames are generally so tight that you must rely on rules and borders. They're probably getting overloaded with information and trying to convey too much at once. Try spreading the content over more frames. Be generous with the materials you need to get the job done. You can move through four succinct frames as quickly as one that's complicated, and your audience will enjoy the pace as well as the sense of clarity.

Motion And Animation

Electronic presentations—from simple programs to multilayered Web sites—offer designers the fantastic—and diverting—tool of motion effects. Movement and change in an otherwise static environment really grabs attention. On the other hand, you need substantial, organized graphics on which to focus all that attention. In other words, motion is an enhancement, not a substitute for the hard work we've been talking about here. You can give an animation party where everybody has fun, but nobody will go home any wiser.

First, allow your audience a chance to become oriented to the frame before the motion begins. They'll miss the point if they can't catch the headings and main ideas before the bars start to grow or the flame transforms into a phoenix.

Because of the power that the idea of transformation holds over our psyches—from the Greek myths forward—you can engage your audience in a process with animation. Concentrate doubly hard on focus and reserve movement for the central ideas or concepts of the sequence. Don't allow this device to turn counterproductive just because it's new and cool. If you find a canned effect that you want to use, be sure it's on target. Plan and justify each effect, then orchestrate the presentation with movement for emphasis within frames and for maintaining continuity between frames.

Ground Relationships

Whether they're electronic media or overheads, presentation graphics are by their very nature flat and two-dimensional. An oil painting, by contrast, can create much more physical depth simply by layers of paint and by impasto techniques that show palette knife or brush strokes. Nonetheless, a sense of depth, order, and back-to-front definition can be extremely important to a presentation. You can achieve this trompe l'oeil by using tools like color, value, hidden lines, shadows, transparency, and perspective drawing.

Think of your frame composition in three levels of depth: foreground, midground, and background. The differences between the figures and ground, or figures and field, form the basis for the relationships between these three levels.

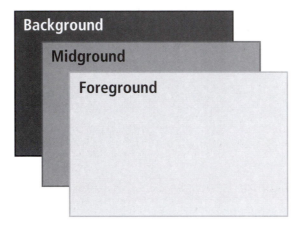

Unlike most of the other techniques for organizing graphics within a frame, the tools that establish figure and ground relationships may work in concert. There's no need to limit your choices; in fact, a combination of attributes is often an excellent solution.

Color

Color suggests distance to our eyes. Position cooler colors like blue behind the subject, and warmer colors like yellows, oranges, and reds in the foreground materials. The cool colors tend to recede; warm colors seem to approach. A world elevation map is a good case in point: lowlands are represented in deep green, with the highest mountain peaks in red. The graduated spectrum of colors between green and red indicates intermediary elevations. This color scheme creates the illusion of bringing the Himalayan peaks much closer to the viewer than low-lying deltas and valleys. The only reason the progression doesn't start with blue, the coolest color, for the lowlands is that cartographers usually reserve blue for bodies of water—coincidentally where the land falls below sea level.

In a monochrome palette, a progression from dark to light suggests movement from far to near. An object viewed at a distance naturally looks darker than the same object seen at close range. When you want to emphasize depth, assign lighter colors to foreground elements and darker colors to the midground. Be sure your up-front colors are full-strength and saturated; colors for the mid- and background can be toned down with the addition of gray tones. That's how we actually experience color in space.

If you want to explore this idea more, take a look at paintings from the Italian Renaissance, like Leonardo's *Annunciation*. Tiled floors or ceilings were often included to establish a sense of perspective. Notice how they change in color as well as shape. The portrayal of depth—way back to a tiny, distant landscape—was a key element in these tableaux.

Opacity And Transparency

A clever way to define or imply relative distance is to hide some of the midground behind opaque foreground elements, revealing only a portion of the midground object's shape.

Below, opaque foreground images (left) block whatever lies behind them. Transparent images (right) reveal the presence of the objects they cover.

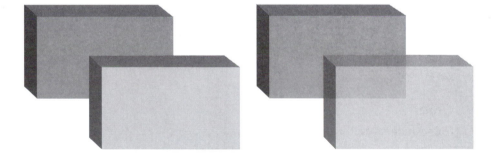

Semitransparent foreground objects create veil-like effects that demonstrate layering even more clearly but can become confusing if the viewer has to deal with a number of objects or sort out too many layers quickly. In presentations, your objective is usually to create a clear hierarchy of importance, rather than to play with our perceptions of order, a la Escher.

Shadows

A standard in the personal computer world, shadowing is an extremely useful technique for generating dimension. Shadows must be cast in a consistent manner in order to be effective, and they must really look like shadows—not duplicate images.

Imagine a light source that's shining onto the frame from a position close to the front corner of the monitor. Foreground objects catch the light and cast darker shadows on objects lying behind them. You can see and manipulate this to good effect in many presentation programs, as long as you remember that the function of shadows on foreground objects is to bring them closer to the viewer and to separate them from the background.

Shadows can be drawn as either flat areas or using a perspective technique. The flat variety, drop shadows, imply that foreground objects are floating above a flat background plane. They work best when offset very slightly from the objects or type they shadow; you may find that standard offsets are too confusing for titles and text, so feel free to adjust them. Outrageous drop shadows, especially those with fuzzy edges, have become something of a visual cliché and can produce more problems than they solve for the viewer. They should be hardly noticeable—working to enhance legibility and bring objects to the fore without calling attention to themselves. Here, too, less is better.

Each shadowing style creates a different effect. Below, notice that flat drop shadows (top) float objects over a plane, 3D shadows (left) imply volume, and graduated shadows (right) provide a convincing "stand-up" illusion.

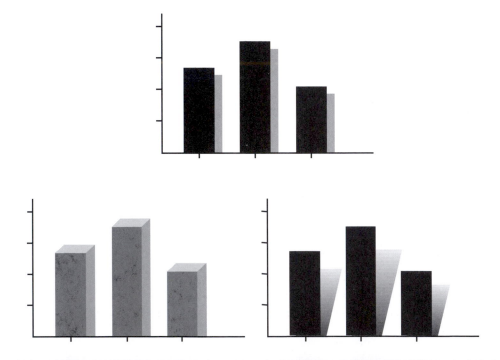

Three-dimensional shadows are drawn in perspective to suggest shapes with volumes and flat planes at angles to one another. Many programs create these shapes automatically and allow you to adjust their depth and angle. By now, you already know what's coming: adjust for the effect that gives you the substantiality you want without shouting about technique.

Graduated shadows can successfully re-create the effect of light patterns cast by real objects. They take a bit of effort in drawing, however. The angle of graduation must be carefully calculated, as it's critical to the success of the illustration.

Perspective

Perspective techniques can be applied to presentation graphics, creating the illusion that elements occupy different planes in space. Frequently, drawing tools are able to give you the shapes you need, as long as you're clear on the frame-wide plan for perspective. It helps to sketch this out quickly with pencil and paper before beginning your computer rendering.

Below, you can see that parallel projection (left) provides a simple sense of three dimensions. One-point perspective (right) draws the eye to a vanishing point.

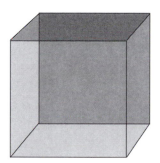 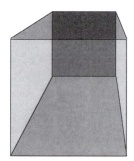

Simple parallel projection is probably the easiest method with the greatest relevance for presentation graphics. Occasionally, one-point perspective comes in handy, for situations like a pattern that disappears into the background. Consider whether this vanishing-point technique is too elaborate for your information graphics, however. Highly detailed perspective illustrations simply aren't necessary for most presentations. Concentrate on your original objectives, and render them with the techniques that support them most directly.

Restraint: Say It Again!

Most audiences sincerely appreciate graphic simplicity, which helps them concentrate on the message. People decide to attend a presentation because they want to reach a new understanding of the topic, not to be wowed by fancy pictures.

Software programs are loaded with features that can seduce you into graphic overload. The vast array of color choices and graphing formats, for instance, makes it tempting to go wild and use more features than necessary to get your point across. Reserve these tools for the times when you really need them, not for each and every frame. Developing a truly effective and memorable design style is a highly selective process. Just because you have the capabilities for unlimited typefaces, shadows, patterns, decorated corners, borders, and tapered lines does not mean they'll contribute to your communication.

For instance, graphic overload (left) can lead to indigestion. Effective communication (right) promotes action after an enjoyable meal.

To test for graphic overload, stand back and start paring down the visual effects. If you can remove anything without sacrificing content or clarity, keep going!

Moving On

Good graphic design is invisible. Well-made images are never contrived or forced. They call attention to the focal point of the content rather than to themselves. They serve simply to convey the message without distractions, but with enjoyable style. In fact, the better you do your job as a designer, the less your audience will be conscious of your craft and skill. Practice a light touch.

The next chapter looks at typography. Typefaces and type styles are important graphic elements; your choices can make or break the effectiveness of your design. Now that you have lines of type roughed in and positioned on a grid, go ahead and give your thumbnail sketches their final form.

UNDERSTANDING 5 TYPE

Words—to identify, list, label, and clarify— are a staple of presentation graphics. Knowing how to design with type is equivalent to knowing how to chop vegetables— you can't make a balanced presentation without it.

Almost every frame of a presentation makes its point with text or numbers. When you create a presentation, it's inevitable that you'll need to manage type. Envision yourself as a typographic designer, structuring your message through type choices.

An overwhelming proportion—something in the neighborhood of 75 percent—of presentation graphics relies on type exclusively: bullet lists, tables, key phrases, and titles. Even frames that are primarily graphic—charts, diagrams, photographs, and illustrations—would be meaningless without type for titles and labels.

Carriers Of Content And Style

Words and numbers carry the message; they're absolutely fundamental to your presentation. The more you understand about typographic design, the more effectively you'll be able to harness the tremendous, vital power of the word. In a presentation, the word is more than a set of meanings—it's also a visual element. Good design allows the meanings to surface effortlessly, through the visuals, as the viewer peruses the frame. Choose your typefaces and styles wisely, and you'll set a flawless tone for the entire presentation, supporting both the content and the design concept. In this best case, you, as a designer, can fuse form and function into a single, powerful element.

Type Talks

Typefaces differ radically in detail, and yet we're able to recognize and read each letter immediately in all but the most far-fetched designs. As we decode the type, abstracting the basic form, we receive subtle design messages. Our reactions to the presentation as a whole are influenced by details like the relative sizes of the letters, how tightly the lines of type are packed together, what weight and force the letterforms carry, and whether the strokes get thinner as they round curves. We notice if the lowercase letters are nearly as tall as the capitals, and whether the individual letters look round and fat or thin and spindly. Our eyes take in the delicate cross strokes that finish some letters. Most important, we respond to legibility: how easily can we read this type? How much of the total effort we're willing to expend on this frame goes into simply reading the words—before we even start to grapple with their meaning? Is the face easy and familiar, or slightly challenging but interesting, or has it crossed over into the hackneyed and cliched?

In this chapter, we'll explore typographic terminology and basics, the main categories of typefaces, rules of thumb for their effective use, and the fundamental reasons behind those rules.

Setting Type Is Not Typing

Because most presentation programs use proportional typefaces, you should follow the rules professional typesetters observe. These will give your presentation typography a distinctive polish and keep it from looking amateurish.

Real Characters

The most important typographic differences are the use of special characters, especially for certain punctuation marks. Set your program preferences for *curly*, or *smart*, apostrophes and opening or closing quotation marks. The long *em* (—) and shorter *en* dashes (–), and ellipsis marks (…) can be accessed through special keystroke combinations: Option+*keystrokes* on the Macintosh, and Alt+*keystrokes* or *ASCII code* on the IBM platform.

Always, always single-space after a period or colon. Rather than indenting the second and third lines of a single entry, work with extra between-line spacing to separate two or more ideas. Instead of relying on default tabs, manually set the space between a bullet and the left edge of the text that follows to give it just the right amount of breathing room. True fractions can be difficult to set correctly in presentation programs, but you can usually specify a smaller type for them.

Type Terminology

Typography has been a profession since Gutenberg, and it has developed its own rather arcane vocabulary. In order to understand the ways type can enhance your message, it's important to grasp an overview of the world of letterforms and characters.

Typefaces

A typeface interprets the 26 letters of the alphabet, 10 numerals, and punctuation marks with a particular style and an individual set of design rules. The "face" originally referred to the printing surface of metal type. Hundreds of electronic versions of traditional and newly developed typefaces are available. Each one has design strengths and weaknesses; no single face can work for every presentation situation. One face might make efficient use of space; another was created for legibility and to prevent eye strain. Faces that create clear, precise labels might be very boring as bullet lists. Each type family has characteristic strengths: Some faces are crafted especially for certain papers and inks, and others work best in long, dense documents. Each character has its own anatomy.

SCANNING FOR GREAT TYPE

A good way to learn about typography is to examine a pleasing brochure or annual report that seems especially attractive typographically. Have the typographer's choices in subtle areas like special characters and quotation marks made a difference in your perceptions? What else helped create the positive impression: type size, line spacing, open space, relationship between type and art or photography? Keep your eyes open when you find something that suits your sense of style, and examine closely how type is handled.

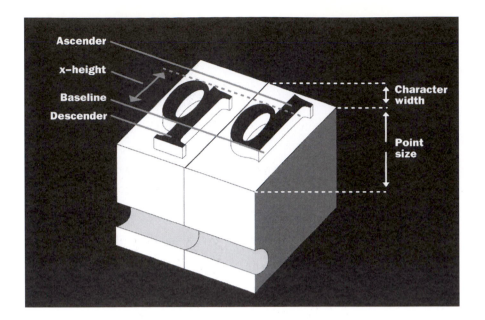

Most typefaces were designed in their first incarnation for the printed page, so we must reevaluate them for presentation media. As a first step toward understanding the vast array of faces available for our choice, we'll group them into general categories and families. Once you recognize typographic guideposts, the journey farther down the road isn't difficult at all—in fact, it's a trip through a varied and fascinating landscape.

Serif Faces

Serifs are the small finishing strokes at the ends of the main character stems. Originally, they were developed to tidy up the rough appearance of letters chiseled into stone. They also emphasize the baseline of a line of type, flaring consistently toward it. This small detail is a tremendous help in keeping the reader's eye on the right line of dense text. In handset metal or wooden type, serifs played an important functional role, bracing the thin letter strokes to keep them from breaking under the tremendous force exerted by early printing presses. One strength of serif type is the ease with which our eyes follow the line.

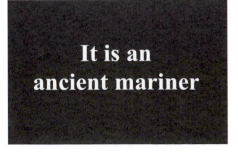

These days we choose serif type because it's easy to read in quantity—newspapers and books are usually set in one serif face or another—and because it's useful for creating certain effects. If you have a presentation that requires your audience to concentrate quite hard on rather dense type, for instance, you may consider a serif face to help establish a baseline and draw the reader's eye along it. Serifs can also play an important role in creating an atmosphere of stable, traditional, trustworthy graphics.

Serif faces can be classified further, according to their place in the history of type design (Old Style, Transitional, Modern, or Contemporary, for example), or by the specific shape of the serif (round, square, cupped, or thin).

And he stoppeth one of three

By the long gray beard and glittering eye,

Now wherefore stopp'st thou me?

Most serif faces combine thick vertical strokes with thin horizontals; this contrast enhances their readability and appearance on the printed page. The tension between the straight and curved portion of the letters also adds to our almost unconscious appreciation of the patterns created by typography. Projected by a strong light source, or displayed on a luminous monitor, however, thin or delicate serifs and horizontal strokes tend to drop out, giving the letter an odd, disjointed look. Robust serif faces work best for presentation graphics, unless the type is set in quite large display sizes. For example, Bodoni Poster (shown on the next page) has exaggerated thick and thin strokes that can become even more exaggerated on screen, reducing legibility.

**And I am
next of kin;**

Another example is Bookman Demi (below), which has more evenly weighted strokes and serifs to convey a steadier, clearer impression on the screen.

**The guests
are met,
the feast is set:**

Sans Serif Faces

Letterforms without terminal cross strokes belong to the sans serif group of typefaces. Because they tend to offer less contrast in thick and thin strokes as well as a more lightly defined baseline, sans serif faces are rarely used heavily in books or other text-intensive materials.

The wide variety of sans serif faces give presentation designers a wonderful array of shapes and tones with which to work. As a group, sans serif faces appear rather heavier or bolder than serif faces of the same size. They stand up to projection and electronic media, remaining legible down to point sizes that would obliterate serif type. For example, Avant Garde (below) has geometrical shapes built on circles and lines, with little modulation in stroke width.

May'st hear
the merry din.'

Many sans serif faces are available in a wide range of weights, from light through extra bold or heavy. Although you'll want to exercise caution at both extremes, this range is quite presentation-friendly. It's a real luxury to increase or decrease in weight as well as size until you find exactly the right combination of heading and text type for your material, size limitations, and line length. Italic or oblique versions of sans serif faces will prove to be useful when you want to convey a sense of dynamic forward motion, or when you want to loosen up the tone of the presentation. Italics in sans serif fonts function somewhat differently from serif italics: they're frequently able to stand on their own as a useful choice for headings or bulleted type. For example, Helvetica (below) moves toward slightly more oval shapes and modulated width where letter strokes join.

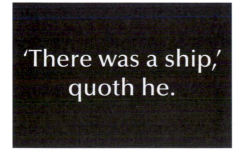

He holds him with
his skinny hand,

Optima (below) is a hybrid, considerably influenced by modulated stroke width and even a serif-like thickening of the line as the stroke ends.

'There was a ship,'
quoth he.

The simplicity and neutral style of many sans serif faces make them perfect partners in presenting information in a business or scientific setting. Some, like Optima, retain the grace and inflection of serif faces with a suggestion of flare at the end of the letter strokes, and a modulation in width around curves. Others, like Avant Garde, maintain a strictly uniform line and geometric shape. Look closely at the faces available to you, so you can match their personalities with your messages.

Script Faces

Script typefaces are modeled on handwriting, with letters that appear to connect. They're slanted like italics, but script faces serve an entirely different purpose—one that's generally well outside the milieu of presentation graphics.

It's usually good advice to save scripts, with their flowing lines and flourishes, for wedding invitations and other occasions when an embellished ornamental face looks just right. They are typically hard to read and even more difficult when presented on an overhead or slide in a presentation. Like all rules, however, this one should be broken when the content and design demand it. We've designed some very effective presentations that use simple, legible brushstroke script fonts for short headings, choosing them as design elements that reinforce the content.

Display Faces

We usually sacrifice a degree of legibility in favor of style when we incorporate a display typeface into a presentation. These faces are designed to be printed in large point sizes for elements like headlines and initial caps. In presentation graphics, they're suitable for titles and other special applications, provided they work harmoniously with the overall design and the text type. They're definitely not the workhorses you'll need for graphs, diagrams, and bullet lists, but they can add a real flair when used sparingly and thoughtfully.

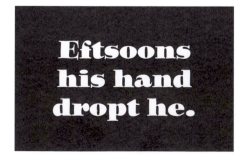

What's In A Font?

In Gutenberg's day, a font meant a drawer full of characters made of lead or carved wood in a given size and style. The printer's devil sorted the letters into the proper compartments of the font drawer after each page was printed, so they'd be ready for the next job. The specifications for printing a document might include a typeface—Garamond Book, for instance—and two fonts—perhaps 10-point and 16-point Garamond Book.

Nowadays, digital type has taken over from lead, and although the world of typography is still full of characters, we hear the terms *typeface* and *font* used interchangeably. In the era of computer-generated type, a font is the binary file of geometric coordinates defining the form of each character.

Your software probably uses PostScript or TrueType fonts. These describe the geometry of the characters' outlines, so they can be imaged at extremely high resolutions. A single outline file can print any size of a particular font and weight. These desktop industry standards produce extremely smooth curves and fine details.

Along with character outlines, the files also contain intercharacter information, which proportions the space between letters to produce a smooth and readable visual effect. This is especially important for *kerning*, the process of adjusting the space between certain character pairs that would look awkwardly spaced without special tweaking. Following are examples of kerned (above) and unkerned (below) Palatino.

He holds him with
his glittering eye—

He holds him with
his glittering eye—

Type management utilities like Adobe Type Manager allow you to see clear PostScript letterforms on the screen, no matter what their size. The program refers to the PostScript printer files for information on how to draw the sharpest letters possible at the screen resolution.

Families

A type family includes several fonts that are variations on the same typeface design theme. Smaller families include roman (regular-weight type, not slanted), italic, bold, and bold italic. When you select from these four family members, you can give special treatments to headings, subheads, or particular words and phrases without using a second, "outsider" typeface.

Some far-flung type families, like Helvetica or Frutiger, have many members; others are more tightly knit and rely on only a few weights. Some families include condensed and extended versions, which may be available in many weights—the second-cousins-once-removed branch of the clan. Other families are more tightly knit and rely on only a few weight choices.

The Wedding-Guest stood still,

And listens like a three year's child:

The Mariner hath his will.

The Wedding-Guest sat on a stone:

Restrain yourself when you assign roles to members of a type family. Too many weights, sizes, and italic variations can clutter your work and confuse your message. Make sure the combinations you settle on for various roles are easily distinguished, as well as compatible. Don't combine hairline, outline, inline, condensed, extended, and extended bold italic simply because they all carry the same family name. Maintain consistency throughout a presentation by using the same face for the same function from frame to frame.

Your Best Face Forward

Be practical. Out of all the hundreds of typefaces available, you really need only one or two at a time. So, how do you choose?

Type—especially presentation type—is meant to be read. Legibility is priority number one. Second, you don't want to call attention to the type itself during your presentation. The type's job is to communicate ideas, facts, concepts, or statistics in an energetic and nearly transparent manner. Style that contradicts the message undermines the presentation; self-conscious type misdirects attention. When people notice the type rather than the content, you're drawing them away from the central concepts to a peripheral element. And finally, the letters must fit, both vertically and horizontally, into the space you've assigned them in your sketches.

We'll run through some examples and descriptions of particular typefaces to help you get going with the selection process.

Helvetica

Helvetica makes a logical starting point, because it's the most widely used typeface in the Western world and it's probably already available on your computer system. Designed in Switzerland in 1957, soon after the introduction of phototypesetting, it has a bold, clean look that is easy to read in lowercase with initial caps. All-uppercase Helvetica is so uniform that it reads rather poorly.

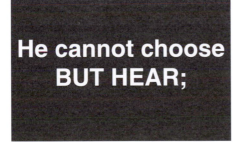

Neutral in shape and restrained in tone, Helvetica includes no distracting elements. Of course, that makes it less interesting for some applications, as well as less memorable. Its very omnipresence means that Helvetica has begun to wear a bit thin for some audiences. But for many purposes, Helvetica remains an excellent choice. Even in small point sizes, the lowercase letters are relatively large when compared with most other typefaces. As a result, though, it sets fairly wide.

The Helvetica family offers another advantage: scope. It's one of the largest type families around, including condensed, extended, true italics, and weights from light through black. As you expand your typeface library, remember to add depth to your Helvetica holdings. You'll be amazed at the versatility and freshness added by the less common weights in your type arsenal.

If you refrain, as I highly recommend you do in presentation work, from setting successive lines in all-uppercase or justified type, Helvetica makes a safe, unimpeachable type solution. Just remember that hundreds of other presenters are choosing it for the same reasons. You'll have a bit more latitude, then, to work with another design element—color or texture, for instance—to individualize your presentation when working with Helvetica. If you'd like a break from Helvetica while staying in a similar realm, take a look at the Frutiger family.

Optima

Nearly contemporary with Helvetica, Optima brings grace, clarity, and stylistic subtlety to the sans serif arena. Herman Zapf modeled this type on the lettering of Renaissance sculptor Luca della Robbia, and it retains a clear, classical flavor, particularly in the capitals. Close observation of the letter stems shows that they flare just a bit where you might expect a serif. The strokes modulate between thick and thin without going to extremes.

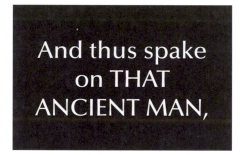

For short headings, Optima works well in all-uppercase. Try setting them with loose kerning for an open, airy look to the letterspacing, showcasing the forms. The combination of upper- and lowercase generates energy and interest. The characters are generous and full, but they combine to set fairly compactly without looking rushed. Large or small, the letterforms hold up quite well; the purity of their shapes tempts you to use individual letters as design elements. In an extra bonus for presentation designers who often rely on heavier weights, Optima's useful bold successfully translates the intriguing subtleties of the face.

Futura

Although designed some 30 years before Helvetica and Optima, Futura still looks modern and functional, Bauhaus-style. The precision of its rigidly geometrical letterforms based on straight lines and circles can work to your benefit; on the other hand, you can find it detracts from your overall design by insisting on its unmistakable shape.

Where Helvetica tempers strict geometry toward more traditional letterforms, Futura will have no compromise. That's both a strength and a danger.

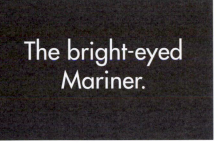

Select Futura for presentations where you aim for cool, crisp lettering surrounded by plenty of space. Avoid it when working with a text-heavy presentation.

These letterforms demand balancing open areas, or else they'll appear to compete with other design elements and appear disproportionate. Apply Futura carefully, and it will reward you with its unique style.

Times Roman

Widely available with software programs, Times Roman was originally designed to set legible, compact lines of type in newspaper columns. The very attributes that make it effective for the press—legibility at small sizes through shapely serifs and carefully modulated thick and thin strokes, along with a tight set and relatively tall x-height (the height of lowercase letters like "x"; see "Type Measurement Terms" later in this chapter)—limit Times' usefulness as a presentation face.

'The ship was cheered, The harbour cleared,

In presentation graphics, every word counts; we're not concerned primarily with how many characters we can fit into a line of type. Times Roman can look awkward when asked to do the kind of work demanded by presentations; the headings don't seem strong enough and the short, telegraphic bursts of type essential to bullet items can appear cramped and stiff.

When you're designing page graphics, posters, or flip charts, however, look to Times for help in dealing with text blocks.

Century

If we characterized type as we do wines, Century would be called vigorous, pleasant, and lively. Because of low contrast between thick and thin strokes and generously sized characters, Century makes a legible, open presentation face. It's a serif face, so it offers the possible advantages of stability and a more traditional appearance. It sets a bit bulkier than some of the other serif faces, but that can help establish its presence in the frame.

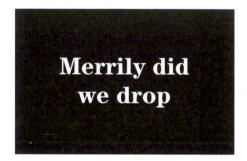

Century's lowercase italic font is somewhat ornamented, so you might plan to avoid it for engineering or scientific presentations. Take a look at Century for clear, traditional, and unremarkable serif text. If you want to branch out, consider one of the faces I recommend next.

Some Of My Favorites

So many exciting typefaces are available as PostScript or TrueType fonts, I encourage you to branch out and try some of my favorites. Start with Palatino, which may be familiar, because it's resident on many systems. Palatino's lively letterforms are based on calligraphic shapes, gracefully translated.

It's easy to see the influence of the pen in the serifs and contrasting line weights. And yet Palatino hardly ever looks too informal or lacking in seriousness. The italic and bold fonts are interesting in their own right and add depth to the roman fonts.

Choose another serif face, Stempel Schneidler, particularly in the bolder weights, to add elegance and to borrow the authority of the printed word. The original letterforms have been reinterpreted for digital imaging, and they translate graciously and beautifully. Even the serifs are shapely, echoing the curves of the letterforms without becoming overbearing.

The Stone family was designed specifically for personal computing applications. Stone Sans fonts make engaging presentation faces. They are proportioned generously and require plenty of space around each line to set off the large x-height. The italics preserve the open, clear shapes while adding a sense of forward motion.

When you'd like your type to speak colloquially, try the Stone Informal fonts. The semibold weight makes an interesting choice for very casual or "work in progress" presentations. If you want to take a couple of steps farther along this route, check out Tekton, based on an architect's distinctive handwriting.

Gill Sans breathes life into sans serif letterforms, making it an excellent alternative when Helvetica and Futura start to look repetitious and mechanical. Because it was developed as signage for a railway, Gill is very much at home in presentation environments.

Following are examples of Palatino, Stempel Schneidler Bold, Stone Sans, Gill Sans, Tekton Oblique, Helvetica, Frutiger Condensed, Optima, and Futura Extra Bold Oblique.

Palatino: Aa Bb Cc Dd Ee Ff Gg Hh Ii Jj Kk Ll Mm Nn Oo Pp Qq Rr Ss Tt Uu Vv Ww Xx Yy Zz

Stempel Schneidler Bold: Aa Bb Cc Dd Ee Ff Gg Hh Ii Jj Kk Ll Mm Nn Oo Pp Qq Rr Ss Tt Uu Vv Ww Xx Yy Zz

Stone Sans: Aa Bb Cc Dd Ee Ff Gg Hh Ii Jj Kk Ll Mm Nn Oo Pp Qq Rr Ss Tt Uu Vv Ww Xx Yy Zz

Gill Sans: Aa Bb Cc Dd Ee Ff Gg Hh Ii Jj Kk Ll Mm Nn Oo Pp Qq Rr Ss Tt Uu Vv Ww Xx Yy Zz

Tekton Oblique: Aa Bb Cc Dd Ee Ff Gg Hh Ii Jj Kk Ll Mm Nn Oo Pp Qq Rr Ss Tt Uu Vv Ww Xx Yy Zz

Helvetica: Aa Bb Cc Dd Ee Ff Gg Hh Ii Jj Kk Ll Mm Nn Oo Pp Qq Rr Ss Tt Uu Vv Ww Xx Yy Zz

Frutiger Condensed: Aa Bb Cc Dd Ee Ff Gg Hh Ii Jj Kk Ll Mm Nn Oo Pp Qq Rr Ss Tt Uu Vv Ww Xx Yy Zz

Optima: Aa Bb Cc Dd Ee Ff Gg Hh Ii Jj Kk Ll Mm Nn Oo Pp Qq Rr Ss Tt Uu Vv Ww Xx Yy Zz

Futura Extra Bold Oblique: Aa Bb Cc Dd Ee Ff Gg Hh Ii Jj Kk Ll Mm Nn Oo Pp Qq Rr Ss Tt Uu Vv Ww Xx Yy Zz

Typographic Design Elements

Although Zapf Dingbats, Whirligigs, Wing Dings, and other iconographic fonts aren't exactly typefaces, they are delightfully useful shapes that can be set just like letters. Dingbats make bullets more fun and interesting; they give you control over spacing and sizing. You can create lots of great effects for backgrounds, too, with dingbats. Print out the whole font and keep your type chart close at hand to remind yourself of the endless design possibilities made available by shapes that act like letters. Following are examples of Galliard Bold, Times Roman, Century Bold, and Zapf Dingbats.

Galliard Bold: Aa Bb Cc Dd Ee Ff Gg Hh Ii Jj Kk Ll Mm Nn Oo Pp Qq Rr Ss Tt Uu Vv Ww Xx Yy Zz

Times Roman: Aa Bb Cc Dd Ee Ff Gg Hh Ii Jj Kk Ll Mm Nn Oo Pp Qq Rr Ss Tt Uu Vv Ww Xx Yy Zz

Century Bold: Aa Bb Cc Dd Ee Ff Gg Hh Ii Jj Kk Ll Mm Nn Oo Pp Qq Rr Ss Tt Uu Vv Ww Xx Yy Zz

Zapf Dingbats: ✿❀ ✛❂ ✜❃ ❉❄ ❋❄ ❈❄ ◆❄ ◇❄ ★❄ ☆❄ ✪❄ ☆❄ ★● ★○ ☆■ ☆□ ☆□ ✳□ ✳□ ✳▲ ✳▼ ✻◆ ✦❖ ✳◗ ✳◖ ✳◗ ✳◗

Type Distortion

Many drawing and presentation software programs include features for skewing, shearing, stretching, or reshaping graphic objects—including type. Please save these features for occasional special effects. Don't rely on them for condensing type to fit the space available—a common quick-and-dirty solution to type fitting. Check the fit of the longest line of type before you begin layout of the presentation; if you have irretractably long lines, you might try a condensed font that's been designed for legibility. Excessive electronic distortion can easily detract from the quality of your work. Your audience may not know exactly what seems odd about the frames, but they'll be disturbed by stretched or skewed type, even when it's less than obvious.

MEDDLE NOT IN THE AFFAIRS OF TYPE WIZARDS

You may think that condensed or extended fonts are merely compressed or stretched versions of a basic typeface design. In fact, type designers actually create a complete new set of drawings for condensed and extended type, adjusting each character stroke to the proper weight, angle, and shape. Likewise, italics are much more than slanted versions of roman faces. It will pay off handsomely in your overall frame design to respect the original type proportions. When you find you must adjust them electronically, do the least possible with care, paying close attention to the changes in counters (the enclosed spaces in letters like "b" and "g").

Type designers work at an exacting level of detail. They consider the geometry of each angle and the curve of every letter, numeral, and punctuation mark. Tiny refinements of stroke width or arc can make the difference between letters that look lumpy or static and those that flow gracefully from one to the other. Distorting carefully designed characters may easily degrade the aesthetics and readability of any typeface.

Although distortion often works against good type design, it can enhance individual frames when used for specific purposes.

Electronic manipulation entices us with features like outlining and shadowing; evaluate these effects by asking whether they contribute to the overall legibility and power of the frame design. Make sure you're not turning to these bells and whistles to disguise a more fundamental design problem. Use them sparingly, to further a clearly conceived visual purpose. For example, letterform distortion can work effectively when the type maps with a background object that's skewed or slanted, or when the letterforms themselves are used as three-dimensional objects with shadows or other depth-enhancing graphic treatments.

If you find yourself about to distort type simply to fit the words into the space allocated in your design, go back to the drawing board to redesign the frame layout and—brainstorm!—edit the text. You could also try resizing the type rather than distorting the letterforms.

upon the left, Out of the sea came he!

And he shone bright, and on the right

When you distort type, you create a separate typeface that no longer matches the type in the rest of your frames. For the sake of consistency, you must distort the equivalent elements of each frame in the presentation—quite an undertaking. It's not worth it! In addition, the distorted face counts toward the limit we recommend of two typefaces per frame, with no more than two or three weights or versions of a single face in each graphic.

Type Sizing

Despite the dramatic changes the digital revolution brought to typesetting technology, we still use most of the original terminology, including the units of measure. Specifications for printed materials are given in points and picas: approximately 6 picas or 72 points to the inch, with 12 points to the pica. Picas are often used to specify line length; for instance, the maximum measure for lines in the text column you're reading is 27 picas. Type is sized by its height in points. The minimum vertical space required for a 36-point line of type is roughly half an inch, because 36 is half of 72. As a frame of reference, the text you're reading now is set in 12-point type. The following shows Helvetica at 36 points, which measures about half an inch in height.

Right

Most drawing and presentation programs allow extremely fine tuning in type size. You'll become familiar with these sizes as you work with type, selecting a standard size spec for each category of typographic element in your presentation.

TAKING CHARGE
OF LEADING, PT. I

As type size increases, leading requirements do not increase proportionally. Optima set in 24 points might work well with 4 points of extra leading (24/28), but type twice that size would not require 8 points leading. In fact, it may work well with only 5 points at 48/53.

Line spacing is a matter of proportion, finding a pleasing relationship between type size, line length, and leading. It's safe to start by looking at the computer's default 120 percent of your type size, but be sure to experiment with decreasing the leading for closely related lines and increasing it to help individual lines or groups of lines stand out. After a certain point, more isn't necessarily better. It's not easy to follow type from line to line when the leading is more than half again the character size. When you want to separate ideas, more space is a relief.

Line Spacing/Leading

Years ago, when type was set with individual metal characters, printers added spacing between lines with thin strips of lead. Although line spacing is digital today, the term *leading* (pronounced "ledding") is still standard. The increments of space between lines of type are usually expressed in points. Extra leading in the text of this book makes it much more legible and accounts for the fact that six lines of 12-point type fit into an inch and one-eighth rather than in a single inch as they would if set *solid*—that is, without extra leading. Each line here has 3 extra points of leading. This type size and leading is expressed as 12/15, or 12 (-point type) over 15 (-point leading).

Most drawing and presentation programs allow you to choose the amount of space you want between lines of type. If you don't specify the amount of leading, the default will be approximately 120 percent of the type size in points. Usually you'll want to change this to take into consideration the x-height of the type you're using and to allow slightly less leading between multiple lines of a single bullet point or other style text entry, and more space between different points or entries.

Till over the mast at noon—'

- The wedding-guest here beat his breast,

- For he heard the loud bassoon.

Minimum leading requirements are influenced by the characteristics of the typeface you've chosen. To appear open and uncrowded, faces with tall lowercase letters or large x-heights require more leading that those with small x-heights. For example, 18-point Helvetica or Stone Sans requires at least 4 extra points between lines of type in presentation graphics.

Went down into the sea.

Higher and higher every day,

Type Measurement Terms

The following terms, and many others used in the typographer's lexicon, originated in the printing trade. However, they have stuck over the centuries and are still used widely today.

- *baseline*—The imaginary line on which type rests. Descenders fall below it, giving variety and character to lowercase type.

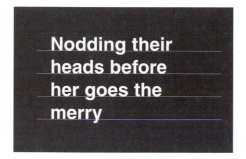

- *x-height*—Literally, the height of a lowercase "x" in a particular typeface. The ratio of the x-height to the body size determines the visual importance of lowercase letters for a given typeface. Different faces set in the same size appear to be larger or smaller, depending on their relative x-heights. Goudy, for instance, has a small x-height when compared with Avant Garde.

- *point size*—The distance from the lowest point of the longest descender (such as p or g) to the highest part of the tallest ascender (such as b, d, or a capital letter) is known as the *type* size. Because metal type couldn't be cast to the very edge of the block it was mounted on, the *point* size includes a small additional space for the "shoulder" of the block that carried each letter. We retain this margin in our point size today.

- *em space and en space*—A blank space equal to the point size of the type in which it appears. An em space in 12-point type measures exactly 12 points by 12 points (based on the size of the letter M). Because this measure is proportioned to the type itself, it's a very handy term. An en (based on the letter N) is half the width of an em. Ems and ens are convenient measuring units for paragraph indents (one em is standard), dash lengths (em or en dashes), and bullet size (12-point or 6-point).

Sizing Type For Projection And Display Media

Specifying type sizes for printed materials is an art in itself, but it seems straightforward when compared with sizing type for projection or electronic media. We review presentation frames as screen displays, as laser-printed proofs, as slides or overheads, and as projected images. Through it all, we must evaluate the effectiveness of our typographic choices in communicating critical information to the audience.

Proportional Sizing

One way to start designing typographic elements is by working out percentages of the overall image height. This will give you a guide to their relative sizes, rather than the exact point size of each element. Keep in your mind's eye a vision of the way the displayed image will look to your audience.

Some designers and presenters prepare and image sample charts of type sizes to use as references when specifying type for off-screen applications. These samples can give a good idea of how various sizes, weights, and fonts look when imaged on different media and projected to various sizes.

Figuring height by percentages isn't as complicated as it might sound. Work with the frame in your presentation that contains the most type, solving the worst-case scenario first and applying the same type specs throughout the show. For example, you might be making an overhead with nine lines of type. One of those lines is the heading, which you decide will be larger as well as bolder than the others, and will be followed by more leading than separates the following eight bullet entries. Each of the eight will be weighted evenly. Count this basic type size as 10 percent. If the heading will be half again the size of the basic bullet entries, it counts as 15 percent. Follow the heading with a 5 percent space.

Minstrelsy
- The Wedding-Guest
- he beat his breast,
- Yet he cannot choose
- but hear;
- And thus spake on
- that ancient man,
- The bright-eyed
- Mariner.

Minstrelsy
- The Wedding-Guest
- he beat his breast,
- Yet he cannot choose
- but hear;
- And thus spake on
- that ancient man,
- The bright-eyed
- Mariner.

Measure the overall height of your "live" image area in printer's points, picas, inches, or whatever measurement system is most convenient with your experience and software. Multiply this height by the percent value for the maximum type size. Work down from this size to allow for leading, extra room at the bottom of the frame, and other spatial considerations.

Finding The Right Size

Audiences shouldn't have to strain to read your message—and many people won't make the effort. Be sure your type specifications result in words that are large enough to read easily. As a rule of thumb for determining minimum type size, keep your point size larger than 2.5 percent of the height of the image area. On a horizontal overhead transparency 8 inches (576 points) high, this means the smallest letters should be about 14-point type.

For a quick legibility check, hold your slides at arm's length. If you can read the type without magnification, it will probably be clear to your viewers. Be sure to stand back from your computer screen and check legibility from a distance of 6 feet or so.

Copy Fitting

A further wrinkle in type specification is the fact that the various typefaces set differently, so they're not interchangeable. These rules of thumb are quite general and need adjustment to each presentation design. The same line set in five different faces will measure five different lengths and heights.

The designs of some faces make more efficient use of space, but others require plenty of room for their knees and elbows. For example, a heading composed in 16-point Helvetica bold italic upper- and lowercase might produce a line 20 picas long; the same words composed exactly the same way in Century bold italic would set 22 picas long. When space is tight and text long, choose a compact face.

And now the STORM-BLAST came, and he

And now the STORM-BLAST came, and he

Was tyrannous and strong

Was tyrannous and strong

You'll find quite a wide variation in height between different fonts because of their internal proportions; this is true, even comparing the same characters at the same point size. Look closely at the height of the capitals and the length of the ascenders and descenders. These individual qualities influence your typeface selection and sizing decisions; once you've chosen your typeface, they help you plan how much leading you'll need to set off the lines most effectively.

Spacing

Judicious spacing between individual letters and words, as well as between lines, contributes significantly to the legibility and the overall success of your presentation graphics.

Letter Spacing

Most software programs offer an adjustment for tighter or looser spacing between letters, through *tracking* choices. Although you may routinely set your type for print fairly tight, presentations frequently benefit from some generosity of space between characters. Unless your type is extremely large, it's easier to read when set a bit more open, especially when you're dealing with monitors and projectors.

He struck with his

He struck with his

These increases should be tiny, hardly discernible. If the type comes out looking as if it has lost a few teeth, go back and tighten up the tracking again. Occasionally, you may notice a disproportionate gap between two letters, especially in heading type. When possible with your software, go in and make *kerning* adjustments to this particular pair of characters. Kerning takes a tuck in the letter spacing and helps bring the letter pair into harmony with the rest of the frame. When you're working on precise kerning, check your results frequently on a laser-printed proof; it's hard to see exactly what's happening on screen at this level of detail.

Word Spacing

The space between words created by pressing the keyboard spacebar is tied to the tracking adjustment. When you can adjust tracking, you'll see that word spacing increases as letter spacing expands. You can also add or remove minute bits of space manually through kerning controls, when the software allows. Here again, check results on a laser proof. Your goal is to provide enough space to indicate the end of one word and the beginning of the next—not to isolate each word more widely.

Line Length

Long lines can be awkward to read and can defeat your goal of working with key words that the audience will absorb at a glance. Newspapers and magazines use columns to help the reader stay oriented. Presentation graphics should be written for the screen, in short bursts of information. Consider the reduced line length a tool to assist your viewers as they take in your material.

Occasionally, a heading, attribution line, quote, or other statement should be broken into more than one line. Carefully position the line break to follow the sense of the text, avoiding a very long line followed by only one or two words on the second line. Experiment with your typographic choices for stacking the lines to find the best length for the face and size you've selected. Use your grid layout system to help position these type blocks.

As a quick rule of thumb, consider 40 characters per line as the outside limit for screen graphics and slides, and 60 characters the maximum for overhead transparencies. That's considerably longer than the ideal tight, condensed phrase, however, so please exercise restraint.

Moving On

Typeface selection and specification exerts a tremendous influence on frame design. The right type treatment will enhance delivery of your message; an inappropriate choice can cancel out lots of hard work. Tread carefully and experiment with a sample frame before deciding on the type styles for the whole presentation.

The next chapter concentrates your attention on another important design element that works hand in hand with type: color. We'll consider why, when, and how to use color in presentation graphics, based on the inherent properties, emotional effects, and effective combinations of colors. As you apply these principles to your presentation media and overall design scheme, you'll amplify the effectiveness of your communication.

EXPLORING COLOR 6

Color can be the most engaging design element of your presentation if you choose your colors carefully. It can add richness and depth to your message and allow you to put your own personal stamp on your work. We live in a full-color world, so why not let your presentations reflect this colorful reality?

Go For Color

Using color in presentations used to be a time-consuming, complex, and costly process. Today, with the widespread use of color inkjet printers, color laser printers, and color copiers, you can load every screen of every presentation with all the colors of the rainbow.

The most obvious reason for using color in your presentations is to reflect to our audience what's in the world around us: green trees, blue water, and multicolor sunsets. That's simple and straightforward. It's also fun.

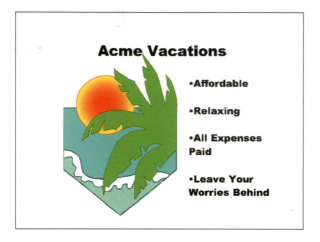

Another, less obvious reason is that color allows us to establish meaning through association. Abstractions, such as statistics, ideas, and proposals, have no intrinsic colors, but we can add meaning through color. Red means warning, blue means calm, green means growth.

Color Palettes

A *palette* is the board an artist uses to hold and mix colors and it's also the term used to refer to the set of colors on the board. In either case, the word implies a set of colors chosen with care. There are so many colors you can use in your presentations, it's easy to go overboard if you don't take the time to select and plan your palette.

Before you start producing a presentation in color, take some time to think about the colors you will use and select a few (just a few) for use throughout the entire presentation. You want to select colors that coordinate well on screen or in print and can be used in a variety of ways in the presentation.

What's Your Favorite Color?

Everybody has a favorite color, and for most people it's blue. Surprisingly, though, it's not the same shade of blue for everyone. According to a recent color study done by Roper and Pantone, 35 percent of those polled chose blue as their favorite color. Spectrum Blue, a strong, vivid blue was the favorite among men, while women chose the lighter, more serene sky blue.

If you're ever in doubt as to what color to use in a presentation, the results here say you can't go wrong if you include some blue. To help you further, here are highlights from the study:

- Green was the second most popular color, especially favored by the group the study called *influentials*. These are people to whom other people go for advice. This group is also fond of most shades of orange.

- Purple was the third most favorite color, narrowly edging out red. People between the ages of 18 to 29 like purple because they consider it sexy. The influentials like it, too, because it strikes them as powerful and sophisticated.

- Red and black are popular as well. *Achievers*, people who are economically stable and who are not afraid to take risks, like red a great deal, while wealthy, achievement-oriented women like black. It's not so popular with blue collar and middle-aged men or women who associate black with mourning.

- Adolescents like purple, orange, and a shade of green they call *slime green*.

- The most disliked colors by all the groups include a strong yellow-green, bright orange (although other shades of orange are liked by some groups), fluorescent pinks, and fluorescent colors in general.

These tips will help you most if you remember you can use different shades of all these colors. You don't have to use the most vivid shade of a color in order to work it into your color palette. In fact, all these colors are so vibrant at their peak of strength that you wouldn't want to use them full strength.

Imagine using a light lilac background with dark teal or dark ivy green text for a multimedia presentation for women 30 to 45 years old who work part-time. Or, you could use a dark purple background and slime green text in a slide show presentation for college freshmen.

A Few Examples

One of the major take-away lessons in this chapter is that color can make or break a presentation. Another lesson is that it isn't that difficult to understand how color affects your design. To give you a better idea of how color can change the whole look and feel of a presentation, a few examples follow.

The first example is three screens that are basically the same. The only things that have been changed are some of the color selections. The text and images remain the same. Even some of the colors remain the same. Yet, each screen has a different look. See if you can spot all the color changes in each screen.

The second example is how differing the amount of color can change the look of a screen or a presentation. In this example, the first screen is shown in grayscale, then one color is added, then a few more, and finally another. In the last screen, only a few colors have been used, but the screen looks alive with color because all the colors used are vivid shades.

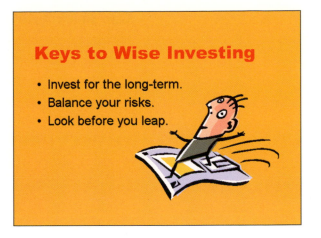

Before choosing your colors, there are two considerations to take into account beyond simple aesthetics: how the colors affect your content and which presentation media you plan to use.

Considering Your Content

The colors you select for your palette can affect the audience's comprehension of your content, so you must take your content into consideration when choosing a palette. If you are making a presentation to a group of wealthy senior citizens about a new, upscale retirement village, you would not want to use strong, vibrant Day-Glo colors. Instead, your palette may consist of warm, strong earth tones or may even have a few tropical colors if the facility is located in a tropical area.

To help you consider your content, take a moment and decide how you want the audience to feel when the presentation is finished. Do you want them to feel comforted, energized, excited, satisfied? List a few feelings and then choose colors that convey those feelings.

Think About Your Media

The medium or media you choose for your presentation will affect your color choices—at least it should if you want to have the best-looking presentation possible. You can use less highly saturated colors if you are printing your presentation, but you may want to use more highly saturated colors for a presentation that you are projecting on screen inside a large auditorium. The ambient light in the room may wash out less saturated colors and make details on the screen hard to see.

So many factors are involved in choosing colors for various presentations, you're better off keeping the media choice in mind when making color choices. The rest of this chapter, plus the material in Chapters 10, 11, and 12, will help you make wise choices.

Can Black-And-White Be Read All Over?

It's tempting to say reassuringly that black-and-white presentations are still acceptable, but we're not sure that's true anymore. They may be perfectly acceptable in some environments, such as nonprofit and academic settings where presentation budgets are traditionally low. However, in the business world, color is becoming the standard for all types of communications and especially for presentations.

Having said that, there may be times when you want to turn the tables and do a classy black-and-white presentation with lots of interesting grayscale images. You would do this kind of presentation to stand out in a crowd and gain some extra attention. It's not the norm, but it's an option to keep in the back of your mind.

Coding With Color

Color-coded file folders and labels are a quick and easy way to organize your work. Color can also be a good way to organize your content in a presentation quickly. There are several ways you can use color this way:

- *Color associations* are a good way to add depth and meaning to abstract material. Advertisers and corporations spend a lot of money coming up with custom colors to associate with their products and services. You can do the same without the expense by coming up with custom colors for your presentations or by using your corporation's colors.

- *Color differentiations* are a good way to quickly show the difference between items. Similar classes of items can be shown in subtle variations of a single color. Distinctly different items can be shown in markedly different colors and hues.

- *Color hierarchies* indicate levels of importance or progression of data. You can use dark to light or gray to bright sequences to show increasing significance. To show development in a series, you can use different colors of the same levels of brightness.

- *Color emphasis* helps focus the audience's attention to a specific element on screen if you make that element a brighter color than the rest. In a flock of pigeons and one cardinal, you see the red cardinal first. In a bowl of pears and a single banana, the banana stands out. Use this attention-getting principle to draw attention to any item, such as highlighting one item on a bulleted list with bright yellow.

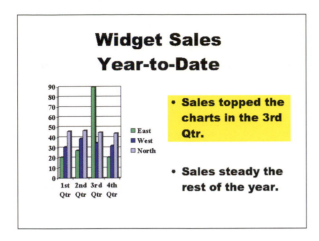

Audience Appeal

Advertisers and graphic artists gravitate toward certain colors, and their choices affect the rest of us. You wouldn't think of making a modern kitchen avocado green, yet sage green would be a good choice today. Be aware of popular color choices in the world around you as you choose your presentation color palette.

If you're oblivious to such nuances as popular colors, head off to the local large car dealership and pick up some brochures on the latest models. Or check out the paint selection display areas in the paint store around the corner. Between the two, you'll find the latest, hottest colors for almost everything, including your presentation.

Here's a tip: If you know your audience's likes and dislikes but aren't sure what color scheme would work best for the presentation, choose a car or two you think your audience would like to own. Then study the brochure for those cars. Look at the exterior paint choices and even the colors used in the brochures themselves. Finally, pick a few colors from the mix for your presentation.

Legibility

Never sacrifice legible screens for color. Legibility is a key component of comprehension, and easy comprehension is essential to your message. Pure black text on dark backgrounds is difficult to read under even perfect lighting conditions, so stick with dark text on a light background.

Proceed With Caution

Unless you were born with a flair for design, using color well is a difficult skill to master without sufficient practice. So be patient with yourself as you experiment and learn about color. Remember, too, to budget time for experimentation.

Doing thumbnail sketches of each screen will help. Sketch them in black and shades of gray, then use colored markers and highlighters to sketch in your color choices. Once you've got a color palette or two you like on paper, use these palettes in your computer presentations. Believe it or not, for brainstorming color palettes, a packet of colored highlighters and a stack of photocopied sketches works better than all the computer programs out there.

The Language Of Color

To say that color speaks to us is obvious. What it says to us is less obvious because so many factors affect the meaning. Our culture, our heritage, our education, and even our eyes all affect our perception and conception of color. A color-blind American carpenter thinks and feels about color differently than a sharp-sighted Chinese mystic or even a sharp-eyed American homemaker. To help us gain common ground for a discussion of color, let's start with some of the basics and then examine some of the differences that will influence our color selections for presentations.

The Color Wheel

You're probably familiar with the color wheel, the circular presentation of the basic colors in the color spectrum and their relationships to each other. Primary and secondary colors alternate to form the wheel. Red, blue, and yellow are primary colors, and green, orange, and purple are secondary colors. Combinations of the primary colors are used to create the secondary colors.

Complementary colors, colors that work well in pairs, appear opposite each other on the color wheel. Each complementary duo consists of a primary color and a secondary color. Red with green, blue with orange, and yellow with purple are all complementary color combinations.

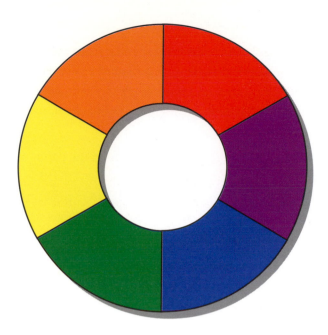

Seeing Color

Whether it's projected light or ink on paper, every color can be described by its characteristics of hue, value, and saturation. Each color in the spectrum or around the color wheel represents a hue—red, blue, yellow, green, orange, and so forth. Value is the shade of the color, and saturation is the intensity of the hue.

Unless you have spent a great deal of time working with color for design or some other kind of visually oriented work, chances are you are not comfortable with these terms and may not even be able to recognize the difference. Spend some time looking over the color charts in an art supply store or gather up some swatches from the paint store. Educate your eye about the differences—subtle and striking—in color characteristics.

Computers And Color

The colors you see on a computer monitor are created using three colors: red, green, and blue (RGB). On paper, process color is derived from inks in four basic colors: cyan, yellow, magenta, and black (CMYK). Getting the two schemes to coincide and work together consistently is not easy. In fact, designers and printers deal with the difficulty on a daily basis.

Fortunately, you can leave most of these technical difficulties in the hands of print professionals. Don't be surprised, though, to see some color differences such as shade and intensity shifts when you take a printed presentation and put it on screen and vice versa. Professionals can minimize these differences and changes, but they cannot eliminate them entirely.

You can help minimize them yourself if you routinely create presentations that will appear on screen and in print. Use a color reference book from a color matching system, such as Pantone's, choose your colors from the book, and use these colors in your presentations. Because of the way screens and projection systems present colors, you won't see an exact match between the printed item and the screen, but you'll get a closer match than if you pick your colors from the screen.

Making A Palette

To make your palette, choose a group of colors (anywhere from two to ten) that you think would work well in a single presentation. Think of this set as your box of crayons or set of markers. Then decide how the colors will be used in the presentation. You'll need to make specific choices for the background and text, and then decide upon a subset of colors for other uses.

Sequencing

Organize your palette according to graphic function. When you specify and use a certain color for each type of design element, such as body type, headings, bullets, and rules, your audience will recognize the associations. Using the same colors consistently will help the audience understand the content more easily than using random color assignments. In fact, switching colors randomly may even confuse the audience.

Start by choosing a color and a shade of that color for the background of your screens; remember that text looks best against lighter shades of color. Then work your way through the elements and the colors, assigning a color or shade of color to each element. Many presentation software programs allow you to set up these relationships and save them so you can reuse them. This is always a good idea because you'll have something to start with on the next presentation.

Color Relationships

At this point, you need to start looking at colors in combination with others in the palette. If it helps, print out a few screens with the background color in place and everything else in black and white. Then choose colors for the rest of the elements and try out a few combinations. Choose one or two fully saturated (bright) colors for the palette and plan to use them sparingly. The rest of the colors in the palette should be a mixture of less saturated colors. Here are a few more pointers:

Spectral Neighbors

Spectral neighbors are not ghosts who live next to each other—they are hues that sit next to each other in the color wheel. Blue and green, red and orange, and yellow and green are examples of these closely related colors. The visual contrast between these pairs is low, so reserve them for low-contrast and subtle effects, such as creating drop shadows.

Complements

Complements are opposite each other on the color wheel. If fully saturated, these colors actually appear to move or vibrate when placed next to each other. Avoid using these combinations at full strength unless you like this kind of look. You can use the colors together if you reduce the saturation of one or both, or separate them with a thin black or white line or a small amount of space.

Triads

A triad is a group of three primary colors, three secondary colors, or any other set of hues located equidistant on the color wheel. Triads can be very pleasing to the eye, as they balance each other nicely, especially when all three match in value and saturation. Blue, red, and yellow, and orange, green, and purple are examples of triads. Using triads is a quick way to establish the basics of a pleasing palette.

Color Contrast

Contrasting colors appear markedly different from one another, particularly in value. Black and white provide the greatest contrast. That's why most printed documents use black type on white paper. The smaller the graphic element, the more contrast it needs to stand out. The same is true for complex elements. Use the concept of contrast to help determine background colors and colors for foreground elements.

The Misfits

The sight of someone wearing three kinds of checks and a paisley jacket with a striped tie is enough to make the most fashion-unconscious person groan inwardly. There are combinations that are equally unappealing in presentations, such as blue type on a black background. High-intensity backgrounds are another example of a presentation misfit. Let your inner design sense be your guide; if you put two or more colors together and find yourself wincing in pain, it's time to try another combination.

Multiple Background Colors

In a word, don't. Multiple background colors in a single screen can wreak havoc on your presentation. The various colors draw attention to the background and can distort the appearance of text and graphics. If you must use different background colors, use a single solid color for each screen and change the colors only when you change screens.

Some Winning Combinations

If all this color theory leaves you a little bit unsure about what colors work well in different kinds of presentations, don't despair. It's time to talk about the specifics of color palettes for different kinds of media, including on-screen presentations, overheads, slides, and Web sites.

On-Screen Presentations

Deep, rich backgrounds create good contrast with dark type, but you will find darker shades look lighter when presented on screen. Experiment with mid-tone backgrounds that offer enough contrast for your foreground elements if you want an even lighter overall look. Teal and blue-gray backgrounds are good choices for black type and colorful graphics. Use shadowing techniques behind less colorful graphics to help them stand out more.

If you are sure your presentation will be viewed only on good-quality computer monitors at normal viewing distances, you can be more creative with your color choices. Because most people have their monitors set for viewing black text on a white background, you can use highly contrasting colors and not overwhelm the audience. You can experiment with deeper purples and brighter blues; even some browns and red tones may work for backgrounds. Stick with bold, simple dark text and bold colors for your graphics. (Remember, deep doesn't mean dark: Think of it as using cherry furniture in a dining room with burgundy velvet drapes.)

Overheads

Most overheads are transparent, because people tend to add the type and the graphics and forget about backgrounds. This can work well if the over-head projector is bright enough and the room dark enough. Use highly saturated and bold colors for your graphics and dark colors for your text. Grays and lighter shades of any color will tend to wash out on overheads.

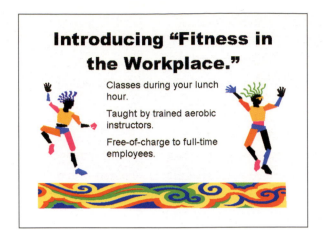

You can use colored backgrounds for overheads if your printer can generate smooth-looking colors over a stretch of space as large as an overhead transparency sheet. To find out, place a page-size block of your background color on a page and print the page on a sheet of overhead film. If the background looks streaked or blotchy, you're better off purchasing a translucent-colored background sheet and using that for your overheads.

Slides

You can use a lot of different colors in slides because they are imaged directly on high-quality film that can capture many levels of color. You can also use darker colors if the slides will be projected onto a wall from some distance away and ambient light will lighten the colors. You can choose either a dark background and lighter-colored text or a lighter background and darker text. You can even mix them in the same presentation.

Darker backgrounds are great ways to frame color graphics that dominate a screen. A large, colorful pie chart looks great up against an eggplant-colored background. It would not be as dominant if placed up against a bright yellow background. The same blue background, however, would wash out any dark text unless the text was so large it became a graphic itself.

To make the most of color in slides, make sure the background colors and foreground colors provide a high degree of contrast—more than you would use for any other media. If the contrast seems a little extreme on paper, you're probably on the right track with colors for slides.

For graphics with lots of mid-range shades or with shades of gray, choose a background color that is a darker or lighter shade of a color used in the graphics. The audience will focus first on the colors in the graphics, and then their minds will notice the link between the graphics and the background. The graphics will seem to project slightly forward, ahead of the background. You won't see this effect on paper, but it will be noticeable on the projected slide.

If your presentation contains a lot of graphics and a few short lines of text per screen, experiment with creating two-tone backgrounds. You can create these by layering two backgrounds: one a solid block of color and the second, top layer a subtle, yet discrete, pattern made of lines a shade or two lighter than the background. This kind of a background gives depth to the screen if you keep the contrast between the two colors very low—only one or two shades difference in color.

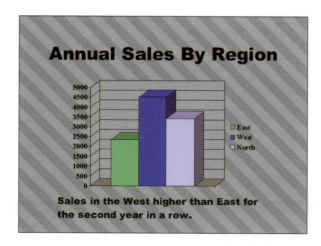

Web Sites

Many Web sites use backgrounds made of patterns, swirls of color, photographs, and even scans of fabric and paper. Web designers can do this because most of the time the Web site is viewed on a small, high-resolution color monitor. It helps them grab someone's attention the minute that person visits the site.

Use this same idea in Web presentations, only turn down the volume a little. No one wants to stare at vividly colored backgrounds throughout the entire presentation. Use backgrounds with subtle textures, and combine them with strong foreground colors. Don't be afraid to use unusual color combinations, as long as you stay within the Web-safe color palette.

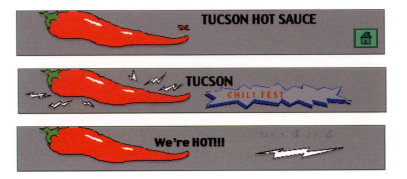

Graduated Color

Graduated (or ramped) color refers to a special effect image editing software can generate that allows one color to dissolve into another color or move from one shade to another of the same color. Colors can blend vertically, horizontally, or even radially depending upon the capabilities of your software.

Usually you choose your two colors or shades, and the software takes care of the rest. You may be asked to specify the number of gradual steps in the process, and the more steps, the more graduated the effect.

Graduated backgrounds are appealing if you use them carefully. Don't use them for busy screens, as they only add to the noise level of the visual picture. Don't run text across areas of visible color shifts, either. Use graduated backgrounds to enhance a simpler, slower-moving presentation, and stick to colors that are close together in intensity.

In addition, keep these backgrounds subtle and smooth by moving from a medium tone to a darker or lighter shade of the same color or to black. Spectral neighbors make good ramping combinations.

Backgrounds aren't the only places to use graduated effects. Try placing the blend area in a corner or as a band at the top or bottom of the frame or some other confined area. When the final color of the blend is the same as the background color, the blend and the background join seamlessly. Graduated fills for bars or pie chart slices can be very sophisticated-looking. Even rules and bullet symbols can be filled with graduated color.

Getting smooth printed images from blended colors is not easy unless you are imaging in color with a high-resolution imagesetter or with another commercial printing process, such as computer-to-plate. Inkjet and laser printers do not have enough color imaging capability to image blended backgrounds smoothly. You end up with visibly stepped blends instead of smooth ones.

Black, White, And Gray

Although color is expected in business presentations these days, you can choose to create a black-only or grayscale presentation. Aside from a few technical considerations, the principles of color design remain the same whether your palette has 20 colors or 20 shades of gray. Content is still king; readability and contrast are still paramount.

In laser printers and printing presses, black toner creates the illusion of gray or ink laid down in various patterns or screens, ranging from finely spaced dots to coarse blocked or crosshatched fills. Screened areas of black indicate shading and shadow, helping to create what we see on paper.

Black Patterns

The most common screen pattern is tiny round dots, although other screens are possible. The size and spacing of the dots determine the shade of gray and coarseness of the screen. Resolution is fixed in dots per inch, with many laser printers printing at 600 dpi or higher. Common offset printing resolutions are 1,270 or 2,540 dpi.

Imaging devices use the patterns and screens as guides in laying down toner or ink to create images. Black is 100 percent, whereas dark gray is around 80 percent and light gray around 20 percent. This means that 100 percent, 80 percent, or 20 percent of the area is covered with toner or ink; the remainder of the area is the paper with nothing on it. The result is black or gray—black when no spaces are present, gray when some are.

Ready-Made Patterns

Software programs let you specify the density, or resolution, of an image when you print it; most often you make this choice when you activate the Print dialog box. You can choose the highest setting for your output device or choose something lower. The lower the resolution, the larger the dots and the coarser the printed image.

Coarse patterns are attention grabbers, so limit them to one or two images. Fine patterns can render detail so minute they disappear in large screen-projected presentations. When in doubt, aim for a resolution of 400 to 600 dpi for informal printed handouts and higher resolutions for important printed materials. Use no more than 100 dpi for on-screen presentations, because most screens can't display resolutions higher than this.

Type Over Screens

Screens with screened patterns as backgrounds aren't legible with large blocks of text unless you create your own colored two-tone backgrounds as described earlier in this chapter. The screen pattern confuses the eye and the mind; you're never sure where to look, and you always have the feeling you're missing something.

You can use short (two- to four-word) chunks of large text on screened backgrounds if you are working in black and white only. The weight of the text overcomes the busy nature of the background. Once you're sure you've mastered the ins and outs of color in presentations, experiment with screened backgrounds to see if you can come up with a few special effects for your presentation bag of tricks.

Moving On

Color is great fun to use and a challenge to any designer, novice or pro. You'll be successful with color when you take the time to select appropriate colors and arrange them in your presentation before you begin your design. Focus on reinforcing the message with color and make sure your screens are readable and attractive.

Now that you've learned about using color in presentations, it's time to learn how to create presentation text screens. In the next chapter we will focus on the design details of using text effectively in presentations.

TEXT FRAMES AND MORE

7

The majority of presentation frames contain words and only words—beyond the design elements common to all frames in the show. This fact is both challenging and inevitable.

The challenge is to create text frames that aren't boring, word-heavy, and thick. We don't mind the familiar if it's streamlined and well thought out. The inevitability rises from the extreme usefulness of text frames, which condense an idea, provide transitions from one point to the next, and interpret information.

Terrific Text

Even though text frames are the mainstay of business presentations, they don't have to look dull or read monotonously. In fact, the audience's high level of comfort with text can work to your advantage, allowing you to bring more depth to the topic. You can familiarize members of the audience with the basics, preparing them for graphic representations of ideas, facts, or data so they're ready to interpret your visualizations. Similarly, text frames allow you to summarize the material presented in detail in your charts, graphs, and other illustrative frames. When you run a video clip, text frames can help anchor the audience's attention on the salient points.

Tell It Like It Is

Text frames reveal sloppy reasoning and spliced ideas. They take some time to write and edit well, but the clarity they bring repays this effort many times. Most of us enjoy making text frames because we're more familiar with words than with pictures—we write proposals, work summaries, letters, and reports all the time. Remember, however, that a text frame is a picture itself, a visual entity that requires choices of color, focus, placement, balance, and style. On the Web, this is particularly obvious when we compare sites with excellent typographic design—created by treating text as a graphic—with their "text only" versions.

Show It Like It Should Be

The text frame or Web screen is *not* a page. Written pages must stand alone, introducing key topics, explaining and supporting particular views, and finally reviewing and clarifying the issues. In a presentation, the designer has far more control over the flow of information. With live delivery, the presenter can manage the pace and modulate the tone of the show. With delivery through a technological interface, the presentation screens can encourage viewers to follow a number of alternative paths. The trick is to design each branch to unfold in a way that maintains clarity of communication. In any delivery, the words themselves work in tandem with the visual support structure for the words to create meaning.

While you tell the whole story in your live presentation, your visuals complement your words and give dimension to them. They outline, keynote, and emphasize. An idea "boiled down" to its essentials in a succinct phrase becomes memorable, especially when elaborated and interpreted by the speaker. Find a visual style that reflects your verbal delivery. Don't ask people to read lots of words—in doing so, most viewers will lose the thread of the ongoing presentation. It's hard for many people to switch gears between listening and reading, so make sure the "reading" frames are punchy and distill verbal content, so that they enhance rather than distract from the speaker's stream of words.

Intelligent Editing

Concise wording doesn't mean oversimplified content. People will forgive the occasional confusing graph or diagram, perhaps, but they're much more demanding and familiar with the written word. Keep your concepts specific and your verbs active. Avoid generalizations and passive construction like the plague.

Most important of all: make it interesting. Your audience will feel patronized by the "Dick and Jane" style of copywriting. One-syllable words alone cannot tell a complex story. Aim to present the essence of a subject, stopping well short of information overload. When you have lots more to say about a particular point, create a deeper level of the presentation that the interested viewer can access. In live presentations, you can move to these detail frames when the audience expresses particular interest or to answer a question.

List Making

Because everybody makes lists—lists of tasks to accomplish, people to call, supplies to order, chores to complete, groceries to buy—we're used to this telegraphic style of communication. I urge you to go beyond this technique, to engage and please your audience with excellent organization. Show not just the components, but the structural way they fit together. Communicate confidence by drawing on your experience. You're putting this presentation together because you know what works and what doesn't; make sure your frames reflect the insights you've gained by grappling with the issues and understanding their relationships. Generate audience interest by giving evidence of your own passion and involvement.

When you create outstanding text frames, you're well on your way to success with presentation graphics. However, the words and phrases of text frames aren't working to their top potential if they're merely wan, verbatim reflections of the presenter. Work for text that reinforces rather than repeats the live presentation. And not even the liveliest design can save a presenter who merely reads from the visuals. Consider these frames as a form of secret communication with your audience, and your live delivery as the cracking of this code.

Opening Titles

Because they're the first frames or screens your audience will see, take advantage of your opening to set the visual style and engage your audience. Introduce the color palette, background treatment, underlying grid structure, alignment, typography, and illustrative elements here. Because there's less information in titles, and it tends to be simpler than in the bullet lists or tables that will follow, you're free to work out a pleasing arrangement to focus attention on the most important elements.

Build Anticipation

Think of the way your favorite film opens. Although you don't have as much latitude to intercut titles with opening action, you do want the titles to offer a seamless, energy-generating segue to the presentation. Sometimes it's easiest to design titles if you have at least one important section of the presentation roughed out. Titles work best as frames with a close relationship to the content frames, allowing enough variation and surprises to keep things interesting.

Anchor The Information

While you're mapping out title frame design, consider the information you might include: the name of the presentation, program, or Web site, of course, and perhaps an explanatory subtitle or snappy positioning line; the speaker's name, title, and affiliation to lend credibility (and because we're incurably curious about the person speaking to us); the company name and corporate logo; the name of the organization or meeting and the date; and funding agencies and other attributions or acknowledgments. At this stage, consider also the graphic elements that you've designed for frames throughout the show, like special rules or shapes for bullets and other highlights.

When you choose to include a good bit of this type of information up front, by all means don't try to squeeze it all onto a frame or two. Build a sequence, replacing information smoothly while keeping the focus on the title itself. Start with the basics, which can remain on screen for a long time—even for several minutes as your audience comes in and settles down. Unless the speaker is especially well known, the title of the presentation is usually positioned as the featured element.

Starring And Supporting Roles

Contrary to what you might imagine, the type size need not be tremendous to imply the importance of the title. It's more important to work with a size that's easy to read and to use contrast in weight and color, along with open space, to emphasize the title. The subtitle, if any, and the speaker's name and affiliation come next, followed by company name, relevant dates, organization or seminar name, funding sources, and other essential information.

To make the title of your presentation concise but simultaneously hook the audience with an interesting aspect of the material, you may find an explanatory subtitle—or a crisp positioning statement—helpful. Subtitles allow you a bit more freedom to indicate the tone of your presentation, or to clarify a brief title while still keeping attention fixed on it. A number of graphic techniques create a subordinate position for the subtitle, without making the distinction heavy-handed. Draw a rule, allow extra leading space, or try a subtle variation in typography. Without changing typeface or size, try one of these subtle differences shown in the table below.

Small differences create clear distinctions in importance.

Title	Subtitle
All uppercase	Initial caps
Large and small caps	Small caps
Roman	Italic
Bold	Text weight
High-contrast color	Mid-contrast color

Distinguish the title and subtitle of a frame by experimenting with subtle variations in typography to indicate the two levels of information.

Of course, you may find that the contrast in length between a brief title and longer subtitle necessitates a smaller type size. That's fine. Reduce the potential for graphic overkill by changing only the size at first. If that doesn't give you enough contrast between title and subtitle, work with a second variable. Remember to note the choices you made in these frames so you can apply similar qualities to text frames throughout the presentation.

Closing Up Shop

Frequently, the opening title sequence can be adapted for closing titles to wrap up the presentation with polish and pizzazz. In one or two frames or sequences, repeat the essential information, such as title and subtitle, speaker, and date. Your goal here is to round out the time you've spent with this audience, giving them the sense of a satisfying "click" of the presentation closing. Bring back the graphic elements of your opening, but keep the tone a bit more restrained to signal that it's almost time to clap and stretch. Ah! You did it.

Section And Conquer

To introduce important new topics within your presentation, consider creating a special format for section divider frames. Base these frames or short sequences on your design for the opening titles, notched down a bit to convey that they're secondary in importance. The anticipation and excitement generated by your opening titles will spill over to the section divider frames. Your audience will recognize a section divider as a road sign in the flow of information and will appreciate the signals you're sending to aid understanding and provide continuity.

Elements Of Identification

Consider creating an identity for each content section by using a visual that heralds the information you're about to present. You could design a simple graphic for each section divider, or you could find a visual element from the frames in that section that represents a condensed version of the content. A simplified graph showing earnings over time, for instance, would make an excellent element for the "History" section. Try a small video image or photograph for presentations that rely on these media to convey their message. The more coherent you make your sections, the more credence they'll lend to your conclusions.

Chris Potter.

Although separate section dividers work easily for slides or electronic presentations and can help organize Web site access, they can add fuss and bother to overheads and flip charts. If you're preparing an overhead presentation and plan to launch directly into the topic without spending too much time on a transition, you might incorporate the section heading into the first frame of the material.

Running heads are helpful guides providing continuity throughout a complex presentation. The running head identifies the section topic in a small line of type near the top of each frame. It integrates the set of frames and reminds the viewer of the presentation's larger structure.

Invite A Following

The segue function of the section divider makes it an ideal place to present a pithy quote or an authoritative claim. Because it's already in an overview position, the section divider sequence can provide some perspective to the presentation. A humorous quote adds sparkle to the flow of ideas; a provocative citation adds spice.

Your presentation need not be top-heavy with loads of information coming at the viewer in a constant barrage. Pace yourself through a long presentation with changes in the density of information as well as changes in tone and intensity. Your audience will appreciate the relief and heed the emphasis.

List Winners

The best list frames are the kind of notes each member of the audience would write as a personal reminder if they really understood the material: tight summaries of each idea. Lists are perfect for presenting material that lends itself to grouping and itemizing, such as names, procedures, sequences, or features.

The Golden Thread

The essential ingredients of good bullet list frames are excellent organization and the consistent presentation of concepts. These lists help members of the audience key into the speaker's points, orienting them to the subject matter at a glance. For this reason, bullet lists are effective only to the extent that they're brief and clear. If they're overwhelming in detail or length, they become discursive and distracting.

Think of the subject of the list as a kind of golden thread running through the content. Never let one idea strand grow too far from the central thread, or it may obscure the others. Try to connect each idea to its thread with the same kind of knot. Your golden thread is strong enough to support four or five strands, but it starts to stretch and distort as more are added. Allow the soft gleam of the golden subject thread to remain visible and strong, attracting and engaging the audience.

• • • • • • •

Birds of a Feather

- Nesting habits

- Song pattern

- Migratory route

- Food preference

Headings

The headings for bullet lists should be lively and focused. Whenever possible, use active verbs that support and energize the topic. Steer clear of clichés and tired lines. Write each frame heading in a particular group using a similar style and consistent grammatical construction. Make each heading a short phrase, a single word, or a very brief sentence.

You may be tempted to put a colon at the end of the heading, but the format of the frame will clarify the relationship between the heading and the bulleted entries. The extra colon can dilute the graphic tension created by the contrast between the heading and bullet items. Avoid punctuation in situations like this, when you might end up with a colon for every heading. Reserve it, instead, for those special situations that need extra clarification or emphasis.

Consider using a subhead rather than a longer heading when meaning must be augmented. Headings and subheads are a good way to maintain consistency without sacrificing content. Visually distinguish these headings and subheads, as you did in the opening titles.

Bullet Entries

Reduce each item in a bullet list to a few key words or a tight phrase. Don't worry about complete sentences or the traditional outline format, but do keep points on the same frame grammatically consistent by using the same type of phrasing or structure. Work for this kind of consistency from frame to frame, as well. It conveys a sense of authority and polish, with a convincingly in-control tone.

Move repetitive words or phrases to the heading or subhead. For example, when discussing regional sales, pull the word "Reports" from each entry and use it in the heading.

By Region

- West Coast Report
- Central Report
- Southern Report
- Northeastern Report

Regional Reports

- West Coast
- Central
- South
- Northeast

Condensed language will help you keep each entry on a single line for a more streamlined visual effect. When you come across an idea that simply won't be cut to less than two lines, work it into your format gracefully. Set less leading (line spacing) between the two lines of the entry than between bulleted items, so a viewer perceives the units at once. "Hang indent" the second line the same amount as the text of the first. Choose the spot where you'll break the line to match the content or phrasing, rather than running the type to the maximum line length and dribbling a few leftover words onto the second line.

It's essential to separate the last line of one bulleted item from the first line of the next bulleted item. Otherwise, the visual effect will be confusing and unorganized, even when bullets signal the beginning of a new idea. Make the extra effort to plan wise use of the space between lines of type and between bullet points. The resulting graphic sophistication will more than repay your fine-tuning.

● ● ● ● ● ● ●

Gourmet Hoo!

- **Spring**
  – Snake jerky
  – Bunny burgers

- **Summer**
  – Bar-b-que squirrel ribs
  – Stir-frog

- **Winter**
  – Hearty rat stew
  – Chipmunk chowder

How many bullet entries can each frame hold effectively? That depends on the complexity of the ideas presented and the format of the entries—whether they're one-word quips lightly passed over, or full phrases representing ideas considered in some depth. In general, though, you should consider breaking topic headings with more than four or five bullet items into two or more frames. Group the items logically so the frame breaks follow your content. You might even keep the same heading for this series of frames and write different subheads to indicate the more detailed criteria within the broader topic.

Bullet entries rarely need punctuation, either within the line or at the end. In fact, the discrete quality of the phrasing and line breaks creates its own rhythm, and commas, semicolons, or periods can distract from the open flow of information.

Bullet Symbols

The bullet symbols themselves can make interesting, subtle graphic elements. Traditional printer's bullets—dots, squares, arrows, or pointing hands—serve to set off individual entries. Each has a distinct personality that contributes to the overall frame design and to the typographic flavor. Squares, for instance, are sharp and bold, dots more subtle, and right-facing triangles imply motion. Checkmarks indicate checklists. Long em dashes make excellent bullets for secondary points.

Zapf Dingbats and other specialty fonts provide a wide variety of ready-made bullet shapes. Experiment with the size of your bullet symbols as well as the shape. Frequently a bullet set in a slightly smaller point size will balance well with the text that follows, without overwhelming the frame. Foreground colors will emphasize the bullet symbols and call attention to their sequence, whereas midground colors will convey an attitude that's calmer and steadier. Variations of standard shapes and colors, like square bullets with a graduated fill, can be extremely effective additions to text frames.

For a special presentation, create your own bullets with simple shapes that reflect the subject matter. Slight variations of the standard symbols work more effectively than complicated drawings. Often these details aren't noticed on first glance, but as you move through the program, the audience will begin to observe the fine points and move to a greater level of engagement. When you make your own bullets, however, use caution. Whimsical shapes can become tiring and dull when used frame after frame. If your shape is particularly distinctive, you might decide it's best used once per frame, in concert with more standard shapes, to convey special emphasis for the most important point.

Bullet Subentries

When the concepts under discussion are complex, bullet lists may work best with subentries to break out more detailed information about a particular point. Limit the layers of information in each frame to two—three at the very most. Otherwise, your audience may become tangled in the structure of the frame and lose the anchoring connection. Make use of follow-up frames and more detailed layers of information to supplement the primary flow.

On any particular frame, subentries should be the exception rather than the rule. When many points need further clarification, don't try to squeeze lots of levels into one frame. Instead, devote an entire frame to a major point, including three or four subentries of detailed information you plan to emphasize in the presentation. If necessary, return to an overview frame and pick up with the next major point.

It's a good idea to offer the viewer a visual distinction between principal entries and subentries. Try indenting the subentry, choosing a secondary size or weight or type, or working with a subsidiary bullet shape and color. Em dashes work especially well as bullet symbols for subentries, because they convey the sense of a list with less drama than squares or circles.

Summaries

Summary frames take the audience in the opposite direction from detail frames, up for an overview rather than down for a closer inspection. Sum-

NUMEROLOGY

Numerals can be viewed as a specialized kind of bullet symbol. Numbers convey a particular meaning: they prioritize and rank the bullet entries. When you choose to work with numerals, be sure the items are part of an ordered sequence, related by time or hierarchy of importance. Consider also that numbers can imply such an order, even when you don't intend it. A whole series of numbered frames can grow tedious and overbearing, so be sure to take the context into account when you opt for numbers.

maries can recap the major topics in the presentation as a whole, or they can work with a particular portion of the program. Try using them right after a section divider frame to orient the audience, or following a segment to give your viewers a quick review of the points you've made on that topic. Offer them to Web surfers to provide an idea map of the site. You might even label them "Summary" or "Overview" to distinguish them from other bullet lists and to allow the audience to reflect on the overall shape of the material you're presenting.

Build Sequences

To keep your audience following the flow of information through the presentation, think of building your points by revealing them one by one on the screen. This method encourages viewers to focus on the current topic and prevents them from reading ahead to your next points (and getting confused). Build sequences work very well with slides and electronic presentations, because the changes are smoothly animated. Overheads and flip charts are less easily orchestrated as build sequences and require other highlighting techniques (see Chapter 3).

There are many different variations on the theme of building bullet list sequences. Experiment with several to see what works best for your content material and overall design, then continue to use it wherever appropriate throughout the presentation.

Because they're dynamic, build sequences help to keep your audience involved visually with the screen. At first, viewers will see only the heading and subhead, and possibly the first bullet item. Many presenters like to highlight the text of each new point as it is added to focus the viewers' attention on it. All previous points are then lowlighted for contrast. Create highlight and lowlight effects through brighter and duller color combinations, boldface and roman type weights, larger and smaller typefaces, or different bullet symbols. Experiment to find the contrast that works best for your frames, but keep it fairly subtle. Your audience will recognize the new information quite readily—no need to use your loudest voice.

For build sequences to work effectively, you should have something to say about each point as it's added. This technique is excessively intrusive and interrupts the flow of information if you're planning to build the whole frame immediately and then talk about the points as a group. Web pages and interactive presentations can adapt the idea of a build sequence by presenting all points on the screen at the same time, then highlighting one or two of the most important.

After you've added all the points for a particular topic, it's a good idea to pause for a moment on the full frame so the audience can review the points. This overview can also be a good starting point for the discussion, introducing the larger picture before concentrating on each component piece.

Variations on the standard build sequence are legion. Your choice will likely be a matter of matching content and delivery style to the technique as much as an issue of design. For instance, you might stay with an overview frame, keeping the entire list on-screen while you move through the bullet items and highlighting each entry as you consider it. At the opposite end of the spectrum, you might decide it's more important to focus attention entirely on the point at hand, so that only one bulleted item appears on the screen at any time until the final review frame recaps them all.

Detail-reveal sequences provide a means of incorporating subsidiary entries into the flow of the bullet build. These sequences allow space for subentries to support each point as it is highlighted. When the presenter adds the next bullet, the detail from the previous point drops away and new detail appears. Details in interactive pop-up windows or linked Web screens work like reveal sequences. The effect is flexible; detail-reveals are elastic, expanding and contracting with the content. The final frame summarizes all the major points without subentries for a clean overview.

Setting The Table

Although they're often misused or overlooked, tables make great tools for organizing the way two variables interact. Tables are multicolumn lists that present a matrix of items and subitems arranged in two directions. The calendar is a fine example of a table: It allows you to see at a glance which days will be Tuesdays in a particular month (reading down a column) and which days will be included in the second week of the month (reading across a row). At the meeting point of the variables represented by the two directions, you find the second Tuesday of the month. Tabular entries aren't limited to numbers, either—excellent matrices are constructed to show the relationships between ideas, represented by words or short phrases.

Identifying Correspondences

In cases where graphs don't present information specifically enough and verbal descriptions are too long and cumbersome, tables offer elegant solutions. They can show exact numeric values, and language can be condensed because the variables are identified in labels outside the entries. Tables can be quite visually appealing and provocative. When the relationship between two elements (like time and money, sleep and health, food and season) falls into place, people experience the "Aha!" sensation. Our job is to design tables that make these exciting correspondences visually appealing and available.

Making Connections

Start designing a table by determining the primary motion you want the audience to follow—across a column, down a row, or hopping from one entry to another. Create a matrix format that allows easiest access to this connecting motion. Transition effects within a series of frames—wipe down or wipe right, for instance—will help provide the momentum to underscore these connections.

Separate the vertical columns of a table with enough space to keep the entries from running together (about an em space or two is enough), and resist the temptation to create a strong gridwork of vertical and horizontal lines that isolate the bits of data and work against the connections and comparisons you want to generate. One good design technique is to build the matrix out of midground color blocks, then reverse the type for the entries to white or another high-contrast color. The "lines" between the color blocks remain the background color. The entries, rather than the gridline structure, should be clearly the most important elements.

Up Till All Hours

Sightings:	Night	Day
Jan–Mar	42	18
Apr–Jun	36	13
July–Sep	21	16
Oct–Dec	32	24

Allow plenty of room between horizontal lines to open up the grid. Thin horizontal rules or subtle horizontal bands of color can help the viewer follow the information across categories, working with the natural motion of left-to-right reading. If a particular column holds the key to your ideas, highlight it with a vertical band of color or set the entries themselves in a bright foreground color.

Simplifying Structure

Because you don't want your frames to look like pages from the tax tables, hold down the number of rows and columns to the bare minimum essential for making your point. A matrix with only four or six entries can convey lots of useful information. If you want to show the vast scope of the information you've considered, try starting with a small-scale table of just a few entries for the initial explanation, followed by a larger-scale table for impact and reinforcement.

As a general rule, set columns of words or short phrases flush-left, and set columns of numbers flush-right or by decimal alignment. Of course, you'll certainly find exceptions, such as a flush-right/flush-left combination for a two-column text table that enhances readability by keeping the related entries in adjacent columns close to one another.

Some very effective tables are made from matrices of yes/no answers or small icon-style symbols that indicate a particular response to the variables in the rows and columns. This condensed visual presentation allows you to convey a large amount of information in a relatively small space and is perfect for Web pages and other reference materials. Provide a well-organized key to the symbols so viewers aren't left guessing and perplexed. For live presentations, remember to break this matrix into bite-sized chunks for the audience, and be sure you focus attention on a particular area. The challenge of table design is to make a very clear point while drawing from what can be rather dense information.

Doing Decimals

Figures that include long strings after the decimal point can be as intimidating as a long row of spoons set to the right of a knife at a fancy dinner party. When your numerical entries include decimal points, help your audience to read and compare the quantities by aligning columns on the decimal, and by carrying out or rounding all values to the same number of places—preferably, the lowest-possible number. When all your values are whole numbers, don't bother with decimal points. Rather than looking impressive, all those extra zeros are likely to be confusing and misleading. Remember that the decimal point is by far the smallest element in the numeral and can be hard to see on screen. Follow the clutter-reduction principle and opt for clarity.

● ● ● ● ● ● ● ●

Feast or Famine

Per Day:	Mice	Rabbits
Jan–Mar	10.3	.8
Apr–Jun	8.9	1.4
July–Sep	21.6	2.3
Oct–Dec	15.4	1.9

Labeling Columns And Rows

Labels for tables are often radically different in kind or length from the information they mark. The words labeling vertical columns can follow the alignment of the column below, especially for text-based tables, or they can be centered over the column when that defines the column area more clearly—especially for numerical tables. Exceptions abound, of course. Much depends on the length and size of the label. When columns of figures are presented decimally aligned with a noticeably ragged left edge, flush-right column labels may look perfect. On the other hand, a thin column of checks or visual symbols calls for a label centered above it.

Typographic design choices for labels should reflect the type size and style used in the body of the table, with subtle differences to set them apart. Bold-face column labels over lightweight type provide a good solution; if the labels are much less important than the data, decrease their point size as well. Thin rules between the labels and data entries provide another good way to set them apart. Decide whether your content calls for an emphasis on column labels or on row labels. In a successful table, viewers have no trouble distinguishing labels from entries, and they move from entry to entry with ease.

The Nest Egg

Species	Eggs	Survival
Snowy	1	1.2%
Barn	2	1.3%
Screech	2	1.9%
Horned	1	1.2%

The Nest Egg

Species	Eggs	Survival
Snowy	1	1.2%
Barn	2	1.3%
Screech	2	1.9%
Horned	1	1.2%

Long, complex horizontal rows with many entries require extra line spacing between them, which will help hold them together as a unit. When space is tight, thin horizontal rules can accomplish the same purpose with just a bit more clutter. Experiment also with low-contrast, alternating background bands like the paper that accountants use to assist in line tracking. Only a subtle shift is needed, and the light touch keeps attention focused on the entries themselves.

Illustrated Text Frames

Occasionally you'll find a situation that benefits from a combination of text with a graph or diagram. A classic image of this type shows both a graph to illustrate relationships and a table to provide exact data figures. Both parts of the frame contribute significantly to the viewer's understanding, and neither would work as effectively alone.

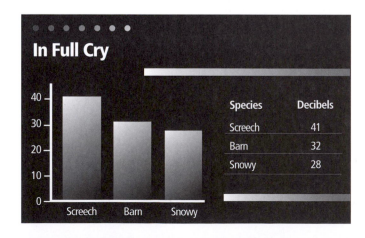

Species	Decibels
Screech	41
Barn	32
Snowy	28

Pause to reflect before including a graph or illustration in a text frame. What is the message you're delivering, exactly? Simply because they're visually interesting, these elements may draw attention from the point on which you want to focus. The illustration alone won't tell your story—or you wouldn't have felt it required the table. Is the effort to link the two worthwhile? Would they be more effective if presented individually? Presenters sometimes assume that they should always graph numbers; actually, there are many instances when a table can make the point more strongly. Don't include both forms just to hedge your bets. Convince yourself that the elements will be working in concert before packing your screen with words and graphics.

Question Frames

When a speaker plans to pause and ask for questions, a simple text frame can signal the event. It provides a neutral background for the question-and-answer format and avoids the awkwardness of displaying a screen on one topic while discussing another. Be sure to let the audience know you have set aside a time when you'll welcome questions, both because people will make an effort to remember their ideas and because they'll be less likely to inter-rupt during the rest of your presentation. When the question frame comes up, the audience sees that the speaker is ready to entertain their inquiries and will feel encouraged to speak up. These question frames provide a rather formal invitation to participate. Because they help with the technical issues of lighting and continuity, question frames tend to be more useful with slides and electronic presentations. Speakers using overheads have a bit more latitude in dimming the projector and interacting with the audience.

Follow the graphic rules you've established for the rest of your presentation when designing a question frame. One small question mark or the word "Questions" will certainly convey the point. No need for the overkill of an assortment of jumbled question marks in different sizes, colors, and type-faces. When you anticipate several question-and-answer pauses during the course of a presentation, you can use the same design each time.

Blank Frames

Sometimes there will be a part of your presentation for which no text or graphic is required, or even appropriate—delivery of an anecdote, joke, or story, for instance, or even a performance in the form of a skit. If this visual break is long, you'll probably want to turn up the houselights and reestablish personal contact; but for a short break, you can use a screen that's "blank," except for the graphic elements common to all your frames. This way, the audience won't keep staring at the old news of the last slide while new material is introduced.

Design blank frames to match the presentation's overall design. A combination of graphic elements already familiar from previous frames will make a relaxing, nondistracting "place-holder" frame. An empty plane of your background color can also make a good break. If your background color was black, be sure to use some defining elements like a box, rules, or symbols to avoid an all-black screen. (Otherwise the audience may think there's been a power failure!) Conservatively and sensibly designed, blank frames will help to pace a presentation.

Moving On

Distilling your message to its very essence will help you create simple, effective text frames. They quickly communicate the key ideas you want the audience to absorb, freeing them to hear and understand the more detailed live presentation or to locate the thread they want to investigate further in an interactive program or Web site.

8 USING GRAPHS

Graphs give physical form to abstract data. They show relationship, comparison, and change. Their magic is in being able to present several concepts simultaneously, demonstrating at a glance the ideas that linear language must take up laboriously, one at a time.

A graph's strong suit is the representation of numbers and quantities—over time, by place, or any other factor. In translating the conceptual into its visual equivalents, graphs make your ideas more easily accessible to the audience.

Focus On The Data

You can create your own graphs with sophisticated drawing programs, or save time by using automatic rendering software features. Whatever production technique you choose, the design basics will stay the same. First, make sure you start by understanding the data completely. What are the variables? What sort of comparisons do they imply? Are there any unexpected values?

Next, be certain that you're clear about the conclusions you're asking the audience to derive. Are you demonstrating relative size, change over time, or typical values? Will one event predict another? Let each graph support one particular point; focus attention on that crucial segment of the visual interpretation.

Most software for presentation and financial analysis includes automatic charting and graphing features that organize and automatically plot data into a wide variety of graph formats. Producing this kind of visual interpretation is easy, but the automatic nature of it takes many design decisions out of your control. In many cases, these are merely program defaults that you can—and should—modify and customize.

To regain power over the frame design, it's essential that you have a clear visual concept sketched out. That way, rather than meekly accepting the predetermined "factory" design offerings, you'll be able to ask the program to create the best graphs for your particular needs. No reason to settle for bland, generic interpretations of your data when you can customize to enhance communication. This effort is especially important for maintaining continuity in the graphs throughout your presentation.

By all means, take advantage of the automatic charting features for their terrific production capabilities—who wants to figure out all those angles for a pie chart, for instance? But direct the charting wizard to select your choice of colors, size, and position of the pie. Decide where labels will work most effectively, how big they should be, and what typeface will read best. Tie the pie chart frame to the rest of the presentation by using the same background, grid framework, and heading style.

Graphing Terminology

Graphs have their own language, and speaking in their lingo will help you take control of the design process. Throughout this chapter you'll encounter words with specific graph-related meanings that are very useful to know. Just to get started, I'll introduce a few important terms.

Presenting Data

In relation to graphing, the term *data* means counted or measured information. To be graphed usefully, data should vary over some regular interval of space or time, from definable group to group, or in some other clear-cut way. Population density represents the kind of data that varies over space, whereas population growth figures change through time. Comparing total population data by age group demonstrates the shifts in proportional representation. In addition, it's often interesting to track a particular category of data to show how it depends on a related factor. For instance, data points can reveal the way bird populations change in relation to food supply.

Collecting Data

Many graphing terms are drawn from the process of data collection. Each measurement or value is called an *observation*; each observation becomes one plotted point on a graph. A *variable* refers to the set of observations for each activity; a *plotted variable* means a collection of points used to shape a trend line, a set of bars, or other graphing symbols.

The *range* of the data is the extent of spread between minimum and maximum data values. This range determines the optimum graph size, shape, and scale, allowing room to plot the values in the data set. *Units* give the terms of measurement for the data—dollars, percentage points, or millimeters, for instance. A *scale* of units with appropriate reference values gives meaning to each axis of a graph. The *grid* is formed by the intersection of the two scales.

Setting The Scale

To represent quantities, time, or space, graphs must be drawn to one or more scales. Normal scales use direct relationships: When 1 inch on a graph represents $1,000, then 2 inches represents $2,000, 4 inches $4,000, and so on. Logarithmic scales, on the other hand, compress or expand time, quantities, or other values according to a progression based on a mathematical logarithm.

Graphs with one scale usually answer the simple question, "Which is biggest?" You can plot more complex, two-variable graphs with two scales: one along the horizontal x-axis, the other along the vertical y-axis. Graphing conventions lead us to expect time-related data on the horizontal and a second variable, such as quantity, along the vertical. In charting annual rainfall by month, for example, the months are typically scaled from left to right and the inches of rain from bottom to top.

Define Your Purpose

In designing a graph, your first decision will be choosing the best format. To start with the right type of graph, focus on the core relationship or pattern you want to depict in that frame. For example, when you plan to show your audience past trends as indicators of future activity, the ideal graph will emphasize the time-related aspects of the data. The two variables of a time-series graph will plot variables like employment figures or revenue against the appropriate units of time. Keep the horizontal and vertical scales consistent from graph to graph when you're building a comparative series, so the audience can count on a constant frame of reference.

On the other hand, not all information is related to time. The relationships between values associated with different places or things, frozen at a given point in time, also make elegant visual stories. You might decide to focus on productivity by shop or by individual employee performance. To detail this information without charts might well require several boring or confusing text frames; a chart can make it crystal clear in a snap.

Of course, our world is interconnected, and frequently you'll find that the ideas you want to illustrate in a graph are based on interdependent values. It's worthwhile to ask yourself the hard questions before you begin graphing. Are you showing how market share and budgetary allocations influence total sales activity and profit outcome? Decide which of these areas provides the clearest background, and build this information first. Gradually add visual representations of the other factors that influence the results, coaxing the audience from the simple toward the complex.

Similarly, it's very helpful to articulate the purpose of each graph. You may be showing how the size of a house relates to household income or asking whether education influences the amount of fat in the diet. What about the relationship between rainfall and plant growth in various climactic zones? Sort out these sets of interdependent relationships carefully to make the best choice of graphing formats.

Types Of Graphs

Each type of information has a best graphic form. Your audience will respond best to data that's presented in its most clarified state. Some simple rules of thumb will simplify your decision-making. I'll examine the design of each format in detail later in this chapter.

Bar Graphs

Compare one quantifiable aspect of places or things at a particular moment in time with single-scale *horizontal bar graphs*, the simplest format for information graphics. Typically, these graphs are scaled only along the horizontal axis; the vertical distance between bars and the thickness of the bars themselves are not scaled, but based on design considerations. These unscaled aspects must be the same for each bar, however, or an unsupported comparison will be implied. Because these graphs don't include a scale of time, it's never appropriate to connect the bars with a trend line; allow your viewers to draw their own conclusions from the clear evidence.

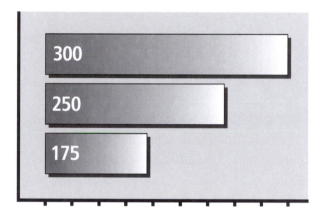

Time-related *vertical bar graphs* show the activity of one or several things through a particular time period. Single bars or sets of bars, some taller and some shorter according to the values on the y-axis, but all the same width, are spaced at distinct intervals through time. This arrangement along the horizontal axis is fairly subtle and understated, as long as observations were made regularly, each month, quarter, or year. When data is missing for any period, however, a gap for the missing period indicates the passage of time without an observation.

Line And Area Graphs

Bar graphs represent things counted at distinct intervals, like production units. Choose a *line graph* to show changes in quantities that vary continuously through time. Line graphs start with points plotted relative to scales on the horizontal and vertical axes. Each point marks a known occurrence.

Connecting these data points with a straight line gives a representation of what probably occurred between observations. Usually line graphs indicate *rate*—the relationship between change (scaled in the vertical axis) and time (scaled on the horizontal axis). Bar graphs are limited in the number of data points they can portray effectively, but line graphs can accommodate any number of data points.

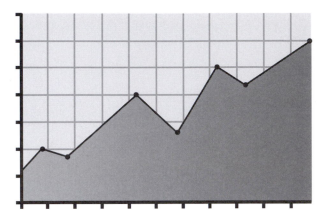

Building area graphs is similar to building line graphs, with one important addition: The space between the horizontal axis and the plotted line is filled in. This fill implies volume, so you should use area charts to present information that measures magnitude.

Pie Graphs

To show proportions in relationship to the whole, pick the pie graph. Each wedge represents a percentage of the total. Viewers comprehend pie graphs quickly and easily—provided a reasonable number of components are being compared—a pie chart with more than six or seven categories can appear cluttered and confusing, and may be difficult to "read" correctly. Pies are best at giving rough impressions of proportions; even so, unless each wedge is labeled legibly with an amount or percentage, it's impossible to make the proper comparison. Other shapes can work to show parts of the whole, as you'll see with divided bar graphs, but the circle continues to be the most popular and universally understood.

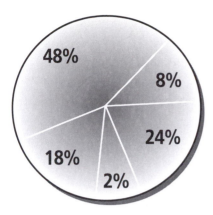

Anatomy Of A Graph

Four distinct elements are used to build any type of graph: The graph window, reference values, data symbols, and text.

The Graph Window

Technically, the graph window is that portion of the Cartesian plane on which you render your data. It is defined by the *origin* and *extent* of the plane necessary to plot the data.

The origin is the starting point of the information, the conjunction of the lowest positive values on both the vertical and horizontal axes. Typically, the origin is found at the lower-left corner of the graph window, although negative quantities can affect the placement of the axes within the graph window. The extent refers to the end of the graph window, the highest and longest space that must be opened in order to display the data. The extent is usually found at the upper-right corner of the graph window, except when negative values open an area to the left and/or below the origin.

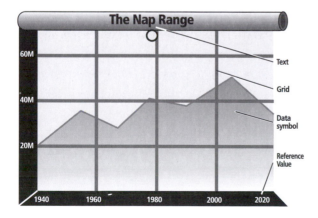

SETTING—OR SKEWING—THE SCALE

Be sure to select the true starting point for your data scale and to make this starting point obvious to your audience. To avoid distorting the data, it's vital to include the full progression from the reference value to the plotted observations, even when the reference value is zero. Suppose your data takes a jump from $6,000 to $9,000. If you start the vertical scale at $4,000 to save room, the bar representing the $9,000 will be twice as tall as the $6,000 bar—quite a misleading and unexpected graphic result.

Set the origin and extent of your graph window to accommodate the range and reference values of your data. Design graph frames to allow a generous graph window size, so data symbols can be large and prominent without distortion. Take a close look at the data itself to determine the scale and shape of the graph window. The graph symbols should nearly fill the window. Avoid extents that overrun the data and create large, empty spaces that dwarf the symbols. Make an exception to this guideline, however, when you're preparing a series of graphs comparing the same variables. In this case, use the graph with the largest range of data to draw a standard graph window. Keep the scale the same from graph to graph, creating a consistent context for the series.

In addition to size and shape, the color of the graph window itself is an important design consideration. Keep the color contrast low between the background and the window to emphasize the importance of the data symbols. Consider using slightly lighter or darker shades of the background color, or choose a midtone gray or neutral for the window. If you graduate the background, try graduating the graph window in the opposite direction. Remember that for the graph itself, the window color is the background and should provide a basis for clear display of the data.

The Window Grid

Any graph depends on a grid within the graph window to present the scale and reference values that give meaning to the visual treatment. This grid can be obvious, defined by lines, or it can be more subtle, implied by tick marks and labels. The grid orients viewers to the starting point for observation counts and measurements. It clarifies the numeric progression from that point. In most cases, the starting point reference is zero, but it can be another value appropriate to the data, like the freezing or boiling point for a substance.

When reference values don't include the true starting point (for instance, zero on the numeric scale), the column sizes can be misleading. In the following figure, at left, the difference between the 2011 and 2012 values seems to be a factor of 2. This impression is rectified when the correct proportions are generated by the full scale, at right.

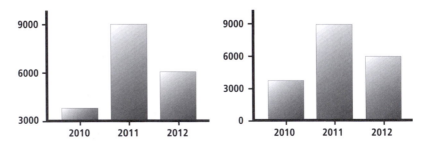

Sometimes you'll want to emphasize very important increments on the graph window grid. "Break-even level," for instance, may deserve a special bright grid line because it's an essential reference value for certain types of information.

There are many ways to handle the grid itself. At the most fully realized extreme, there are graph-paper style squares with supplementary ticks between the ruled lines. At the most minimal, no reference marks are present at all, and the observation value labels do all the work. In between, there are scores of choices, all dependent on the sophistication of the audience, the familiarity of the information, and the nature of the data itself. Some graphs work best with just horizontal grid lines, or tick marks alone, or the vertical scale alone. Some data sets depend heavily on individual values, whereas others only make sense with a comparative scale.

Thin horizontal grid lines can help the viewers read data points in formats like line graphs, where it's awkward to label observations with exact quantities. When time is important, light vertical grid lines orient viewers to the critical moments. Consider choosing colors for the grid lines that are in low contrast with the window itself—just enough difference to be clear, but not enough to steal thunder from the data.

Generally, graphs in scientific or formal presentations can use tick marks to avoid cluttering the graph window. The edge between the graph window and the background of the screen can imply an axis, so that tick marks can be placed right along the edge of the window. Give your audience just what's necessary to communicate the data with integrity, avoiding support overkill. Clear results count more than following some hard-and-fast rule.

Reference Values

Your viewers will expect scale values to break at familiar intervals, increments of 2, 5, 10, 25, 50, 100, or 1000, depending on the scope of the data. For very large scales, reduce the bulk of the figures by representing values in thousands, tens of thousands, millions, and so forth. Note this convention near the reference values, never in the heading where it may not be noticed or understood.

The standards for labeling time increments in graphs have been refined over the years by practical considerations. If you're pressed for room, there's no need to include all four digits for each year in annual data; for most graphs, include the four digits of the first observation year and only the last two digits for subsequent years. Abbreviate months to save space. When you're using familiar time increments, there's no need to spell out "Time," "Years," or "Months" under the horizontal axis. Avoid filling space with the obvious.

Data Symbols

Symbolized data forms the main part of a graph. Points, bars, pie wedges, lines, and graphic symbols illuminate statistics and clarify their relationships. The graph window, grid, reference values, notes, and scales are all "support staff," helping viewers make sense of the data symbols.

The lines connecting plotted points show what probably occurred between observations. The points, which show what you actually know, should be bright and sharp; the line interpolates what you suppose about a trend through time and needs to be quite bold, with sufficient contrast in width and color to pop it out of the graph window background.

Many presenters distinguish between magnitude and rate; they use bars and areas to imply magnitude, reserving lines for rate over time. Areas tend to have large presence in the graph window, so the bright colors necessary for a thin line can be overwhelming. Tone down your color palette slightly, and when you're dealing with more than one area, be sure that you reserve a particularly vibrant color for the specific area you want to emphasize.

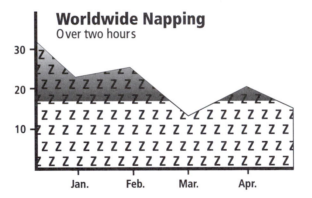

Whether bars are oriented horizontally in single-scale graphs or vertically in time-related graphs, they are linear symbols that should change size only in one direction. In other words, your bars can grow longer or taller, but no thicker or thinner. This is true for the presentation as a whole, as well as for all the bars in an individual graph. Think through the entire presentation before you start with very thick or very thin bars as part of your design style. How practical will they be for all the bar graphs you'll be making? What would you communicate with a radical change in bar thickness from one frame to another?

The one-dimensional change rule is easy to remember for simple bars, but it's also important to apply for more complex pictorial symbols. Stack small symbols instead of increasing symbol size; otherwise, you will inadvertently imply a shift in volume.

Stack symbols (as on the left-hand graph that follows) to show growth along one scale. When the symbols themselves increase in size (the right-hand graph), volume is misrepresented by growth in two dimensions.

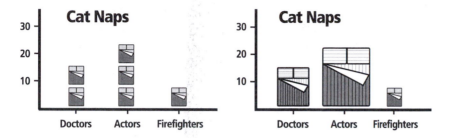

Bars are symbols for comparing measurements, whereas pies show component parts of a whole. The round form inherently conveys completeness; the angle of the wedge, sharper or more open, gives an immediate indication of size. When you tilt a pie for a three-dimensional effect, be sure that the data supports the idea of volume. Avoid radical tilts that foreshorten the circle and distort the proportions.

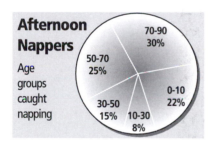
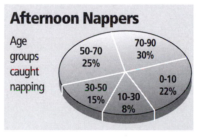

As you design the graphs in your presentation, remember to maintain consistency from frame to frame by using the same color palette and keeping the same placement of headings, subheadings, and the graph window. Bring the data symbols to the front of the visual field. Use strong color contrasts to make these symbols—bars, points, lines, or pie wedges—bold enough to stand out from the background. Animated effects can focus attention on the data symbols, but be sure to allow your audience a moment to become oriented to the graph's context before beginning the motion. Take care that the window grid recedes to the midground or background, explaining but never competing for attention with the core symbols and labels.

Text Annotation

Graphs wouldn't make much sense without titles, labels, scale indicators, and other annotations. A great heading will encapsulate the idea behind the graph in a way that the audience finds both clarifying and interesting. Every graph needs some text labels to identify exactly what is illustrated. If you think your audience will want to know where the information comes from—either to ensure its validity or to support your conclusions—be sure to include your sources. Avoid overload, however; the more you add around a graph, the more you distract from the symbols themselves. Find that balance between a stark graph and over-elaboration, where you require no more of your audience than is absolutely necessary.

Time-Related Graphing

Much of the information you deal with falls into the category of time-series graphs, which work with variables that are counted or measured as time passes. The two major families of time-series graphs are line graphs and vertical bar graphs.

Line Graphs

Typically, the subject of a line graph is rate: the measurement of quantity over a particular period of time. Line graphs "fill in the gaps" between plotted observation points to illustrate trends. You can symbolize individual observation points emphatically or subtly, depending on your message. When you draw a line between the points, you imply that the quantity measured was continuous throughout the time period. The jagged trend line clearly shows the intervals between measurements. Be sure to design lines that are thick enough to convey the important information they represent.

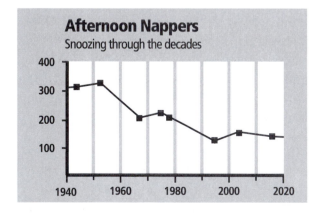

When observations have been made at uneven time intervals, or at intervals not consistent with the time increments on your horizontal scale, it's conventional to plot them as clearly marked points along the trend line. The line by itself is adequate otherwise, unless you'll be making a special point about the time intervals or data collection process. In any case, be sure to convey the measurement intervals.

Sometimes your meaning may be best served by plotting individual observation points, then showing a curve by drawing a trend line through those points. Rather than connecting individual points, this curve illustrates the relationship between points as a flow. Because it provides a sense of the pattern rather than of the precise measurements, it may be more convincing to combine this type of graph with a table that provides more detailed information. When data points are missing, a dashed or straight line will indicate your interpolation.

Line graphs can compare the rates of several different entities—from products to people—with a line for each. The design danger in these graphs comes from the tangled web they can create. Draw up each line independently, and give each the weight and color it needs to stand out from its fellows. Avoid this method for presenting data with many complicated crossings and convolutions, unless that sense of interplay is important to your message.

Motion effects can make line graphs more interesting to the audience. Draw the line from left to right; emphasize the individual data points by pausing slightly at each observation. You may even pop up the data points first, left to right or high to low, depending on your message; then draw the trend line to connect them.

Area Graphs

Whereas line graphs concentrate the viewer's attention on a single stroke, area graphs demonstrate volume by filling in the area from the baseline of the horizontal axis to the graphed line. Areas are flat and bold, eliminating many of the design difficulties associated with creating impact with points and lines. Lightly marked grids on the graph window can help differentiate the graphed area from its background.

If areas are impressive, three-dimensional areas are even more striking. Use these mountain-range images selectively to emphasize volume even further. You see the "tops" of the area blocks, so it's usually less confusing to keep them narrow. That way, the value of a particular plotted data point can be read much more easily against the vertical scale.

Vertical Bar Graphs

Vertical bar or column graphs provide another way to visualize time series; they represent a count of the same group or groups at various moments in time. Each observation in the series is marked by a bar that rises or falls from the horizontal axis. The change in bar heights demonstrates the difference between the values over a period of time The upward energy of vertical bars rising skyward lends an optimistic outlook to the graph. Electronic presentations allow you to reinforce this motion by growing or wiping the bars up from the horizontal axis. Grow all the bars at once, or add them gradually to follow your content.

Bars work well for counts of production units, orders and returns, intensities and concentrations, or populations. Where exact figures are important, they can be included at the top of the bars themselves, or below the horizontal axis. The time intervals can be days, weeks, months, quarters, years, decades, or centuries—so long as they're consistent units spread evenly across the horizontal axis with a bar or cluster of bars at each interval.

In contrast with line graphs that can display a nearly unlimited number of data points, bar graphs work well with data sets that include a discrete number of observations. As a rule of thumb, show six or fewer observations with bars rather than a line.

Too many bars will make comparison difficult. Unless pertinent information is only revealed with the more detailed treatment, it's easier for an audience to grasp the implications of 4 quarterly bars than 12 monthly bars. When you must present bar graphs with many columns, use them as overview frames, then follow with detail frames that zoom in to concentrate on particular sections of the overview. As you strategize to work toward clarity, this type of sequence thinking will become an important ally.

Three-dimensional effects, drop shadows, and bars shaped like pyramids or octagons look intriguing at first. Maintaining accuracy and easy reference to scaled values are the major difficulty in working with these unusual bars. Sometimes adding depth makes it hard to tell which part of the bar represents the top, so it's impossible to read individual values against the scale. Visual comparisons can be distorted by pointed shapes like pyramids that are squat when small and needle-like when tall. If you're considering a design that relies on a particular effect, try it out on several sample time series drawn from the beginning, middle, and end of the presentation—then you won't have a continuity crisis late in the day.

Time-Series Combinations

Think of points, lines, areas, and bars as the basics of time-series representation. Variations and combinations of these building blocks—such as multiple lines, several areas, or lines and bars together—convey more complex information and relationships. Audiences see certain patterns in data more readily through combination graphs than when they're following a set of single-subject graphs. For instance, how did monthly projected sales compare with real sales over the past year? Neither the projected sales line nor the real sales line alone is enough to assess the accuracy of your prediction methods. The two lines in combination—and the space between them—will tell the story.

The more information you pack into a single frame, or the more complex and multifaceted the comparisons, the more vital it becomes to be absolutely clear about the message of the frame. Decide which information is essential to convey that message, and which is secondary—interesting, but a step or two removed from the first level of understanding. Spin off these collateral ideas into separate frames, or animate the graph to add them once you've established a firm groundwork. Otherwise, you can quickly develop an impenetrable jungle of graphic symbols and scales. Combination frames are particularly prone to information overload, because they're a balancing act to begin with. Just remember to limit each graph to a particular point, so that your audience can easily follow the development of your analysis or argument.

A look at your data will help you determine whether you can chart it clearly. How subtle is the relationship you're trying to establish visually? Try a preliminary test for a multiple-line graph, for example. Are your lines tangled and entwined, or separate and distinct? Can you adjust the vertical scale to pull them apart? Do different, bright colors help you follow them visually? Label each line close to the right edge of the graph window, and align the labels to keep the frame as clean as possible.

Multiple-area graphs work only when smaller areas can be placed in front of larger areas. If the values for one area fall below those of the area in front of it, the information will be blocked and lost to view. Label areas within the graph window whenever possible. Reserve legends in line and area graphs as your last resort, because they take up space you'll need for the most effective graph window and they require the viewer to take a further interpretive step.

Clustered bar graphs generally do require a legend to identify the elements, so if your presentation lends itself to this type of format, design a space that can be reserved consistently for the legend without interfering with the audience's focus on the graph symbols—outside the graph window. Try spreading the legend horizontally across the bottom of the frame. To relieve confusion, represent similar types of information with the same colors throughout the course of the presentation.

Sequences help enhance and develop the complicated messages presented in combination graphs. Start with the first and most basic line or set of bars; then add layers of information in a way that reflects normal learning patterns. Animate the frame to start simply, then build in complexity. By the time the image is complete, your audience will already understand the message, and you won't find yourself trying to untangle a Celtic knot of lines and bars for them.

Most combination graphs show data collected over the same time period and using the same unit measurements, so the scales on both the vertical and horizontal axes remain constant. Occasionally it's useful to compare the trends or general shapes of data measured in two different categories of units—money and widgets, temperature and weight, rainfall and volume. In these cases, keep the time values on the horizontal axis constant, and draw a double-scale graph using two vertical scales. A graph that demonstrates the relationship between the product price and the number of products sold requires this kind of double scale for each pair of variables measured in dollars and product units.

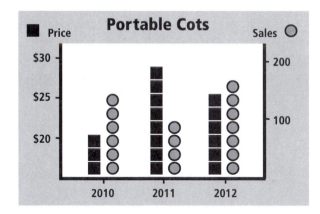

Double-scale graphs require clear, concise labels, and scale indictors to help the audience identify the variables quickly. Label the scale for one variable on the usual vertical axis at the left side of the graph window, and create a second vertical axis on the right for the second variable scale. Link data symbols to the correct scale with color, shape, texture, labels, and other graphic devices.

As your graphs grow more complex, attend closely to annotation and scale identifiers. Are they absolutely clear? Can viewers make the right connections quickly and easily? Keep your language terse, and make every word contribute to the meaning.

Comparing Component Parts

When the parts of a whole are presented successfully, the audience grasps their relative importance intuitively. Any shape can be divided proportionally into component parts, but circles are the traditional favorites. The wedges cut from a pie graph make sense to use, as long as they're not too small. Squares and rectangles can be divided, but audiences don't recognize them immediately as parts of a whole. Reserve these shapes for shows that allow the luxury of setting up and maintaining the context over several frames. There's also the chance that viewers might interpret these boxes as area or bar graphs—especially confusing when your presentation includes both types of graph formats.

Budgets are excellent subjects for pie chart representation: Visualize total revenues as the entire pie, cutting a separate wedge for each expenditure category.

Pie Graphs

With their simple, flexible structure, pie graphs make interesting and elegant charts. Be sure your data supports this format, however—pies work only when the parts add up to a whole, with the percentages totaling 100 percent. The scale is actually a single quantity, starting at zero and going around the circle that represents 360 degrees, 100 percent, or some other appropriate whole value. To determine wedge size, convert each observation's value to a percentage or fraction of the total, which the graphing program will plot as a portion of 360 degrees.

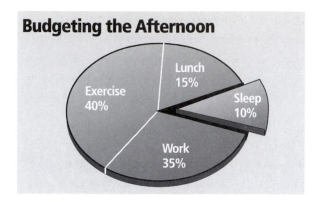

Pie graphs work best with relatively few slices—more than seven components can be confusing for the viewer and difficult for the designer to
distinguish and label. In fact, labeling is a challenge and often a frustration
in creating a pie graph; sometimes it takes a lot of work to rotate the pie and
to position and size labels for maximum clarity. If any wedge is small, as
usually happens, labeling inside the pie won't work. With more than four or
five wedges, labels look too scattered and diffuse when they're positioned
next to the appropriate wedges, outside the pie.

One solution to the labeling dilemma is to create a callout list to the right of the
pie, aligned flush left. Connect each label with the appropriate wedge by drawing a thin line, jointed if necessary but never crossing another line. A small dot
at the end of the line will anchor it to the wedge. Labels, values, and percentages can all be included in the callout list when they enhance the content. A
row of small bullet-like squares, colored to correspond with the wedge colors,
makes a nice addition to the callout list, but avoid a true legend if you can
find an alternative. The main idea is to allow your audience to read the chart
at a glance, rather than jumping back and forth between pie and legend.

The conventional way to organize the pie segments is from small to large,
starting at the top (12 o'clock) or the right (3 o'clock). In a graph with only
two observations, center the smaller segment at 3 o'clock. Handle the color
palette with care so that contrast draws attention to the most important
sections. Pies can be drawn directly in the background of the frame—a
graph window is not necessary—but position the circle in the area you've
designed for the window to fall in other frames of the presentation. The
simplest color combination is merely a high-contrast color for the focal
wedge, with a medium-contrast color for the remainder of the pie. White
labels and wedge outlines look clean and crisp over saturated colors. If you
find it advantageous to color each wedge differently, work with a palette of
similarly subdued hues, saving the bright colors for emphasis.

Direct attention to a slice you'd like to highlight by choosing a high-contrast color or by exploding it out of the pie. You can even animate this effect to slide it out. When your content calls for you to refer to each pie slice in turn, consider exploding each and adding relevant figures as you go. Here again, a basic context followed by a sequence will simplify the presentation of complicated information.

Designers enjoy working with the pie shape because the form is simple and flexible enough to allow shadowing, tilting, and adding a third dimension. These design treatments can definitely enhance the visual appeal, but run a reality check to be sure they don't distort the relative size of the wedges. Does the graph still express the proportions you started with? Sometimes rotating the pie can help bring the slices back into synch and overcome that perceptual difficulty.

Pies aren't the ideal format for comparing the components of two or more wholes. Although you grasp relative sizes within the same pie, it's harder to compare wedges of different pies unless the breakdown is extremely simple. In that case, let the second and any other pies follow the order established by the first, even if the wedges are no longer organized by size. For more complex information, try divided bars, a series of clustered bars, or a table to communicate comparisons among groups more effectively.

Divided Bar Graphs

Because it can be more precise than a pie, a divided bar graph is a good alternative for comparing the relative parts among several wholes. This format makes it easier to shift attention between corresponding components—over time, for instance—and it's even possible to compare the relative sizes of the wholes as well. Labels fit nicely inside the bars. Because the bars are scaled, they can display certain types of statistical information extremely well.

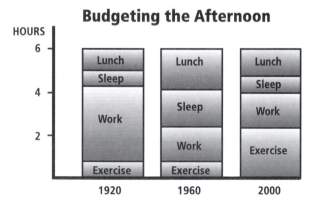

> ### SPLITTING THE BARS—BUT NOT TOO FINELY
>
> You might be tempted to divide the bars into more components than you'd use in a pie graph, but resist the urge. Give your audience only the information they'll be able to absorb during the time they're viewing the graph. Build or animate the bars, division by division, to demonstrate the relationships among them and to make the comparisons more direct.

Comparing Places Or Things

To show relationships between people, products, regions, or companies at a moment frozen in time, bring the horizontal bar graph into action. Because this visual comparison uses a scale only along the horizontal axis, you're free to organize observations vertically in any order that reinforces your point.

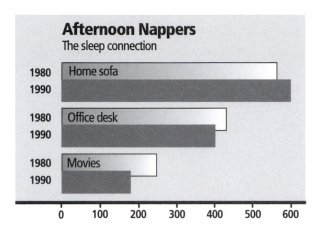

Traditionally, observations are ranked by size, with the largest bar at the top. If another order would work best with your material, however, that should certainly override convention. When you ask the audience to compare information in two or more horizontal bar graphs, remember to keep your observations in the same order in each graph.

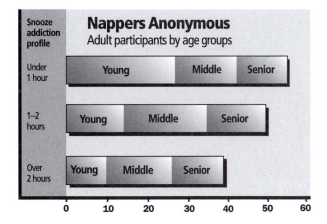

Horizontal bar charts emphasize the observation with the longest bar—it's second nature for us to look for the "winner," the first bar in the group across the finish line. Structure your live presentation to take this inclination into account, and highlight with color or position any other bars you'd like the audience to notice.

Because they start simply, horizontal bar graphs lend themselves to elaboration. Show total volume with some additional detail by subdividing each bar. To direct attention toward specific values or attributes, pair or group the bars.

Pairs Of Bars

The population pyramid is a great format to use for organizing demographic information into the specialized form of the paired horizontal bar graph.

Place zero at the middle of the graph window; then draw one scale to the left of zero to reference the number of males, and a second scale to the right of zero for the female count. The scales should be mirror images, using the same values and increments. Each bar represents an age group. Unlike the comparison of places and things, bars in population pyramids join flush at zero, because this type of data is continuous.

Try this model to represent other paired values, flipping one to the left and the other to the right. Sometimes the butterfly configuration helps the audience understand the data more intuitively than grouping the variables as pairs of bars along a single scale to the right of zero. The wider, shorter structure may also fit better in your available space. Choose the type of pairs that work best with your data and audience.

Animated effects create interesting patterns with butterfly graphs, drawing the bars from the central vertical axis, either one set at a time or all together. Or if you'll be talking about all the female variables first, draw the right side up just like a regular horizontal bar chart. When you're ready to address the male population variables, draw up the left side of the graph.

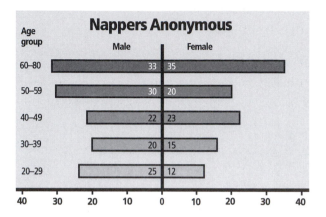

Deviation Bars

Bars to the right or left of the reference axis will indicate the area of standard deviation, emphasizing differences from the expected value. Because position says it all, it's not necessary to color-code observations to the right or left of the reference value.

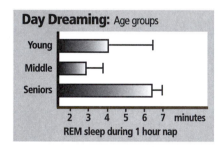

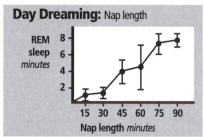

With particular types of information, it's appropriate to use deviation symbols horizontally, as sliding or floating bars. They indicate the beginning and end of each observation, like the visualization of a time line.

Distribution And Correlation

Graphs can show more than a set of observations or a trend: They also demonstrate what's typical or exceptional about an event. Statisticians apply precise mathematical measurements to determine the parameters of data sets, and they use specific graph forms to express them. You may find that you need to incorporate statistical analysis in your presentation; here's a guide to handling such data accurately.

Frequency Distributions

Statistical studies start with raw data, which must be organized for analysis. One method of arranging data is by dividing it into groups that are easy to compare and quick to reveal interesting relationships.

The *frequency* of a variable is the number of times it occurs. The *frequency distribution* measures size (quantity or magnitude). The classic example of frequency distribution is a group of student test scores. Let's say a test had 50 possible points. Some number of students taking the test scored between 40 and 50 points; some number scored between 30 and 40 points, and so on. The number of students scoring within a given point range represents the frequency of occurrence.

Chart a frequency data graph as a *histogram*. The shape of the histogram reveals the distribution of measurements along the horizontal scale, which is divided into bins.

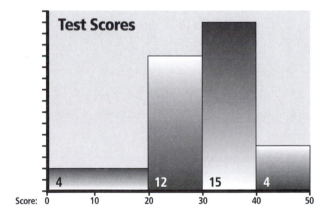

The height of each bar shows the number of measurements that fall into a particular bin. The normal curve, or bell curve, is a good example of the histogram. The curve of a normal distribution of test scores confirms what we suspected: Most of us are average, a few are slightly above or below average, and even fewer are far above or far below average.

Unlike the bars in time-series graphs, the rectangular bins in histograms are scaled in two dimensions. The width of each rectangle represents the class interval (the 10 points between 40 and 50, for example), whereas the height of each rectangle represents the number of occurrences. If class intervals aren't equal, rectangle widths must be varied accordingly, and adjustments to height made to preserve accuracy. The bin symbols are areal rather than linear.

The bin drawn for the first class, scores ranging from 0 to 20, must be twice the width of the 10-unit classes. Next, the height of the bin must be half of what it would be if the width weren't doubled. This accurately represents the data: Four students scoring between 0 and 20. If the height hadn't been cut in half, the histogram would have shown eight students in this bin.

Because histogram data is continuous, the bins are drawn flush to each other and to the sides of the graph. Time-series bars, by contrast, are separated by space.

Until you've made several presentations that incorporate frequency data, you may not feel totally confident about how to visualize the information. Ask the person who made the study or passed the data along to look over your sketches before you go into final production.

Correlations And Scattergrams

You know that some activities are linked to each other by virtue of cause and effect. The degree to which one event can be predicted from another can be visualized in a graph. When linked pairs of variables are part of your story, make it clear to the audience how one variable increases as the other decreases, or vice versa.

A scattergram shows how two data sets correlate. As in time-series graphing, points are plotted in reference to two scales. Each observation in a scattergram, however, is independent of the others, so the points are never linked as they would be in a line graph. The pattern of plotted points alone reveals the nature of the correlation, defining a positive, negative, or absent relationship between the variables. This pattern can be built in a sequence by adding several showers of dots.

Scattergrams are often presented with a regression line. The slope and position of this line are calculated from the data to represent the trend of the data set. Make the regression line a different color from the plotted points. Draw it on the screen or build it into a sequence of frames after you've presented the data points. Include a regression line only when it's statistically derived. If you don't have precise numerical values for plotting the line, don't estimate—just leave it out.

A background grid is rarely helpful in scattergrams. Instead, use tick marks along the axes to leave the data symbol field as clear as possible. Size and color the point symbols so they're readily visible on the background of the graph window.

Beware: The fact that two variables tend to increase or decrease simultaneously doesn't necessarily prove cause and effect. Perhaps the two variables are driven by a third, without which your graph will present an invalid conclusion.

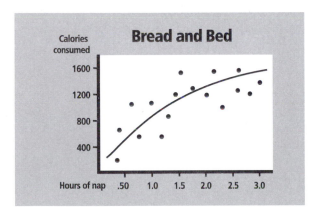

Frequency graphs and scattergrams are not only tricky to construct, they're tricky to interpret. Not all audiences will respond positively to such technical graphs. Ask yourself whether the folks out there will relate to these formats. Would a table or a verbal explanation make the information easier to understand? As strongly as I believe in visual interpretation of information, I still urge you not to create complex statistical images that might be beyond the needs of your audience. When your viewers have a scientific background, such forms are fine, but for general viewing it's usually safer to stay with other types of visual representation.

Moving On

It's vital to choose the right graph for the information you want to communicate in each frame. Keep that information tightly defined so the graph can do its job. Integrate the graph frames with the title sequences and text frames so they're all part of the same story. It's also a good idea to stick with one type of graph—such as pie charts—when you are presenting a series of statistical information so the audience doesn't have to re-interpret graph after graph.

In the next chapter, I'll look at another form of visualization—one that deals with nonnumeric relationships and processes. Diagrams can be simple or complex, but they're indispensable for explaining certain concepts to your audience.

9 USING DIAGRAMS

Communication of key points in your presentation—time sequences, processes, plans, and even abstract concepts—will often benefit from a visual interpretation. Diagrams provide the means for making ideas tangible.

Diagrams are the quintessential visualization tools of our day: They give form to a process or idea so that it becomes tangible and thus quickly communicated to the audience. Neither statistical, like a graph, nor strictly representative, like a traditional illustration, diagrams are a special form of stylized communication. We understand certain types of information much more clearly when we see them presented through the visual metaphor of a diagram.

Diagrams unfold relationships among parts of a whole that aren't necessarily quantitative. When you want to communicate the exact amount of difference between one element and another—the fact that people in the city drink four times as much regular coffee as decaf, for instance—a graph, with its reference values and grid, is perfect. But when your goal is to show how and why people drink a whole lot more caffeinated coffee than decaf, and the scale of difference isn't very important, a diagram is your format of choice.

Each diagram is unique, and there are few hard-and-fast rules. We can, however, visualize concepts by using certain common concepts and elements.

Links And Nodes: Modular Thinking

You can construct a wide range of diagrams using links and nodes as building blocks. Think of nodes as the entities that remain constant: people in an organization, occurrences that happen over time, activities that must be accomplished. Then consider the links between them, aiming to show the process and the flow between nodes. Understanding the basic nature of these links will help you arrange nodes into the hierarchy of positions in an organization, the transitions from one status to another, or the branches of a decision tree.

Begin visualizing a diagram by identifying and organizing the nodes—the fixed points—then allow the more flexible links to follow. Sort the nodes into like and unlike groups, working toward dimension and structure. If possible, reduce the groups to about four major categories. As your diagram takes shape, you can differentiate these categories by shape, color, size, or position.

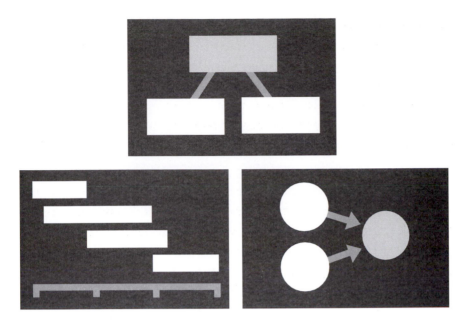

Because all the links between nodes won't indicate the same type of relationship, categorize them as well. When movement is a factor, for instance, separate the one-way from the round-trip, and use different arrow shapes for each. Links may be coded by color or varied in width to imply different types of relationships. Dashed or dotted lines traditionally show intermittent or partial links. Translate the vital characteristics of a link into visual terms whenever possible. Try to make these visualizations convey the essential nature of the link, holding to a minimum any special circumstances requiring a note or key.

Finding The Pattern

Freed from strict quantitative restrictions, the layout of a link-and-node diagram gives you a great deal of freedom to assemble patterns of ideas in the way that will prove most helpful for your audience. In most cases, the arrangement of the nodes is up to you. Don't confine yourself to any particular preconceived structure at this point; sketch and let the natural shape of the diagram emerge. As you experiment with pencil and paper, work out an arrangement of nodes that reduces the number of links that cross or impinge on one another, because those are the points where the risk of confusion is greatest. Remember that we naturally work across the screen, from left to right, from top to bottom, or radiating out from a central point where the graphics focus our attention.

Integrating Design

After you've organized the links and nodes into an elegant two-dimensional relationship, you'll want to incorporate this pattern into the overall design of your presentation frames. Consider setting up an overall grid structure that will help you align the pieces, positioning and grouping nodes across the frame according to the grid's invisible guidelines. This approach will make it easy to incorporate the diagram into the presentation's structure for the heading, subhead, and other consistent elements of the screen. On the other hand, diagrams sometimes work best when the designer relies on a symmetry inherent in the material to establish a balanced internal structure and then positions them within the presentation screen. If the content doesn't allow this sense of even unfolding, don't force it.

Contrast will help your viewers distinguish first between links and nodes, and then among categories of nodes or links. Regular, rectangular nodes are set off to advantage by curving links; heavy nodes can look more elegant with lighter links, and nodes drawn in free-form shapes are helped by geometric links.

Flowing Into Meaning

At every stage of the design process, keep in mind that your goal is a diagram that's accessible and easy to read. In a presentation, the audience must grasp the important ideas in a very limited time period. Representations that take a long time to decipher and break down don't help illuminate the content. Try to simplify complex systems into their component parts, addressing each section separately; then show how they all fit together in a summary diagram.

By enhancing a direction and motion that your audience finds natural, you'll draw them into the diagram more easily. We usually expect time-related diagrams, for instance, to read from left to right. Occasionally they'll unfold from top to bottom, when the events are congruent with this type of organization, but they're almost never successful when they expect the viewer to follow against the grain, right to left or bottom to top.

Authority typically flows from top to bottom, and this structure makes the hierarchy clear. Left to right might also work well and provide a more interesting take on the standard organizational chart. When you're constructing an organizational diagram, be sure to put the big cheeses where they belong!

Because order and timing are major factors in most sequenced information, a big part of your job is to visualize them clearly. Step-by-step instructions and other sequential diagrams rely on a clear directional flow. Consider making the organizing lines explicit in the diagram itself. When you show a long left-to-right sequence in two or more rows, for example, connect them with a device such as a ribbon or strip wrapping from row to row.

Labeling For Clarity

To continue my theme of clarity and the importance of immediate perception, I urge labeling a diagram as directly as possible. Place type right on the nodes and alongside the links rather than in a discrete legend. Fitting the labels to the diagram should be an important design priority. When the diagram itself is too complex to allow individual labels, find an alternative method, labeling the categories or building the diagram so that each new layer can be labeled as it's added. Once identified, the nodes and links can lose their specific labels and revert to category reminders.

Select type for labels that contrasts well with the type you use throughout the program for headings and subheads. Weight, size, or typeface changes will provide a welcome separation. The consistent application of a type style within the diagram will help hold it together as a single unit.

In some diagrams, the label itself can represent the node, without a border or box of any kind. Carefully composed labels allow the type to do all the work, supported by links that connect the labels. Experiment with a rectangle of open space around the label, a kind of implied node box that's the same color as the diagram background. As an alternative, try pulling the node area out of the background just a bit more with a drop shadow or three-dimensional shadow, keeping the face of the node box the same color as the background. This low-key setup allows you to add color and highlight the area of the diagram you're presenting at the moment.

Building In Motion

Showing development and movement between stages is what diagrams do best. That capacity makes them particularly good candidates for motion media or sequential unfurling through animated effects. As you plan each diagram, think of it as a series of small steps moving the viewer forward. The concept of direction is particularly important: Establish a beginning point, a middle section consisting of several intermediary points, and an arrival or endpoint. Adding a step at a time focuses attention on the particular information at hand while revealing the overall pattern.

Motion allows you to underscore the difference between links and nodes. For instance, you might animate the linking lines to draw across the screen in their natural direction, then pop in the nodes. Or, you might wipe on the nodes first and dissolve up the links to join them.

It can be tedious to make each individual node represent a step, especially if this creates an unnatural pause in the presentation. Alternative or simultaneous occurrences can easily be drawn up together. Try working in larger categories, pulling up several smaller steps together. Pause between steps as necessary, or complete the diagram in one smooth motion to give the audience the complete picture.

Process Diagrams: Visual Stories

The process diagram is a particularly satisfying type of visual representation because it tells a story with a beginning, middle, and end. This type of diagram allows you to examine the essential nature of the process itself, in order to find out how it brings together raw materials, acts to transform them, and creates something new—a product, service, or theory, for example.

Processes frequently involve links and nodes arranged in sequences, conditional branches, relationships, functions, and changes. When they are clearly conceptualized and rendered, process diagrams create a universal language for how things work. That's why we're able to "read" something of the processes in pictograms even when the labels aren't in our own language or the culture that created them is far removed from our own in time or space.

To become familiar with process thinking, imagine a very mundane activity, such as cooking an egg. For this task, you need ingredients: An egg and butter are your raw materials. Your tools are a heat source, a pan, and a plate. Once these are assembled, certain steps must take place in the correct order—heat and butter the pan, break an egg into it, allow the heat to cause chemical changes to the protein of the egg, varying the time to match certain predetermined specifications (which means you're cooking it, of course), turn it over, cook it more, and transfer it to a plate. Quite a linear activity resulting in a fried egg.

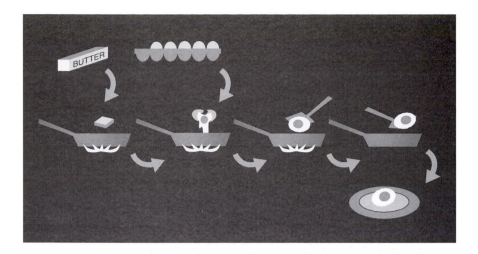

To toast bread, you engage in another linear activity. First you locate the raw materials of bread and butter, as well as your tools: a toaster and a knife. Then you move the materials through the steps required, sliding a slice of bread into the toaster, activating the heating coils, removing the toasted bread, and spreading it with butter.

If you want to make toast at the same time you cook the egg, the process is elevated to a higher level of complexity. Butter becomes a shared resource that supplies both the frying pan and the toast; the plate receives both finished products. The simultaneous activities of this process require a process diagram different from the one we would normally use for a single set of steps. Because of the complexity, motion or animation can act as an important tool of clarification. In our breakfast example, we might start with the central raw ingredients and then move down each chain of events simultaneously. To show even this slight level of complexity, position and timing are critical.

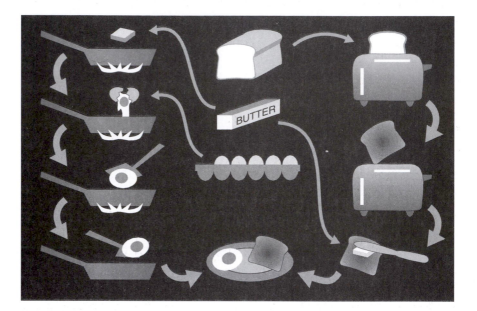

The construction of a building is a process that can be diagrammed successfully. Wall supports must be up before the roof can go on, certain materials must be delivered to the site before the plumbing system can be installed, and so forth. Because it involves many more steps than cooking breakfast—some simultaneous, some with shared resources—you'll have to decide on the level of detail you want to show. It's perfectly possible to present an overview frame, then delve into the particulars of certain phases using a more linear progression.

Diagrams give us a new way to understand and analyze activities, one that's more concentrated—and often more revealing—than a narrative description. They're handy tools for planning and organizing, revealing gaps in our systems. The order of activities, availability of materials, and supply of specialized skills are so essential to many projects that special graphic forms have been devised to handle them: PERT charts, critical path method diagrams, and Gantt charts.

PERT Charts

PERT stands for Program Evaluation Review Technique, and PERT charts are management tools for planning processes and checking to be sure they're on track. Especially valuable when a slew of activities must be accomplished in a certain order, a PERT chart shows the correct sequence and the length of time necessary for each task. Unlike garden-variety flow diagrams, links are drawn to scale so that tasks requiring more time are shown as longer lines.

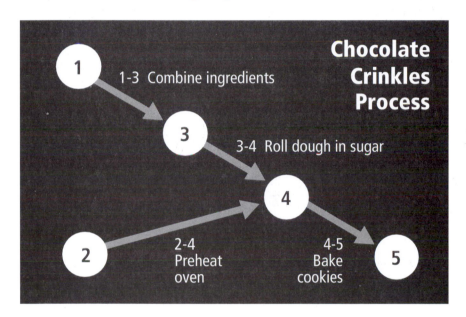

Adapting the typical PERT chart as a presentation graphic will involve choosing the relevant information, simplifying the intricate details of a process, and streamlining the flow from one task to another. Working PERT charts for big projects are usually complex and detailed; the presenter must extract the main points and clarify the underlying concepts. Visualize what the audience needs to know in order to follow the presentation. When details are necessary, separate the facets of the chart into individual frames so the viewers aren't overwhelmed. Presentations and Web sites that allow you to layer information and create hot buttons or areas for details are most effective with highly structured and detailed information like this.

Critical Path Method Diagrams

Another tool from the world of project management is the critical path method (CPM) diagram, which displays a succession of project activities arranged from start to finish along a specially designed "critical path." Arranged like beads on a string, these activities add up to a total time span; if certain activities are scheduled simultaneously, however, the time frame can be shortened dramatically. The critical path diagram can demonstrate the effect of taking these tucks in time. The bars in the following critical path diagram serve a dual purpose—delineating the time required and showing which activities can be "stacked" and which must be done after others because they rely on successful completion of previous steps.

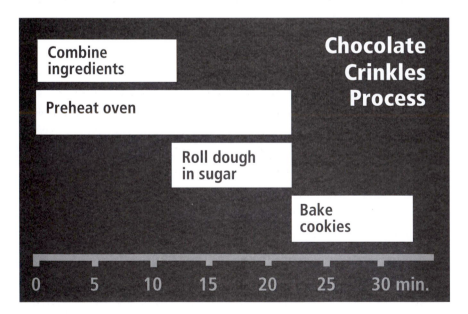

The critical path project schedule often takes a graphic form similar to a Gantt chart—a cross between a horizontal bar graph and a time line—with the path highlighted. Bar length reflects the time required to accomplish each activity. Links or position show the optimal order. If one step is missed or delayed, the diagram can demonstrate the impact on successive stages of the project.

Gantt Charts

Like PERT charts, Gantt charts are usually created originally for management activities rather than for presentation graphics, and they involve activities structured and arranged over chronological time. Your first step will be to simplify and generalize the material, turning it into the type of content most illuminating for your content and most meaningful to your audience. If one streamlined chart doesn't present the project in sufficient depth, divide the overall length of the time line into manageable portions. Aim to make these smaller bites reflect increments the audience will understand intuitively—months, quarters, years, or decades. Don't ask the viewers to study a single labyrinthine image.

Perhaps you'll find it best to open with a simplified version of the big picture, follow with a series of closely focused detail frames, and then close with a return to the overview—modified to reflect the points you've emphasized during the presentation. Motion will help focus attention on each step in order, and changing graphic parameters like color and size as you move through the process will bring the audience along with you more easily.

Processing Other Processes

Process diagrams are extremely flexible forms of graphic communication—they work well for routing plans, telephone networks, decision structures, and representations of logic. Even when the systems they represent are quite complex, the frames illustrating them need not be confusing. Use bold, clear areas of foreground, midground, and background colors just as you would in any effective presentation graphic. Abstract and simplify to telegraph your points to the audience. Elaborate verbally or through detail layers of information accessible to interested viewers.

Specialized diagrams for project management (PERT, Gantt, and so forth) aside, process diagrams are highly individualized in design and layout. Collect examples from your daily life that strike you as particularly effective. Note the attributes that caught your attention: use of color, sizes of links and nodes, typography, shape, and rendering effects, perhaps the inclusion of illustrations or photographs. Which made it easy to follow a set of instructions? Which led you astray?

Remember that it's the structure and relationships you're focusing on, not individual links or nodes. Practice will help you gain the knack of seeing events or challenges in terms of process. Use the graphic latitude of diagram design to show others your own understanding of the elements in context. Let your palette, choice of forms, placement decisions, and use of type work for you to generate outstanding images of processes.

This design flexibility makes diagramming a truly satisfying experience. Without worrying about exact statistical values, you can put your personal mark of creativity on the frame. Explore different layouts, figure/ground relationships, and three-dimensional methods. Work in series whenever possible and use motion to enliven the frame. As long as you keep your message foremost, you can let your imagination be your guide.

Organizational Diagrams: Relative Positioning

Organizational diagrams are pleasantly straightforward. Corporations, institutions, and government agencies use organizational diagrams, or "org charts," to show the relative positions, roles, and responsibilities of individuals and departments. Basically, they resolve at a glance questions of who talks to whom and in what capacity.

Organization diagrams are invaluable management tools; they can be especially helpful in orienting new employees or in troubleshooting communication problems. Names, titles, key roles, and hierarchies are all examined in this type of diagram. Fringe and core groups or figures are revealed. Would the wave of mergers, restructuring, and implementing economies or scale be possible without the workhorse org chart?

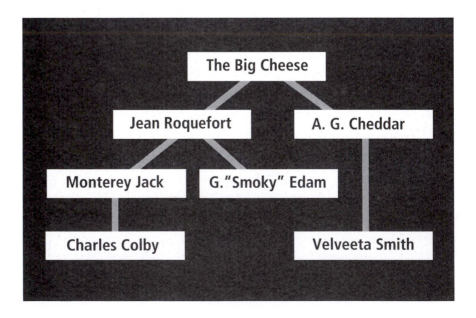

The design of organization diagrams is likewise straightforward, while still allowing the adventurous to have some fun. People or departments become nodes, and the flow of authority or communication among them becomes a network of links. Try a subtle twist to keep your audience from sinking into the lethargy of familiarity. Turn the diagram on its head to show that communication also works from the bottom up, or establish lateral links to show a team network that's different from the structure of bosses and worker bees. Use a traditional structure to demonstrate the unexpected.

Time Lines: Clocking To History

Audiences like to feel they're oriented to the context of the presentation, so at some point, either at the opening or during another opportunity for an overview, many presentations include diagrams that show a historical perspective on the subject at hand. Time lines are the perfect vehicle for bringing the audience up to date, showing them what has happened so far, and pointing out the dates of landmark events, discoveries, legislation, and the like. They set the stage for future accomplishments, providing a structure based on relative timing. They demonstrate the long-term or short-range nature of the subject.

Line and vertical bar graphs use a form of the time line as their horizontal axis, integrated with another variable that's scaled on the vertical axis. The standard time line is really the time part of a time-series graph, freed from the vertical dimension.

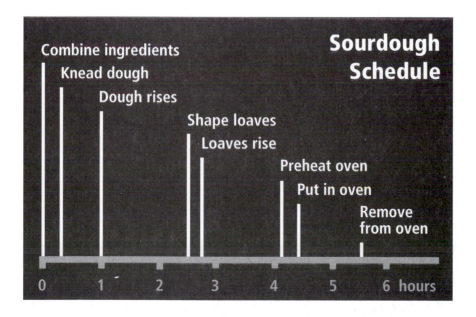

It's possible to show a time line in a variety of ways, depending on the amount of detail and the number of events you want to include. The conventions of reading left to right and top to bottom still hold, unless you have an absolutely convincing argument for turning everyone's expectations topsy-turvy. Even if you're a determined iconoclast, the time line is probably not the place to expect your audience to follow you into graphic terra incognito.

Remember that you're working with symbols scaled to time. Even when there are long stretches during which nothing relevant seems to have happened, you must include these "blank" periods to represent accurately the passage of time. Often the fact that time elapsed between events turns out to be significant in itself—and the time line can help you see this more clearly.

When activities bunch up and you're pressed for space, it's misleading to expand time by elongating the time line out of scale. To fit a lot of activities into a short length of time, try using vertically staggered labels, callout lines with "elbow" joints to create a series of parallel angles, arrows, or (as a last resort) a legend relating events or categories to colors or patterns on the time line markers. Sometimes it's clearer to divide the frame into a series of several frames that each cover a shorter period, or "zoom in" on one particular segment. Choose a scale that will accommodate the content without creating distortions. Audiences will follow more easily the familiar sequence of hours, days, months, and years. When necessary, however, create a logarithmic scale (top) or logical progression (bottom).

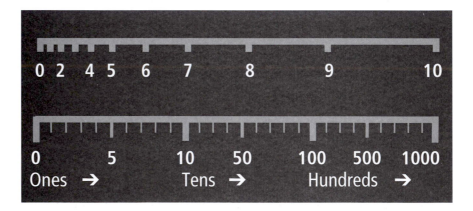

Your scale can make a big difference to the presentation, so choose it carefully and label it clearly. Unusual scales help solve some dire visual problems. Logarithms, for instance, work well for events that are packed closely together at one end and spread widely apart at the other. If mathematical logarithms scare you off, you can create a logical progression for marking time in a way that fits your story, combining tens/thousands/millions or ones/tens/hundreds. If you devise your own scale, be sure to mark the diagram even more clearly than with a standard rendering of time. You want the viewers paying attention to the information and ideas you present, not trying in vain to figure out your terms of reference.

Exploded Diagrams: Disassembling Reality

If you could take a photograph of something flying apart at the moment when everything that had been hidden was revealed, you'd have quite a tool for explaining how things work. Just like the famous photograph of the splash of a milk drop hitting the surface of a table, it's always interesting to see familiar units in a new form. When component parts appear in their separate form, yet still with a sense of how they fit together, you've created an exploded diagram.

The paradigm of explosion creates the illusion of a gravity-free environment that allows you to show details that are otherwise covered or obscured. This sense of bursting apart appeals greatly to the curious child in each of us, giving exploded diagrams a real advantage in engaging the audience. To cash in on this advantage, these diagrams have to make sense and convey the assurance that, yes, the pieces really do come together in this way. Perhaps it would be more accurate—if less dramatic—to think of impending diagrams, showing parts that are just about to merge into a whole assembly.

Often assemblies are rather complex if completely exploded. Instead of breaking apart each and every part, explode only the pieces that are relevant to your story, allowing the others to stay together as the remainder of the whole. Suppose you're creating a graphic diagram to show the next generation of home coffee-roasting equipment. You want to detail one aspect of the unit to show how the safety features work with the rest of the machine. The solution is to draw the assembly and explode only the thermostat and circuit breaker.

Be sure to include guides or arrows that show how the exploded parts fit with each other and back into the whole assembly. That way, the audience can reconstruct the unit in their imaginations. These guides can be lightly screened or dashed, and should be consistent with the perspective of the entire drawing.

Exploded diagrams are actually one style of illustration, and they are almost always rendered as three-dimensional objects. For best results, it's important to be familiar with perspective drawing. Parallel projection is the style of drawing in perspective that's most common in diagrams, as well as the easiest technique for most people to accomplish. One-point perspective, where all depth vanishes to a single point (think of looking down a railroad track), is slightly harder to draw but often looks more realistic. Two-point perspective, where depth vanishes to two points, looks even more realistic. Experiment with these techniques to determine the best way to render your exploded diagram.

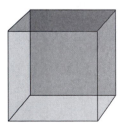

Floor Plans, Maps, And Other Scale Drawings: Demonstrating Relationships

Key points in your presentation may be made most effectively by showing relative size, proportion, or location. Draw these diagrams to a particular scale, and maintain the scale strictly in all portions of the image to maintain credibility. You can loosen up a bit with inserts and details, but set them off in clearly separate areas of the frame, complete with a second scale reference. Alternatively, follow the complete image with a detail or reduction frame, or create layers that offer detail to the viewer who accesses it. When changing scale between these views, be sure to indicate the difference to the audience.

With the variability in presentation media, your scale must show a particular length and establish its equivalent value, rather than stating "1 inch equals 100 miles." Otherwise, when your graphics are displayed on another monitor, your original inch can be tremendously distorted. Relative comparisons make the best presentation scales. You can show two different scales by insetting a detail box with its own size reference.

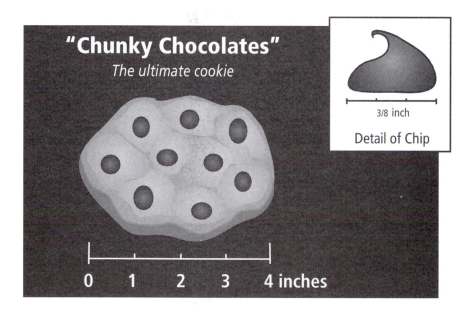

Fair representation demands that product illustrations be drawn to scale. Chocolate chip cookies pictured on a package with chips three times larger than actual size make us feel cheated by the real thing. We expect the cookie to look like its graphic image, with the same relationship between component parts like chocolate chips and cookie dough.

Floor plans are a particular type of scale drawing that shows the scene of a crime, the layout of a building, the room arrangement of a model home, or other such spatial information. We usually represent floor plans from a bird's-eye view, as if we could remove the roof and look straight down into the interior. Elaborate floor plans may include perspective drawings of the walls and furnishings, the type of foreshortened perspective you might remember from the Clue board game.

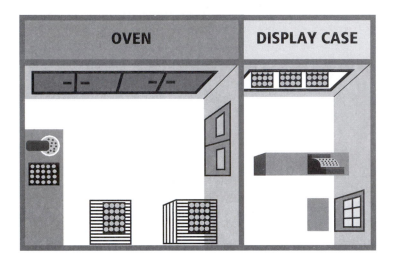

If you're lecturing on fire escape routes and safety exit locations, or if you're orienting new employees to production areas, you'll want to include a fairly detailed floor plan in your presentation to represent the physical context. Floor plans allow us to enter a space imaginatively and follow the speaker through doors, past windows, and into corridors.

Like floor plans, location maps are two-dimensional representations of the physical world as seen from above. Their strong suit is situating a particular building or feature of the landscape—like a river or a mountain in the natural sphere or the company headquarters or a sales office in the man-made world. Strong reference elements will make or break a successful location map. Like good directions, these graphics should include specifics and provide enough familiar features to give the viewer a sense of both scale and place. Consider how well the audience knows the area. Scout the location for interesting landmarks to give your map flair and individual immediacy. Draw a "North" arrow and a simple size scale for reference.

Statistical and thematic maps make great presentation graphics for activities that can be observed by geographical site. They're content-driven designs, showing the prevalence, intensity, or density of target activities, and they're only possible when you have the right data to interpret. On location maps, the symbols represent tangible things, whereas on thematic maps, they represent abstract factors and forces that cannot be seen, even at ground level. The following thematic map associates instances of chocolate attacks with proximity to the chocolate shop.

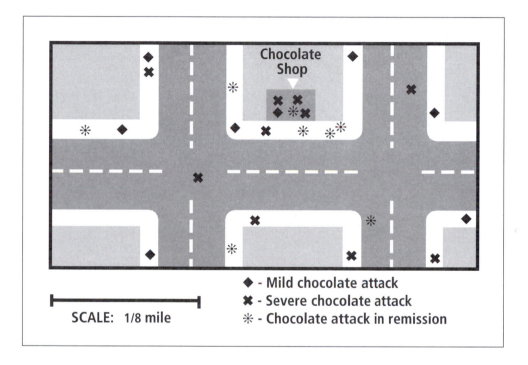

Chocolate Shop

SCALE: 1/8 mile

◆ - Mild chocolate attack
✖ - Severe chocolate attack
✳ - Chocolate attack in remission

Mapping Symbols

Maps can translate data into spatial patterns, as well as locate events in space. Data is represented by various symbols, which can be particularly effective for tracking information like election returns, cultural patterns, demographics, and production activities.

When you're working with data collected at discrete locations, try a dot map. A colored dot represents each occurrence or group of occurrences, just like the colored pushpins on the giant wall maps of old Pentagon movies. The result is something like a scattergram, scaled to place rather than to other variables.

Suppose you're mapping hog production. One dot can equal one hog, or you can scale the data so that each dot represents 100 or 1,000 hogs, depending on your overall numbers. Moving up in complexity, you might want to color-code the dots or replace them with graphic symbols if you'd like to show both hog and cow production. Variations within the symbols can specify the information further to show the prevalence of particular breeds. Scaled bars or columns, like those on vertical bar graphs, work well to show relative quantities; locate the bar bases to correspond with the sites they represent.

Rather than overloading your map with actual count information, follow the graphic with a table to give specific figures, if they're important. If your data was collected by region, use shading or color to show changes in statistical intensity from area to area. For manageable graphics, group values into four or five ranges and assign a visual code to each of them.

Suppose you've just been made marketing manager for Piece-a-Pizza. You want to create a map that will help convince your vice president that your proposed marketing plan will target the right geographical areas. The only sales figures you can find were collected state by state.

First, group the sales values into high, medium, and low ranges. Assign a color to each range, remembering that cool colors recede and warm colors come forward. Try blue for low sales, green for medium, and orange for high. Color each state to match the sales figures. You audience will find it easy to pick up the geographic patterns that emerge from the map; they'll have a new vision of their sales effort, and you'll have demonstrated your knack for knowing what's going on. It's all in the interpretation; you first simplify and group the data, then you interpret it visually. The more people can take in at a glance, the more motivated they're likely to be when it comes time to convince them to act.

Moving On

Diagrams are wonderful devices for communicating priorities, procedures, where things are, and how they work. Especially when your information is highly abstract, your audience will benefit from a visualization of the relationships you want to draw between the concepts. Concentrate on structure and flow to distill a topic to its bare bones. When you devote time to this type of graphic, the payback goes beyond helping an audience understand the ideas and information you're presenting. You also give them a framework for remembering the concepts and incorporating them into their daily practice.

Throughout the overview of presentation graphic design and conceptualization, I've suggested ways you can use motion and media techniques to clarify and enhance your message. Now we'll consider the basics of multimedia, which can add panache to your work, kicking it right out of the majority of ho-hum presentations.

MOVING INTO
MULTIMEDIA

10

Multimedia used to be expensive and time-consuming, so much so it was often beyond the reach of most presenters. Today, multimedia-authoring capabilities are built into many presentation software packages, and quality stock video and audio clips are extremely affordable. So, it's time to learn how to take advantage of multimedia to add an indelible impression to your presentations.

Love At First Sight—And Sound

It's a rush and there's nothing like it. We've all felt it—the shock and thrill of love at first sight. Well, encountering multimedia is a bit like that. At first you're surprised, then delighted. Approached carefully and used appropriately, multimedia in presentations has the same effect on your audience.

Multimedia elements can do more than add razzle-dazzle to a presentation. They can increase retention, make the presentation more persuasive, and make it easier to understand the subject matter. Multimedia can make your audience sit up and take notice.

Although multimedia isn't required in presentations today, more and more people are taking advantage of it to create more effective presentations. If you've never used it in your presentations, now's the time to start exploring and experimenting. If you have used it before, the thrill of first love may be wearing off a bit, so now is the time to let yourself be intoxicated again by new and fresh possibilities offered by the latest in multimedia.

Growing The Seeds Of Change

Because multimedia elements convey a feeling of action, they add a new dimension to any presentation. No longer is the presentation static and staid—it moves in a new way and there are new subtleties. It can be difficult to understand this new dimension at first, but with a little thought and practice, you'll move from novice to professional in no time!

Multimedia can be used to improve all kinds of presentations, although it is most at home in presentations concerning action of any kind, particularly transformation and change. Multimedia motion effects are a natural for showing the visual unfolding of information—such as developing an idea or showing progress over a period of time. You can even use them for process-oriented presentations or when you want to present information in a step-by-step fashion.

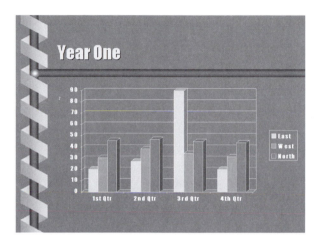

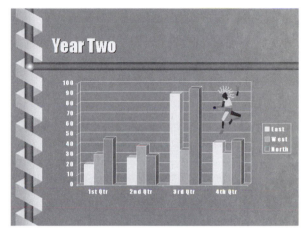

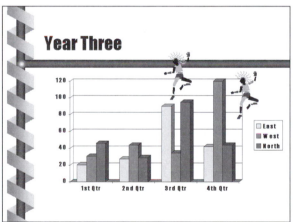

Motion on screen really grabs the audience's attention and engages their minds—at least for a while. It's tempting to keep everything in motion throughout the presentation in an attempt to sustain that level of interest, but it will wear off after a few screens. Audience members may even become annoyed if everything keeps moving as they are trying to understand the core messages. Give them some breathing room to allow your points to sink in.

Upping The Ante

Think of multimedia as a supporting character in any presentation. The minute it takes center stage all by itself, the audience will lose the thread connecting the content together and will focus on the special effects. Use it to support and embellish your message, not to fill in gaps in content.

Live presenters should use multimedia to support their human performance, not to compete with it. Use video clips sparingly, as they, more than any other kind of media, can pull attention away from the presenter.

Audio clips are excellent attention-getters, mood setters, and underscorers in small doses. Try using them only as sound effects to reflect the motion on screen or to help pace the presentation.

You will need to put more time into planning, organizing, and producing a multimedia presentation than a static one. It's vital to first identify your points, then organize, prioritize, and emphasize. Then select multimedia elements that support your content. Know exactly which supporting roles each element will play, and always keep your content center stage.

Complications In Paradise

Multimedia presentations increase the technical complexity of your project ten-fold because they make strong demands on your computer's storage capabilities and speed. For example, a few minutes of digital video can take up five or more megabytes of hard disk space. By comparison, digital audio takes up much less space—an audio clip of the same length can take 30 or so kilobytes of disk room.

The quality of these presentations is also limited by the quality of some of the parts of the computer you will use for the presentation. Unless you have studio-quality external speakers and a good sound card inside the computer, the sound will be played through the system's internal speaker. You can be sure the computer manufacturer did not invest a lot of money in the internal speaker.

The computer display is another part of the computer that can limit the quality of the overall presentation. If your screen is small or the display resolution is poor, the audience will find it hard to appreciate motion effects and video clips.

If you stop periodically during the creation of your presentation to run it, you will find out if you have exceeded the capabilities of your computer. If a video clip plays too slowly or the audio sounds tinny, you can either scale back your multimedia aspirations or invest in a better, faster computer.

If the presentation will be run on several different computers with an unknown range of capabilities, play it safe and design a presentation that runs well on an older, slower computer. You can design the presentation on a newer computer to save time, but take the time to move it to an older computer for a trial run. Then you will be able to pinpoint and eliminate problem areas.

Multiwhich?

So many programs, so many possibilities—so little time to explore them all. There is a wide variety of software packages that allow you to create presentations with multimedia elements. One might allow you to do little more than create slides and add motion effects to a few elements. Another might let you take the process a step further by letting you incorporate stock video and audio clips. Still another might turn your computer into an entire production studio—giving you far more capabilities than most presenters ever need (see Chapter 3).

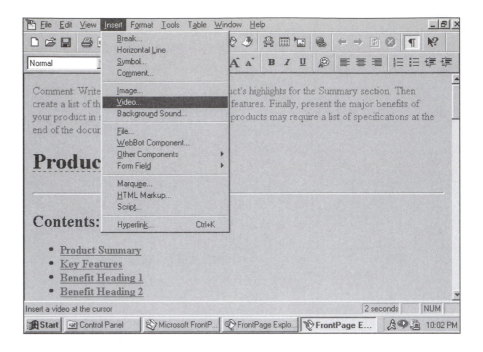

Unless you will be spending a great deal of your time creating multimedia presentations, start with a presentation program that offers some multimedia support. Such a program isn't hard to find—many of the latest versions of mainstream and popular programs will allow you to incorporate multimedia elements. It's also a good idea to look for a program that makes the whole process as trouble-free as possible. A program with limited options that's easy to use is a better choice than a more sophisticated program that can take weeks to learn.

Another item on the list of possibilities is the staggering array of choices for digital audio and video. Stock collections (material gathered and digitized by a company for resale) are available on the Web and on CD-ROM, and new material is being released daily. You can use original materials, as well, with appropriate copyright and performance permissions, but these materials must be digitized before you can use them.

Hear Ye

Audio can be used alone or with animation or video. No matter how you use it, your sources of audio can be stock clips, recorded and digitized voice material, and original sounds and music you have digitized. In order to avoid possible legal problems, it's never a good idea to tape published music or music from the television, radio, or a movie.

If you are good at music, you may be able to create your own sound effects and music clips by using an electronic keyboard. Some models even have digitizer accessories to record and digitize the sound immediately.

Visions Of Delight

Before you create video for your presentation or buy stock video clips, check to see which digital file formats your presentation software can accept. Doing so will allow you to avoid embarrassment (at least) or (at most) costly changes when you get to the production portion of your presentation.

Besides digital video, to add visual interest to your presentations, you can animate entire frames, individual screen elements such as titles and bulleted items, and even graphics. Once again, it's a good idea to be familiar with the animation and video capabilities of your particular software program before planning the use of any of these elements.

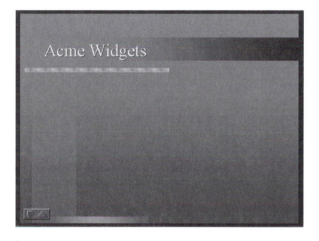

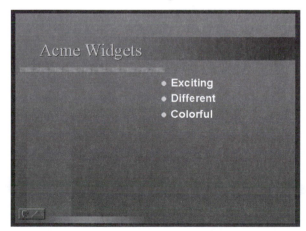

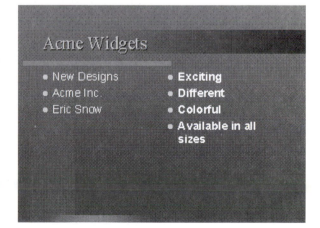

Explore the use of painting, drawing, charting, and other image-editing tools. You may be able to create the same effect inside your presentation software, but these tools are specialized and may be faster and easier for you to use for a particular effect. They also open up a world of new opportunities for creative expression of a thought or idea.

Digital still cameras can be used to capture a series of single images, which can later be put together in sequence and played during a presentation. Make the changes between stills subtle enough and play the frames fast enough and it will look like a mini-movie. A more expensive option is to use a digital video camera to capture original video live. These cameras are more expensive than standard video cameras, but using them lets you skip over the step of having the video you shot with a standard video camera made into digital video.

Mixing It Up In Production

Make sure you have a progression firmly in mind—what elements go where and when—including the starting and ending times for the various audio and video clips. You may want to sketch out a rough time line of the presentation before turning on the computer. Once you have planned and selected your content and multimedia support, it's time to sit down at the computer and put all the elements together into an elegant production.

Leave yourself plenty of extra time for experimentation and revision. A multimedia production put together at the last minute looks exactly as you would expect—thrown together. You can do your message more harm than good that way. A good rule of thumb is to give yourself twice the amount of time you would need for a nonmultimedia presentation.

Combined Resources

You can combine different multimedia elements into one frame of the presentation. An audio clip can accompany the appearance of a box that later fills with a video clip. A video clip can play from inside a more complex static graphic. You can use an audio clip and an animation to preface a particular kind of frame, such as one with questions on it.

The following illustration shows how you can combine these different elements and effects: imagine a screen with an interesting graphic. That graphic expands slowly to fill the entire screen. One by one, four boxes slide onto the left side of the screen. As the box on top begins to slide to the right, a video clip begins to play in that box. As that clip draws to a close, the next box begins to do the same thing, until all four boxes have played their clips while moving across the screen.

Transition Devices

In written documents, there are many different ways of handling transitions between sections of a document. The final paragraph of one section can make a reference to the next section, or the headline for the next section can clue the reader into the main message in the upcoming text. Even headers and footers can be used to guide the reader along.

Transition devices are just as important in presentations unless the presentation is only a few frames long. The longer the presentation, the more important these devices become. They help the audience understand the content by providing them with an unconscious framework for comprehension.

Presentation software has come a long way in both the means and the choices of adding useful transitions to presentations. You don't have to become a multimedia programmer to add slides, dissolves, cross-fades, and other transition effects to almost every portion of the presentation. It's often as simple as highlighting the portion and clicking on an effect in a pull-down menu.

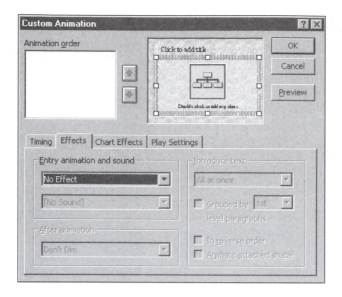

Here are some examples of transition devices to experiment with, but keep in mind that less is more; don't use so many devices your audience is feeling dizzy after a few frames!

- Dissolve one screen into another.

- Add a motion effect to one element of each screen (usually the same element on each screen).

- Fade an image or an entire screen out to black.

- Quick-cut from one frame to another.

- Wipe one screen off from one direction and make the next come in from the opposite direction.

- Close a section or screen with a venetian blind effect.

- Shrink an image off the screen to reveal another image directly beneath.

Animation And Pseudo-Animation

Even if you've chosen the most basic presentation software, chances are it will allow you to add some animation effects, such as making a column in a chart grow upward or having bullet points pop up. You may also be able to move objects around in a frame or make them tumble across the screen.

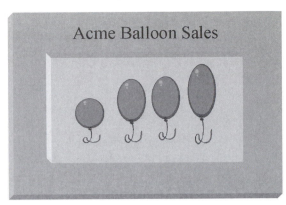

Beyond these basic basics of animation, your software may allow you to do more sophisticated-looking animations. You may be able to move more than one object around in a single frame or even bring in animations you have created in other programs.

You can create the effect of animation without these special effects by using multiple frames. Create a beginning frame and ending frame, then use a transformation device or blend tool to generate a series of intermediate frames. When you play the sequence of frames quickly with a fast dissolve between frames, you will see a convincing display of pseudo-animation.

Motion Clips

Many presentation and multimedia authoring programs come with a library of motion clips you can use. They allow you to add some special effects to any presentation with just a few clicks of the mouse button, and they are a great way to add some sparkle to your presentations.

To check them out, create a dummy presentation and add a few clips to each frame. Save the presentation and review it before you start working on your latest presentation. It's a good way to remind yourself of what you've got at hand before you start looking for other multimedia elements. If an effect catches your eye, keep it in mind for the actual presentation.

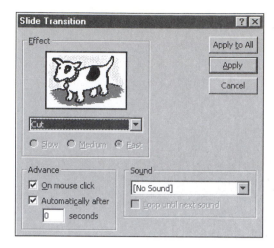

As with any multimedia element, it's easy to add too many motion clips and overwhelm your presentation with them. A sparkle or two plus a star shower may be enough when you add in a few other elements such as an audio and a video clip with transitions between frames.

Sounding Board

Some feature-rich presentation programs and multimedia authoring packages allow you to edit and arrange audio clips. Your computer becomes a digital processing workstation for audio, allowing you to slice and dice sounds to your ear's content. If your software has such capabilities, experiment with them before you need to put a presentation together. Unless you are a musical genius, you'll need a lot of practice to turn out great audio using these tools.

There are also specialty software packages that really do turn your computer into a digital soundboard. To use them you'll need a good sound card in your computer and other hardware to capture and digitize sounds and music. These programs are designed for audiophiles and professional musicians, so they can be expensive and confusing to the non-musically inclined. Still, they are worth the effort if you plan to use a lot of audio in your presentations.

Inviting Interactivity

Although not strictly limited to multimedia presentations, interactivity can be used effectively alongside multimedia in a presentation. If you have a lot of information to delve into but want to be able to tailor the amount of information presented to a particular audience, then consider mixing the two.

Think of interactivity as a means of layering information. The basic information is what everyone sees and hears during each presentation. Underlying the basics can be a whole treasure trove of information and details, waiting for the right audience to show an interest. When a member of the audience asks a question, you can have the answer ready at the click of a button.

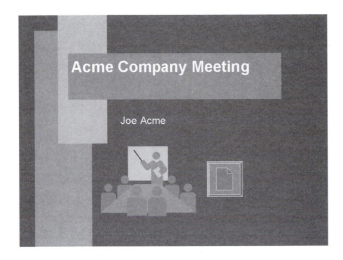

You must use interactivity if the presentation is designed to be complex and self-guided. You won't be there to answer questions and add detail, so you had better build it into the presentation itself. Alternate paths through your information and ideas also allow people to choose their own path through the material, homing in on specifics they find most interesting.

An interactive presentation with multimedia elements is a bigger consumer of computer resources than a multimedia-only presentation. So the same cautions about disk space and computer speed apply to a greater degree. You may also want to consider using CD-ROM technology to hold your interactive multimedia presentation.

Multipresenting

As with any computer-based presentation, you must make sure the right computer equipment is available on-site for your multimedia presentation. With this kind of presentation, you'll need a fast computer with good audio capabilities and a screen large enough and good enough to show off your video.

If your presentation software allows you to create a self-running or fully contained presentation, create one if you are going off-site for the presentation. That way you'll have everything you need to make the presentation in one tidy, not-so-small package. Burning your own CD-ROMs works wonders in such situations.

Technical hitches can destroy your entire high-tech effort, forcing you to watch hours of hard work dissolve into embarrassing delays and apologies. Check out the equipment well before your presentation time, and practice, practice, practice. Have a low-tech version of the presentation available as a backup just in case you need it.

Moving On

Effective multimedia presentations are within the grasp of anyone who can make his or her way through a presentation software program. You'll need to create a few presentations to get the hang of the process, but you'll be a pro before long. Use the multimedia elements to their (and your) best advantage, and use no media for thrill value alone.

Moving to Web-based presentations is only a few steps away from multimedia and interactive presentations. Many of the cautions and design rules are the same, and there are plenty of software packages to help you design a presentation for the Web. In Chapter 11 I'll talk specifically about how to create astounding Web presentations with a minimum of effort and frustration.

MOVING ONTO THE WORLD WIDE WEB

11

You can, and should, take advantage of the unique opportunity the Web gives you to make your information available on a worldwide basis. Anyone with a computer and a modem can access the Web, which gives you an unparalleled means of reaching a huge audience. The opportunity comes with a price, though, because you have to take special care in creating your presentation for the Web.

Visual Punch For Web Sites

Before the Web and Web browsers were created, text was the only means of communicating on the Internet. You couldn't even format the text—it looked like it had rolled off a dot matrix printer. That's all different now; the Web is a visual medium par excellence. Your Web presentations have to be visually oriented to compete with all the other materials available to Web surfers.

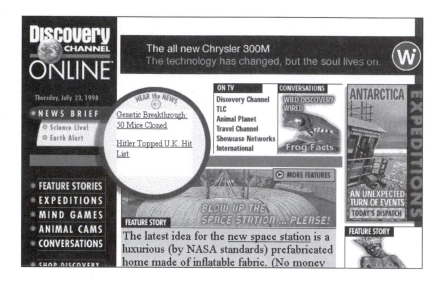

You must also be more creative and more empathetic with Web presentations than with a non-Web-interactive or multimedia presentation. Unlike the audience watching a live presentation, Web surfers are not a captive audience. They're hungry for information and excitement, have itchy mouse fingers, and are easily bored. Unless a site captures their attention immediately and holds it long enough for you to get a few points across, they will be off and clicking.

Fortunately, as more people are drawn to the Web, software companies have devoted themselves to creating easy-to-use tools for creating effective and engaging Web sites. You must supply the advanced planning, strategy, and an in-depth understanding of the magic of the medium, but producing a Web site has never been easier.

Home Pages And Hits

A home page is where your presentation resides on the Web. Many people also refer to it as a site or a Uniform Resource Locator (URL). The exact terminology isn't important—just think of it as the house where your presentations and other Web-accessible information live.

Unless you have a lot of information, such as a database or two, for Web surfers to access, you don't need to go to the time, trouble, and expense of setting up your own Web server. You can rent all the computer power and space you need from an Internet service provider (ISP). You can even set things up so you get your very own URL, and no one will know, or care, where the actual computer files are located.

A Web hit is more like a baseball hit than a Broadway hit (unless your Web site is really spectacular). A Web hit happens whenever anyone visits your site (make sure your ISP collects this information). The number of hits per day or week is important if you want to know how many people are visiting the site. Although the number of visits does not mean everyone who visited stayed for the entire presentation, it does tell you if the site is engaging enough to get people to stick around for the first few scenes. It's also a good indication of how well your advertising is and that people are actually finding your site to begin with.

Organization By Eye

Besides being visually appealing from the start, your Web site needs to be very organized and the organization must be obvious throughout. Such a high degree of organization is crucial, so be prepared to spend all the time you need to come up with a workable and simple way of organizing the presentation.

During a live presentation you control the flow of information, but on the Web your audience does. The presentation is always interactive, and if viewers get confused about where to go next and how to get there, they will move on to another site within seconds. If you do nothing else, make major items such as search capability and contact information for you or your company immediately obvious.

There are two easy ways to organize your site visually. First, select a few (just a few) ways of moving around the site and use those methods on every screen throughout the presentation. The Next Page button should be exactly the same on every screen. Changing the color or shape of a key navigational element may seem like a good way to add visual variety, but doing so will confuse your audience.

Second, use color to organize your information. Color is a wonderful visual aid, as it quickly cues the audience in whether they realize it or not. One way to use color is to use one background color for all sections of a presentation related to product specification and another for ordering information. The two colors used consistently will help the audience understand how the site is organized.

Connective Tissue

It's called the Web for a good reason—the World Wide Web is a mass of digital information connected by networks around the world. You can, and should, use this unique built-in communication capability to make your presentations more interesting and informative.

First of all, take advantage of the Web's ability to let you make lots of content available if your audience wants to delve in deeply to find it. Fill your Web site with interesting information. It's a waste of your time and your audience's time to create a Web site with little more than some great-looking pictures and snazzy animation.

Content-rich sites have to be set up so viewers can zero in on key segments of information quickly. Setting up links between sections of the site is easy; deciding which segments are key elements and how those links should be presented takes much more time.

Navigation	*Sources of Aid*	*Special Interest*
What's New?	FastWEB SRN ExPAN MACH25	Financial Aid Admin.
Mark's Picks	CASHE	International Students
Table of Contents	Scholarships/Fellowships	Disabled Students
Index	Grants & Contests	Older Students
Navigating the Page	Prepaid Tuition Plans	Female Students
Help Using the Page	Tuition Payment Plans	Minority Students
Announcements	Study Abroad & Exchange	Gay & Lesbian Students
Web Search		National Service
	Loans	Sports/Athletics
Assistance	Lenders & Lender Codes	Graduate School
Scam Alert	Servicers & Guarantors	Medicine Law Business
Free Documents	Secondary Markets	Private High School
Glossary	Private Loans	Veteran/Military Aid
Bibliography	Loan Counseling	
Overview of Fin. Aid		*Other*
Answers to FAQs	*Government/Schools*	Personal Finance
Ask the Aid Advisor	US Government Info	Admissions Testing

You should also take advantage of your ability to link your site to the countless others on the Web as a way of adding value to your site. Think of your presentation as a jumping-off point for further investigation. Many live presentations include a section on other resources. Similarly, you can create live links to other resources in your Web presentation.

Wanting It All

Visiting other Web sites is a good way of getting design and organization ideas. So are reading books and magazines about Web sites and talking with other people about exciting Web sites they've visited. Make a list of all the features and design elements you like about certain Web sites and think about whether you'd like to add similar ones to your site.

Designing For Graphic Impact

One characteristic of successful Web pages is their innovative use of images. People love images; they get the point across much more quickly than words can. Images can also convey many different layers of nuance and feeling in a small space. Successful Web designers know this and are always looking for ways to add more images to their sites.

Here are a few ways you can incorporate images to add strength and meaning to your Web site:

- Brainstorm to find new ways to use graphics in the presentation: color images can be enlarged and faded out in image editing programs for use as backgrounds.

- Create graphics to communicate concepts you would use words for in other presentations. Convert a table of information into a colorful chart, or find a cartoon that illustrates a point you want the audience to remember.

- Use pictures of people, especially children, in the early parts of your presentations. Newspapers and magazines use people on the cover to attract newsstand buyers. You can use the same idea for your Web site.

You can also use other graphic elements such as large chunks of vivid color and professional-looking clip art in your Web site design. If you're interested in using any of these elements, make sure to look at them on screen before using them. Something that has a lot of impact on paper can lose that impact on screen when surrounded by other parts of the Web site interface.

If you are going to use images on your site (and you should), take the time to learn about how to handle them properly. A good Web site design book will give you the basics, but you should know to begin with that Web image file sizes should be much smaller than the size of images used for printing. For Web-based information about Web design and some cool resources for Web images, look in the Resource List at the end of the book.

Designing For Text-Heavy Pages

Sometimes you need to put a significant amount of text in your Web presentations, especially if you want to add value by including a lot of content. That's okay, as long as you design the presentation knowing the viewer will read the text on screen but might want to print some or all of the presentation. With text-heavy Web presentations, your job is to make both tasks easy to do.

Break the text into short sections by using subheads. Many books (including this one) are organized this way. Readers are then able to browse through the subheads to find information they are particularly interested in. In your Web presentation, consider creating a detailed table of contents that appears early in the presentation by listing each subhead and creating a link from the table to each section of text.

Use only a few typefaces and stick to sans serif typefaces or serif typefaces that are easy to read on screen. Most of your viewers will be using Web browsers to access your presentation, so use only the typefaces included in those browsers. At several points during the design stage, look at the site using a few different browsers to make sure everything is easy to read.

Use a lot of white space between lines of text and around the edges of the screen. You don't want to crowd text onto a screen—viewers will find that overwhelming and move on to another site. Make each screen look as open and inviting as possible. Dark or highly detailed backgrounds make text on screen hard to read. Stick with black text on a white or lightly colored background.

Adobe Photoshop Plug-ins

- <u>Aged Film</u>
  Add the "Aged Film" Look to Your Images or Digital Video
- <u>Andromeda Series 1: Photography Filters</u>
  The Best in Optical Lens Effects
- <u>Andromeda Series 2: 3D Filter</u>
  99% of Your Daily 3D Requirement
- <u>Andromeda Series 3: Screens Filter</u>
  The Art of Converting Gray Scale to Line Art
- <u>Andromeda Shadow Filter</u>
  The Most Powerful and Flexible Shadow-generating Filter Available!
- <u>Chromassage</u>
  Take Your Color Images to the Extreme

The Devil Is In The Details

The Web is a great place to make a presentation, but there are still technical realities you have to know about before you can make the most of this medium. These realities involve the computer systems used to access the Web, including the screen and the World Wide Web browser software.

As mentioned earlier, anybody with a computer and a modem can access the World Wide Web. That means they may be viewing your presentation on a computer that is five years old. The monitor may not be the latest and greatest, either. The browser software they are using may also not have all the capabilities of the latest version and may not let them see some animations or tables. It may also not let them use fill-in-the-blank forms or other new Web features.

You can't control what kind of computer viewers will use, so you have to compensate by keeping your presentation as technically simple as you can. You can also present two versions of your Web presentation at the site and post a notice to that effect on the first screen. (You've seen Web sites that do this. They have banner messages such as "This site is best enjoyed by users with browsers XYZ, version 4.0 or later." They also include a button that leads the viewer to a much simpler version of the same presentation.)

This site is best viewed by [Netscape Now] or [Get Microsoft Internet Explorer], click either to acquire.

If you plan to do a lot of Web presentations, buy an older computer and collect different browsers, including older and newer versions. During the course of creating a Web presentation, move the presentation to this test computer and test it with the different browsers to spot potential problems.

You should also know about Web-safe colors when designing presentations for the Web. Without going into a lot of technical detail, there are only 216 colors all computer systems and displays have in common. If your viewer's computer cannot display a particular color you have selected, it will substitute one of the 216—which can make images look bad or even make them incomprehensible on screen.

Some image editing tools will mimic the changes for you and will allow you to create images that will be seen the same way on all computers. To learn the nitty-gritty details about how to use Web-safe colors, just use a Web search tool and search for "web-safe colors" online. You'll find all the information you need. In addition, there are several good books devoted to this topic (see the Resource Guide at the end of this book).

Weaving The Web

Several kinds of software programs are available to help you create your Web-based presentations. Some presentation software programs include Web design capabilities, and you can also use multimedia authoring tools. For more specialized features, you can learn some of the Web programming languages such as Java or buy software specifically designed for Web site creation.

No matter what kind of software you choose, look for software you can use comfortably without a lot of training, such as the presentation software in an office suite program. Unless you plan to make a living designing and producing Web-based presentations, you need software that you can learn to use easily and quickly. You may have to forego some of the advanced features of the more sophisticated programs, but at least you'll be able to get your project done in a timely manner.

Keeping In Touch

Include in your presentation several different ways the viewer can get in contact with you to buy your product, sign up for your service, or just ask for more information. At the very least, make sure to include your company's name, address, and telephone number, along with your email address.

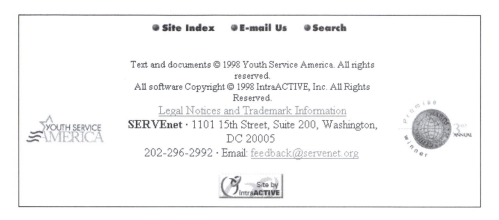

You can also include an instant email connection so all viewers can just click on the address and an email message box opens up for them. Think of it as the electronic version of a pre-addressed, stamped reply card.

A more sophisticated version of the electronic reply card is the fill-in-the-blank forms you see on many Web sites. These are great ways to allow people to order catalogs online or even make purchases. They are also wonderful for collecting information about people who visit the site.

For auto-fill use your ebCARD!

_____ Name

_____ E-mail Address

http:// _____ Homepage URL

_____ Title of your homepage

_____ Where are you from?

If you want to use fill-in-the-blank forms, make sure your ISP can gather the information from the forms for you before you put them in the site. Forms are also tricky for some browsers to handle, so plan on including a non-form version of a reply mechanism (say, an 800 number) if you want to encourage viewers to get in contact with you immediately.

You can track response rates from your Web presentation by setting up different email accounts for the site. One email address can be used to request a catalog, another can be used to ask for a telephone response from your company, and another can be a general-purpose email address.

Make sure to check all the email accounts on a regular basis—at least once a day. Also, plan a procedure for responding to the email promptly and for distributing leads you gather from the site. Some companies are even sending automatic replies to each email thanking people for their interest and telling them how soon they can expect a reply (make sure it's no more than a day or so).

Layer Cakes

During production of your Web site, have someone who hasn't worked on the project sit down and spend some time looking at the presentation. Have that person draw a layer-cake diagram of the site afterward so you can see how he or she experienced your presentations and the entire site. Ask the person to include a detailed representation of his or her experience, including the number of layers of information, how thick the icing is, and whether the person would go back for seconds.

A layer cake is an excellent metaphor for the feelings your audience should experience during and after the presentation. You want there to be layers of cake (content) to satisfy the viewer's appetite for information, yet you want to include enough icing (snazzy special effects and links) to whet the appetite and make the feast memorable. A good Web presentation leaves the viewer feeling well-fed, content, and looking forward to the next "slice."

The main ingredients for such a presentation are great content, effective special effects, and meaningful links to material inside and outside of the site. This is true whether your presentation is graphics-oriented or heavily text-oriented. Remember not to spread on so much icing that the true flavor of the cake (that is, the content) is lost.

Birthday Candles

Not all cakes are birthday cakes, but no birthday cake is complete without the added flourish of at least one candle. With Web-based presentations, there are a few flourishes you can add to customize your message even further. Email response mechanisms and fill-in-the-blank forms are details all Web presentations benefit from, but you can do even more.

If you have a lot of text-based information, you can add versions of the content as separate files that can be downloaded and printed later. These downloadable files can be created with many page layout programs or with software tools (such as Adobe Acrobat), and then posted on the site.

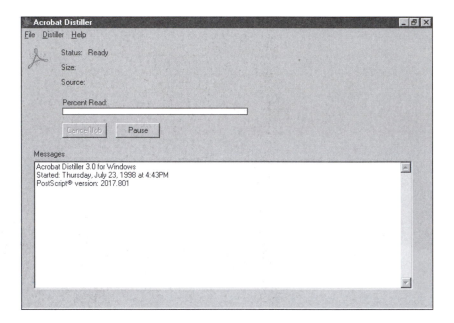

If you have a lot of images or images that viewers might want to see in greater detail, software programs are available that allow you to create several different resolutions of the same image available quickly and easily. The major image editing software programs allow you to create these in Web-ready formats such as FlashPix, GIF, and JPEG.

Online ordering using credit cards is a Web technology that is a very special candle for your layer cake. Although the technology is not in widespread use now, it will be within a short period of time. Ask your ISP about whether you can use it, as it can increase your sales dramatically.

Arachne's Lessons

Greek mythology has given us the legend of Arachne, the young girl whose weaving skills made her bold enough to challenge the goddess Athena to a weaving contest. Athena found Arachne's skills too much like her own and, in a fit of rage, destroyed Arachne's work. Devastated, Arachne killed herself, prompting Athena to regret her temper tantrum and turn Arachne into a spider and her work into a spider web.

Afterwards, Arachne must have had plenty of time to think about her actions and their consequences as she spun her webs and set the table for meals. We, too, can learn a few lessons from her experiences as we contemplate the presentations we can weave for the World Wide Web.

Pride goes before the fall, so the first lesson is to keep your presentations simple. Remember the cake analogy? As with any kind of presentation, you want the content—the layers of the cake—to be what people remember from your presentation and not the frills—the icing and the candles.

Some Web sites are all flash and no substance. They include the latest and greatest Web technologies and involve a lot of money, time, and Web design experience to put together. It's tempting to try to match their razzle-dazzle and risk getting caught up in your own tangled web. Keep your site simple and full of content, and you'll catch enough prospects to keep you happy.

The second lesson is not to let someone else's actions and opinions have too much influence on your work and your opinion of your work. A presentation on the Web is a very public way of exhibiting your ideas, and you're likely to get a lot of comments on your site. Some of them may be as venomous as Athena's and are likely to have a similar effect on your spirit. Again, as with any presentation, know what your communication goals are before you begin creating your presentation, and keep your eye on those goals. If you're happy and the site is doing what you want it to do, you can hold your head high.

The third lesson is related to the heart of the second. Comparing your Web presentation with someone else's is not the best way to keep your confidence up. Some terrific sites cost hundreds of thousands of dollars to create and maintain. Others require a year or more of effort on the part of large teams of highly paid creative design professionals. Unless you know the details behind a site's creation, you don't know how much time, money, and effort someone put into the project. Focus on doing the best you can with your time, talent, and budget.

Moving On

You will surely enjoy creating and producing presentations for publication via the World Wide Web. No matter what level of experience you accumulate, the Web is changing so quickly you will never be bored. There will always be something new to learn and something new to try. Just remember to keep the basic cake recipe handy.

As you learn more about presentations and the wide variety of media available for them, you'll want to learn about the most common pitfalls in presentation design and how to avoid them. In Chapter 12 I'll identify these design mistakes and offer a wide range of solutions.

DESIGN CRIMES AND HOW TO PREVENT THEM

12

We've all seen presentations that made us wish we'd stayed home and read a good book. Most of these presentations make us feel like victims because their designers have committed design crimes while making them. That's a shame, because design crimes are avoidable.

Most presentation design crimes, especially the kinds that make audiences moan inwardly or nod off openly, are more the result of ignorance than blatant rejection of the basic laws of design. Another reason design crimes crop up so often, even in the presentations of seasoned professionals, is that most people believe in the old saying "If a little is good, then more is better." That may be true of chocolate sauce on ice cream sundaes, but it's not the case in any kind of design—especially presentations.

Forewarned is forearmed, and with a little bit of design advice tucked away in your mind, you'll be able to avoid the most common traps (speed and otherwise) that weaken the design and effectiveness of your presentations. As you read through the material presented in this chapter, have a couple of your most recent presentations on hand so you can check your work against the recommendations. Don't worry if you find you're a habitual design criminal—we'll let you off with a warning if you take the information to heart and promise you'll reform!

In the best communications-related design, function is paramount and form, especially form for the sake of form, takes a backseat. With presentations, keep in mind you are constructing a communications device and not a piece of art to be revered and studied. Concentrate your efforts on creating a functional design that delivers your message clearly and simply.

A truly functional design has its own beauty, strength, and serenity that will be apparent to your audience. Picture a large oak tree silhouetted against a dark blue sky—such an image conveys utter simplicity coupled with a feeling of strength and peace. That's how you want your presentations to be.

Functional designs are also economical to create and easy to present. The best way to make money is to save money, and you don't want to put one more penny into creating any presentation than you must to accomplish your goals. Public speaking is a difficult enough task by itself, so you don't want to increase the emotional burden on yourself by creating a whiz-bang, special-effects-filled presentation that you're not sure will work. You will be able to save money and wear and tear on your nerves if you ask yourself what functions each portion of the presentation serves and ruthlessly cut any that serve little or no purpose.

Inexperienced presenters will have the most problems with this "less is more" approach to presentation design. Modern-day presentation software and other presentation tools offer wonderful possibilities, and unfortunately, inexperienced presenters too often give in to the temptation to stuff all these possibilities into a single presentation. Design mistakes such as too many bells and whistles, plus the others presented in this chapter, are sure signs you've got a little more to learn about designing presentations. Fortunately, the rest of this chapter is devoted to giving you the skills for avoiding such troubles.

Type

Typography is a marvelous art and science devoted to making communication more effective and more attractive. Unfortunately, only some professional graphic artists live and breathe type. That's a shame because there are so many beautiful typefaces, and type designers are always turning out new ones.

You don't need to be a type expert to choose good typefaces for your presentations. I cover type in Chapter 5, but will review some basics here to remind you what *not* to do. To begin with, a *typeface* is the term used to denote a family of fonts and types that share a basic design framework. Helvetica is a typeface, Helvetica Narrow is a type; Arial is a typeface, Arial Black is a type. You get the idea.

Times Roman and Garamond are two examples of typefaces commonly used for body text. Besides *body type*, used for the bodies of printed documents (bodies of letters, columns of type in a newspaper, most of the print on a book page), there are several other kinds of type, including *poster* and *display* typefaces, used in print design. Over the centuries, type designers have created hundreds of these kinds of typefaces to help make blocks of text such as headlines and titles stand out. Playbill and Placard are typefaces used for these purposes and may even be on your computer already.

Scan through the typefaces on your computer to find those that convey a feeling of strength, boldness, and simplicity. Start with those whose names suggest they could be used on signs and posters. Experiment with these typefaces in your designs and avoid those you would ordinarily find in body copy. You can still use Times Roman, Helvetica, and similar-looking body faces, but avoid using thin and wimpy-looking typefaces. Type that looks thin and graceful on the printed page will disappear almost entirely when projected many times its original size on the wall of a conference room or meeting hall.

If you're not sure which typefaces to choose, select two or three, use them to create some short sample phrases in a presentation, and produce the presentation as you normally would. Set up your projection equipment or computer, and see which typefaces and type sizes work best. Start with type no smaller than 12 point, and don't be afraid to work your way up into point sizes of 128 or larger.

Finally, when designing your presentation, avoid the urge to fill an entire presentation screen with type. Limit yourself to a few major points per screen and no more than two dozen words. If you've got a lot of detail to give your audience, put the details in the printed handouts and refer to the appropriate section during your presentation.

Stacked Characters

Type designers create type that works together as a harmonious whole when combined into words. Often they start by creating every letter of the alphabet in upper- and lowercase, and then switch over to placing common pairs of letters together and adjusting the shapes of the letters to further enhance their beauty and gracefulness. While doing this, they are keeping in mind that the letters will be used in straight, horizontal lines of type.

Most readers find any other arrangement, such as stacked or distorted characters, annoying because it requires them to tilt their head, scrunch their eyes, or work extra hard to make out your meaning. Any time your audience has to work hard to understand what you're trying to say, it is guaranteed to miss something.

You will be most often tempted to stack letters when you're creating labels for a graph or some other kind of graphic. There are other more viable options that will make your graphics more professional-looking and easier on your audience:

- *Colors*—Use a different color for each set of data, and show the colored legend under or beside the graphic. Use blue for one set of data, red for another, and so on. The audience will get the point immediately. Another good idea is to use the brightest or boldest color in the group to draw attention to whatever set of data is most important.

- *Patterns or shades*—Use distinctly different hash patterns or shades of gray in the same way. You can even create your own patterns—say, with portions of your company's logo—with a computer illustration program.

- *Labels*—Create labels that read left to right in the standard fashion and place them at the top of the bars in a bar chart, or arrange them around the outside of a pie chart. Make sure the labels are large enough to be clearly visible to the entire audience.

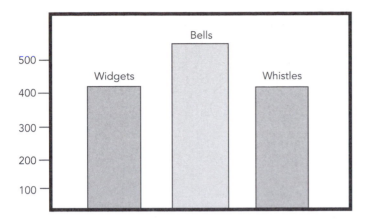

If everything on a chart or graph is not clearly visible, reduce the complexity of your graphic. A good rule of thumb is no more than four bars in a bar chart or six sections in a pie chart. If you have more data than that, try to break the data into smaller sections and make simpler charts from the sub-sets of data. If that isn't possible, you can try using a line graph to present long-term trend data. Use a thick line and not too many ticks along the horizontal or vertical axis.

If all of these alternatives fail and you must include all the data in your presentation, create a simple summary graphic that highlights only one or two major points in the data and include the detail in printed handouts. The audience will have a much easier time understanding complex graphics if they are presented on paper, and they can refer back to them later.

Distorted Baselines

Androids may have no problem following curved lines of text on screen, but humans do; in print and on screen, straight lines of text are much easier to read. Avoid curving or rotating lines of text, such as labels, to fit the curve or slant of chart lines. Let the type play the straight man for the graphics.

Your graphics may seem boring to you, but that may be because you've been looking at the data too long. Let your data as presented in the graphic do the talking for you: Snappy, cute sayings and text mixed into the graphic will only detract from the overall presentation. Remember, function takes precedence over form; make your graphic clean, strong, and clear, and eliminate all unnecessary words.

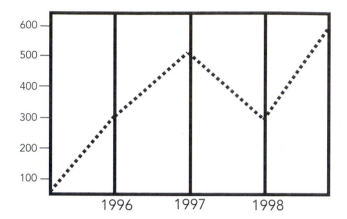

For complex graphics in handouts, you can loosen these rules up a bit. You may find rotating long column labels slightly in a large table actually improves comprehension because you don't have to hyphenate words to make them fit. Be careful, though, and bend the rules only if your audience will gain rather than lose.

Layout

Before almost everyone in the corporate world had a computer sitting on their desks, interesting and colorful presentation graphics were expensive and time-consuming, because they were usually created by design professionals. Now, with office suite software and easy access to computers, you can put your own graphics together in a short period of time.

That's great—you can save time and money by doing the graphics yourself—but unless you are a graphic artist, chances are you never learned the rules of layout design. Here are a few to keep in mind as you create layouts for your presentations:

- Do not underline text or headlines to draw attention to them; use a bold version of the same typeface or an entirely different typeface instead. Underlining text can cut off part or all of the descender (the part of the letter that hangs below the baseline of the type). The line itself is so thin it disappears when projected on a screen.

- Use open space around a graphic, rather than a box or border to draw attention to the graphic. Boxes and borders clutter up the screen, and audiences sometimes have trouble deciding what to look at first. You can also put a box of subtle color behind the graphic to frame it visually.

Background Design

Presentation software packages come with a variety of colored backgrounds, including some lovely ones with graduated tints. Stick with solid backgrounds if you are planning to print the slides for use as handouts. Solid backgrounds are also a good idea because unless you print graduated tints on a high-resolution slide recorder, imagesetter, or printer, the smooth, even transition between the shades and colors disappears, leaving you with ugly chunks or streaks of color.

Solid backgrounds can help you fight the urge to cram the screen full of text and graphics. Your presentations will always look professional if each screen has a few carefully chosen words and images backed up by a tasteful background.

You can also use photographs for backgrounds if you take the time to enlarge them to fit and then use an image-editing program to apply a special effect. The easiest special effect is to wash out most of the color, leaving only hints of the original color but leaving shapes clearly visible. Other special effects, such as changing the picture into a line drawing or embossing part, or all, of the picture, can be stunning—but such effects take more work than simply washing out the color.

Color

Most of us prefer full-color images—after all, we live in a full-color world. At times, though, black and white and tones of gray can make for a refreshing change. If you must choose between fuzzy, lower-quality color images and sharp, higher-quality black-and-white images, choose the latter.

Because it packs so much punch in presentations, you must handle color carefully both from a design standpoint and from a business angle. Strong, vibrant colors such as red and purple may be too strong for your presentation or your audience's tastes. You may also want to avoid using colors associated with a competitor's company—you can bet no one at Pepsi uses Coca-Cola red in presentations!

Black And Blue

Human eyes have trouble distinguishing elements of screens with any but the lightest shade of blue on a very dark background. That's because of the way human retinas receive blue light. Blue text on a dark background looks fuzzy and out of focus.

Of course, blue is a restful, peaceful color that can also connote power—so it, in all its variations, remains a favorite color for presentations. If you want to use blue elements in your presentation, back them up with a swatch of a color other than black and stick to lighter varieties of the color.

Health Club Memberships

Of all age groups, more people 65 and older are joining health clubs.

You can also use blue as a background color; keep in mind, however, that dark elements may blend in too much with the background. Try using type in a lighter color, or in white, if you must use blue in your background.

Speak, Don't Scream

Neon images that scream for attention confuse and tire our eyes—particularly if this is the fifth or tenth Day-Glo presentation your audience has sat through today. Limit your color palette for the major elements in the presentation to no more than six very carefully chosen colors. Only one or two of these colors should be bright, bold colors; the rest should be more muted or lighter shades.

Try constructing a few palettes of compatible colors. Screens constructed of a palette of black, white, grays, warm neutrals, and a couple of brighter colors will look richer and more professional than the fluorescent combinations you may be tempted to use. For more information on color in presentations, see Chapter 6.

Multimedia

Motion can easily become manic if you don't plan carefully and use motion effects sparingly. Animation attracts attention and engages the audience, so choose your effects with these purposes in mind. Never let motion mania overwhelm your content.

Motion Sickness

In some presentations, each screen vibrates, bobs, weaves, shakes, and quivers with seemingly every multimedia and motion effect possible. The most you can hope for with this kind of presentation is making your audience forget about your content and fall in love with the special effects. At worst, they become so bombarded with effects that they turn off completely.

Save major motion effects such as swipes and blinds to signal important divisions in the content (think of them as chapter titles). Between frames and sequences in the same division, use subtler effects such as dissolves and fades (think of these as heads and subheads).

For charts and graphics, some simple and gentler motion effects to consider are animating a line graph, exploding the wedge of a pie chart to highlight an important segment, or gradually drawing in bars on a chart. Keep these effects to a minimum; too many can easily overwhelm. Make sure the content and the screen without animation make sense, then pinpoint one or two pieces of data or points you want to draw attention to and add motion effects as needed. Leave at least half of your screens motionless, and intermix motion-filled and motionless screens.

Web Pages

Web pages call for additional attention, although all the advice given elsewhere in this chapter is equally useful for Web site design. Web pages are almost always unattended and interactive to some degree, meaning the viewer can wander at will through the page or site without a guide. That means you have to make it easy for viewers to navigate—both to find something and to find their way back to other segments or back to the starting point.

Tangled Ganglia

Advanced planning, such as building a road map for your site, is the best way to handle this situation. Take yourself on a mental tour through all the sections of the page, and look for potentially confusing spots where viewers might get lost or have too many options to choose from. In addition, each screen should have a way to go back one page, go forward one page, and go back to the beginning. Some browsers have these features built in, but don't count on them to provide these navigational tools.

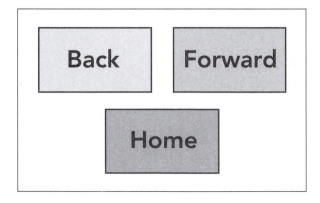

Another way to minimize viewer confusion on a Web page is to limit the page to only a few layers of information—but use at least two. If everything on a Web page is on one layer, viewers will perceive it as a flat, featureless landscape and will feel lost even if they aren't. More than a few levels of information and the viewer can become disoriented ("let's see, where did I see that and how can I get back there?"). If you have a lot of data or text on your page, consider including a comprehensive search mechanism, as well.

Alignment

Make your design time more productive by using a grid structure and one of three text alignment options: flush-left, flush-right, and centered. Early on, establish an alignment plan and text layout rules that you will use for the entire presentation. Odd-numbered grid divisions (three, five, and seven) help foster a sense of open space on screen and, so, are good places to start the planning process.

Stuck In The Middle

If you normally center all your text and graphics on the screen, stop and turn your attention to the right or left. By centering everything, you're creating more design problems for yourself than you are solving. Centering material divides the open space into two equal areas—which is less impressive than larger, asymmetrical sections of open space.

Try aligning the elements along the left side of the screen, leaving a generous amount of white space between the elements and the left edge. (That's what Western readers are most accustomed to. If you are creating a presentation for a Middle Eastern or Far Eastern audience, consider a flush-right alignment.)

Pro Copy

Full color copies

Fast black and white copies

Free delivery

Justifying Justification

Justification (adjusting spaces between words and letters to completely fill a column of space) was invented to help make reading long or narrow blocks or columns of text, such as in newspapers and magazines, easier. Because you should be using only short chunks of text in your presentations, you won't need to justify text.

Because the flush-left orientation works so well in most presentations, you should plan to use it as your standard unless you have a compelling design reason to use something else. Place all headlines and beginning lines of text along the left-hand side of the screen. If you use more than one line of text for a particular point, indent all but the first a small amount so the viewers can easily tell one point from another.

Emphasis

Each screen of a presentation should have no more than one or two key elements, which should be easily identifiable to the audience because of how you've used them in the design. There are several ways you can draw attention or add emphasis to material in a presentation: by using color, by using a larger type size, or by adding white space around the material.

Color With Caution

Color is a great way of drawing attention to something, but as we discussed earlier in this chapter, it must be used cautiously and carefully. Reserve the brightest and boldest of colors in your presentation color palette for material you want to stand out, and use those same colors for the same reason throughout the presentation.

Type designers and typographers talk about another kind of color—the color of type. Although type is usually black or white, when you look at blocks of text and close your eyes slightly, you get a sensation of looking at a gray block. The exact shade of gray depends on the size and density of the type in the block: more text or thicker characters and less white results in a darker gray, and conversely, less text or skinny characters results in a lighter shade of gray. Experiment with this phenomenon (and have some fun) by creating a few sample blocks of text using two variations of a typeface, such as narrow and plain, bold and italic.

Don't Overemphasize The Point

Big objects attract our attention—retail establishments use large point-of-sale and vivid wall displays and banners to get us to notice merchandise. Billboards and stories-high photographic displays on buildings also make us look and (sometimes) make us retain the information.

Size can also help in presentations, and making certain elements larger than the rest of the material in a screen can draw attention to what's important. Headlines, for instance, should be larger than the rest of the text on a screen. Use size in small amounts, though, as it is easy to go beyond emphasis into outrageousness. Vary type sizes by only several smaller jumps—128-point type for headlines and 12-point type for everything else won't work, but 72-point headlines with 36-point type can.

Capital Restraint

In email and in some genres of fiction, setting type in all uppercase letters is a recognized way of adding emphasis, particularly if you want to shout at someone. In presentations, using all capital letters is a sure way to irritate your audience. Here are a few alternate suggestions:

- Change the color of the text for the one word or phrase you want to emphasize.

- Change the type style of the text (bold is good; italic can also work well).

- Make the type size a few points bigger than the rest of the text.

- Experiment with small caps—a type style that looks like all caps but is less strident. This type style is available in most word processing software.

Clichés

Clichés can be visual as well as spoken or written and can crop up easily in presentations if you are not vigilant. Tired, worn-out visuals are ineffective in presentations because audiences automatically interpret them as mental noise. For this reason alone it's worth developing your own set of backgrounds and designs rather than relying on the set that comes with your presentation software.

Take your cue from the visual design effects used in the latest eye-catching commercials and memorable videos and movies. Use your own instincts to guide you and don't overlook some classics. Shooting a scene from an unusual angle, such as from the floor up, was pioneered by Orson Welles—the American actor, producer, director, and writer—in *Citizen Kane* (1941), but it's still fresh enough for today's music videos, television shows, and movies.

Visual Tics

Unless you're creating a presentation for small children, leave the slowly blinking eyes and rotating eyeballs out of your work. Carry the concept a little further and you're back at the idea of using animations sparingly. Start with your content, use special effects and other emphasis techniques to draw attention to the most important elements, and then stop designing.

Punctuation Marks

Punctuation marks are easy to use incorrectly in all forms of communication. Stick with accepted editorial practice (consult a style guide if you need to brush up). Use a question mark only if you want to ask a question, an exclamation mark only if you would raise your voice at the end of the statement if you read it aloud, and a dollar sign to denote currency.

If you want to add emphasis to a line of text or otherwise draw attention to it, use the techniques outlined in the "Emphasis" section of this chapter. Stick with punctuation marks for organizing text—and leave it at that.

Moving On

Allow the material here to help you eliminate any design infractions you may have engaged in before reading the chapter. If you can avoid them, the quality of your presentation design will improve and your presentations will be all the more effective.

With design basics and styles firmly in hand, it's time to move on to some sample presentation scenarios. In Chapter 13, we examine nine situations, including typical presentation environments and audiences, and present appropriate strategies for each.

13 SAMPLE SCENARIOS

As you plan your presentation, content should be your primary concern, but don't forget to consider the practical considerations that the type of presentation and environment will impose. From the boardroom to the conference hall, each setting requires the right mix of medium, environment, structure, and tone.

Delivering The Goods

Some environments offer better room design for presentations than others and seating arrangements more suited to your particular kind of presentation. Certain presentations work best with lecture hall-type seating so everyone can focus on the person making the presentation. Others work better if the audience can see the speaker and the other audience members and act more as participants than passive listeners.

No matter what kind of presentation you are planning, there are several environmental aspects you should look for when you have the luxury of choosing the presentation site. Check for comfortable seating, excellent acoustics with a clear, easy-to-alter sound system and controlled lighting. A booth or similarly isolated area for the audiovisual equipment is a definite plus, as well.

Alas, not every presentation site will provide the best environment. To help you visualize and plan for the environmental challenges you will face, I will discuss some typical presentation scenarios, from ultracasual to superformal. In each scenario I've offered pointers for making the best choices in media, equipment, and site changes.

Peer Group Meetings

Peers are colleagues—not managers or staff on a higher level than you. Presentations for peers are usually small, casual meetings that take place on-site in a conference or meeting room. Many conference rooms are outfitted with overhead projectors, screens, slide projectors, and write-on/wipe-off boards. The company may also have an easel in the room for large flip charts.

Plan to limit your presentation to the time allotted for it. This is particularly important if you are only one of several people making presentations. No one wants to listen to a 20-minute presentation if all the others are less than 10 minutes. If you are not given a time limit, make the presentation no longer than 20 minutes—after that you'll lose your audience's attention.

Media

The attendees will sit around the main conference table and, for overflow seating, in chairs moved into the room. Take advantage of the seating arrangement and presentation options, and design your presentation for overheads or flip charts. Slides can work well, too, in this type of setting.

You want to make sure your peers are suitably impressed with your efforts without feeling as though you've spent more time on the way the presentation looks than on the presentation itself. Keep the style of your presentation in line with those of your peer group. You don't want your presentation to dance and sing while the one the boss did last week merely shuffled a bit.

Start with simple black-and-white transparencies unless your office has a color laser printer available. Such devices have made color much easier and less expensive to use in presentations. Whether you choose color or black overheads, keep a color marker handy (one designed for use on transparency film) to add additional emphasis during the presentation.

Use handouts if you want the attendees to be able to pay attention to you during the presentation. Otherwise, they may be so busy writing, they'll look more at their paper than at you. Handouts are also useful if you want to dim the lights during the presentation—people will get the subtle hint and relax about taking notes.

Making paper handouts from overhead transparencies is easy. You can simply photocopy directly from them or print additional copies of the presentation on white paper instead of transparency film. When making photocopies, try reducing the size of the presentation sheet 15 percent to 20 percent to make the paper version look less intimidating. You can also print more than one (but no more than four) slides per sheet.

You can also prepare handouts based on the presentation but filled with additional data related to the presentation. You can reference, not recite, the detailed material in the handouts to save time during the presentation.

Content And Design

You may be tempted to compromise when creating graphics for a peer presentation, but let your experience be your guide. Some company cultures expect presentations to look a little like works in progress, whereas others expect totally polished materials. Let the purpose for the meeting guide you, as well. If you're briefing a few department members on some brainstorming ideas, you can be more casual than if you're updating several departments on the progress of a major project.

You can usually depend on your audience being interested in the material, so showcase your content by organizing it and presenting it logically. If the group already knows a lot about your subject, you can skip background material. Instead, show them what they are already familiar with in a new way, with particular emphasis on your interpretation and new thoughts.

Keep in mind that your task is to stay within the confines of the corporate culture's expectations for a presentation without letting those parameters stifle your creativity or your content. Here are a few ideas to help you accomplish this tricky task:

- Read a letter from a customer or employee related to the presentation.

- Tell an interesting personal anecdote to underscore a point or two.

- Use flip-chart materials along with transparencies.

- Bring an object into the conference room, put it down where it's clearly visible to all, and ignore it during the presentation. At the conclusion of the presentation, pick up the object and relate it to your content. Make sure you can come up with a good, strong, symbolic connection to your material.

Web Crawling

Web presentations are wide-open. Anyone with a connection to the Web can become part of your audience, which means you have to keep a variety of possible scenarios in mind. To keep yourself focused, keep your target audience in the forefront of your mind while you're creating and planning. Then review the plan to see how well it would work for the possible (and probable) fringe audience.

Media

The only media you'll need to worry about once you've created the presentation is the Web itself. Unfortunately, with the wide variety of browsers and versions of browsers, plus the wide variety of computers accessing the Web, that's enough worry for anyone.

There are two ways to cope with this concern. One, make your presentation choices with your target audience in mind. If everyone you want to reach is sure to have the latest version of a Web browser with all its capabilities installed on their blazing-fast computers, then design the presentation to fit them. You should also include a text-only version of your presentation in case your audience wants the simplest-possible version of the material, no matter how technically up-to-date your target audience is.

Two, you can choose to design a presentation that works well on any moderately fast computer and modem. To do this, you will have to skip some of the latest techno-wizard features and make a simpler presentation that works well with older versions of the major browsers.

Content And Design

Your content and design will reflect your choice of a method for coping with the nature of the media. Include the latest and greatest of everything if you are confident your audience will be able to appreciate it. You can also include such Web goodies as access to online databases and other Web sites.

If you are creating a less complex version of your presentation, limit your content to your major points and graphics. Work hard at applying the axiom "less is more," and think hard before you include extras such as online ordering, fill-in-the-blanks forms, and other features your audience may not be able to use.

No matter what choice you make, spend some time looking for and removing extraneous bells and whistles from your presentation. You need some frills to get, and keep, your audience's attention, but chances are, you won't need as many as you're tempted to use. When in doubt, limit yourself to one special feature per screen.

Make sure to choose graphics that will look good on many different kinds of screens and different browsers (see Chapter 3 for details). You may have to make some changes to existing graphics or create some from scratch in order to do this, so give yourself extra time during the production stage.

Gear your design choices for typefaces, colors, and graphics toward your target audience, but also keep in mind they will be looking at the design on screen. Small type (smaller than 10 point) can get lost on screen, particularly if you've chosen a typeface with extreme serifs (either delicate or bold).

Scientific And Professional Conference Presentations

These kinds of presentations will require more of your time and nervous energy than peer presentations. Much more is at stake, particularly if you are presenting to persuade your audience rather than merely inform. Be prepared to invest more time, thought, and money into these presentations.

Media

Slides are the hands-down favorite for large professional and scientific meetings. In some industries, especially industries where a computer is now an everyday tool, electronic presentations are becoming more popular. These presentations are projected on large screens directly from a computer.

Well-made slides have many advantages over a hastily prepared electronic presentation, so stick with slides unless you're really pressed for time. You'll find it's easier to make your presentation and you'll have fewer technical land mines to step around once you're on-site. Keep in mind that it's much easier to make a last minute change to a computer slide than to make a change to a transparency and have it recopied. Overhead transparencies will not have the same punch in a large room that they have in a smaller conference room. Use them only if you can't create slides or an electronic presentation.

Most of the time you will not be the only person making a presentation at such an event, so make sure you know how much time you will have and plan accordingly. No one minds if you end a little early, but it's awkward if you end much too early, and everyone hates it if you run over.

Unless you have a lot of detail or background material in your presentation, plan on one well-designed slide for every minute of your presentation. Pace yourself and change the slides as you move from point to point. Don't allow one image to remain on screen while you wax philosophical, and don't rush through several in a mad dash to finish. If you fear having more slides than time, put your important points at the beginning of the presentation so you can skip the later portions of the presentations if you're running out of time.

As mentioned in Chapter 3, glass mounts are a good idea and investment, as they will keep your slides intact and unbent. They are a must-have if you intend to use the slides more than once. Keep the slides in plastic sleeves when not in use, and take them out and put them in your own covered carousel tray before you practice your presentation.

If you opt for an electronic presentation, make sure your computer can be attached quickly and easily to the presentation equipment, such as a digital projector, that is available on-site. Hotels use conference rooms and halls for more than conferences, so the technology they have on hand varies widely. The conference organizers should be able to tell you well in advance what will be available. If not, check with the hotel directly.

Always be prepared for technical glitches and have a backup copy of the presentation (with player) on floppy disk or CD-ROM. It's also a good idea to have a lower-tech version (slides, overheads, or even handouts) on hand in case you encounter insurmountable obstacles and can't do your electronic presentation as planned.

Content And Design

To overcome distractions, help your audience out by including plenty of directional material in your presentation design. Use section markers, running titles, symbols, and icons to help them pick up where they may have left off while they were talking to someone beside them.

If the information you are presenting is complex, icons are a great way to help people understand what kind of information they are looking at on screen. Material with references in the handouts can be denoted using a small book icon. Not-to-be-missed information can have a star next to it.

Make one major point with a few subpoints per slide. If you cram more information than that on one slide, you'll end up overwhelming the audience no matter how high their collective I.Q. is. Use more slides, or fewer points, if necessary.

If you are sure you won't be leaving someone in the dark, you can skip over background material in your presentation. This idea is a particularly good one if you are making a presentation to an academic or trade group. If you're not sure of the audience composition, ask the event coordinators or sponsors for their ideas.

Sales Shows

People need to sell and you need to buy. That's a fact of life few of us can ignore. What we try to ignore, though, is the barrage of sales pitches we encounter every day. They come at us via telephone, the Web, the mail, and in person—every kind of media we encounter is used in an attempt to sell. No wonder we feel, at the least, wearied by this effort and, at most, angry. Keep this in mind when creating sales presentations and yours will be more effective.

Media

Electronic presentations are now the most popular kind of presentation for sales efforts. You can impress people with them, and they give you the opportunity to use video and audio to help drive your points home. Self-running or standalone presentations are also effective, especially when you have a lot of information to impart and want to leave your prospects alone to explore it.

Kiosks at trade shows and in retail stores are another more specialized kind of sales presentation. These usually work with touch screens and computers housed inside the kiosks. These are not the kinds of presentations you create by yourself, so if you're interested in doing them, find a multimedia company to handle the nuts and bolts of the job.

You can still use slides and flip charts for sales presentations, and you might deliberately choose to do so if your audience would be turned off by something slicker. Judge for yourself what kind of presentation media will work best for your target market. When in doubt, pay attention to your gut instincts.

Content And Design

Compared with the strict standards you must follow when preparing scientific presentations, you have a lot more leeway with sales presentations. You can be more creative in the presentation of the material, as well as in the design. As long as you're completely honest and straightforward with all your content, you'll be fine.

Polish is essential in sales presentations—fumbling the presentation can often mean fumbling the sale. So, there is only one way you can be prepared and that is to practice, practice, practice the presentation. Test the presentation on sample audiences, including people who do not work in your organization. Make sure your material is free of error and all text has been proofread more than once.

All this preparation and practice means you'll have to devote more than a few hours to creating the presentation. It also means you'll have to do some heavy-duty thinking about your audience—what's likely to hit home with them and what might put them off. Think twice about humor, particularly ethnic humor, and don't tell jokes unless you have a night job at a local comedy club.

Tailor the appearance of the presentation to your audience. You wouldn't use grunge-style fonts and wild colors appropriate for a group of teenagers for a presentation to a group of people 40 years old and older. Stop and think about how your audience would think about the fonts, multimedia elements, colors, graphic styles, and screen layouts you have in mind before you begin creating the presentation.

Traveling Shows

For sales training, internal corporate updates, or customer communication, traveling shows are in a class of their own. Designed to almost run themselves, these presentations are carried in briefcases from place to place, often on floppy disk or CD-ROM. They can be automatic or semi-automatic, meaning they can be delivered without a live presenter or started and shown by a presenter and followed up with live remarks. Because they are self-contained, to be most effective they will require more up-front planning than other kinds of presentations.

Media

You have a few choices for presentation media: flip charts (including table-top flip-chart books), a set of slides or overheads, and electronic media such as floppies or CD-ROM disks. You can purchase a slide projector that advances slides by itself and will run the presentation automatically in the same way a player piano plays a tune by itself. Another way to publish your presentation is to have it recorded on videotape.

Don't overlook the added punch of including handouts and printed materials such as brochures. Design these materials to coordinate with the presentation, not to contain the presentation. That way you'll be reinforcing and expounding on the messages in the presentation and not making the presentation twice.

To help you decide which medium to choose, think about the technical capabilities of your audience. They may have only one computer in the entire office and no one is allowed to load anything new on it. A presentation on floppy disk wouldn't work for this audience, but a nice tabletop flip chart would.

Content And Design

The best way to begin selecting content and design elements for a self-contained traveling show is to place yourself in the audience. Remember, there won't be anyone along to interpret the presentation or to help keep people interested. The content must speak for itself, and the design should help keep them interested enough to sit through the entire presentation.

If you're using slides, plan for more slides than you would if you were standing there making the presentation directly. Plan for two or three slides for every minute of the presentation and use a consistent design to help the audience keep track of where they are in the presentation. Even something as simple as "slide 1 of 15" in the bottom right corner can help.

The idea that "more is better" is true for flip-chart shows, as well. Use all the sheets you need to get your points across in detail, and don't be afraid to reference printed material (if it's sent along). Make the text and graphics on each sheet clearly understandable from a distance of 8 to 10 feet so everyone in the room can see the material easily.

Courtroom Exhibits

The use of specially designed posters, large displays, and other presentation materials are being used every day in courtrooms. Used properly, they can be very effective tools for presenting evidence or someone's theories about what happened. You can use any presentation media in a courtroom, although flip charts and posters are the easiest to use in most cases.

Media

Large, centrally located posters work well in the conventional courtroom-style seating arrangement where a jury and judge are present. They can also be useful if you're meeting in a courthouse room or the judge's chambers. They get the job done without making anyone feel too much time or money was spent on the presentation.

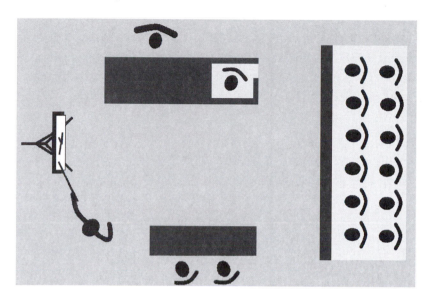

Juries are sometimes taken to the site of an accident or violent crime so they can explore the area for themselves. Such trips help them understand the testimony given in court. If a field trip isn't possible, consider using a short multimedia presentation or even a video clip made at the site. Do this only with prior permission from the court.

Avoid using slides or overheads, as the legal system is much more accustomed to the oral presentation of information, evidence, and testimony. It's also difficult to position everyone in the courtroom so they can see the material. A poster can be picked up and walked around the room if necessary.

Make sure all posters are mounted on a rigid substrate such as foam core board for presentation. Laminating the posters will help preserve and protect them. You will need a sturdy easel to put the posters on during the presentation. If you want to show more than one poster at once, use several easels.

Content And Design

Use overlays on posters to build a complex image. Some attorneys like to use a single base graphic, such as a scale drawing or floor plan, and then cover it with a series of removable clear acetate layers showing details of arguments. You can also use blank acetate sheets so that details may be drawn on them during the trial.

If you are helping the attorney create the presentation materials, rely on him or her to give you directions about subject matter and appropriate presentation. Make sure to label objects with labels that are clearly visible from several feet away. The same is true of any text. Make doubly sure all details are correct and nothing is missing from diagrams and drawings.

Think long and hard about the use of color in these kinds of presentations. You are creating informational displays, not works of art, so use color to inform and guide the audience. Design for clarity to avoid having the audience guess at your meaning. For example, the graphics used for the defendant's car and the plaintiff's car should look like cars but be different colors, and the stop sign should be clearly recognizable.

Financial Reports

Financial reports are all about money—a subject most people find very interesting and important, particularly when it's their money you're talking about. Presenting financial information is serious stuff, and you don't want to offend anyone. Leave your sense of humor at home and make your presentation neat, conservative, and confident.

You must also be completely sure your math and your figures are correct. You can be sure someone in the audience has eagle eyes and a computer brain and will spot any mistake you make.

Media

Financial data is presented in a variety of settings ranging from overheads at informal peer group gatherings to ultraformal electronic presentations at stockholder meetings. Make your choice based on the situation—the more serious the matter, the more money there is at stake, and the more formal your presentation should be.

No matter what media you choose, remember to leave something behind in writing so the audience will have something to review after the presentation is completed. That's a must no matter what kind of group you're talking to and how long the presentation is. Plan to include the data in table and graphic form and hand the materials out before you begin your presentation. Feel free to direct the audience's attention to the relevant material in the handouts during the presentation.

Content And Design

Financial presentations should also be conservative with regard to content and design. Even if the company has the wildest, most innovative commercials on television today, they still want to hear about their money directly and plainly. Here are some suggestions:

- Stick with 2D graphics made up of the standard bars and lines. Save the cute 3D graphics for other kinds of presentations.

- Choose one or two serious, grown-up typefaces such as Times Roman, Helvetica, and Arial for all text.

- Use only a few somber, staid colors. Some financial presenters won't use red because it reminds too many financially minded folk about "red ink."

- Keep all graphics simple and label them clearly.

Boardroom Graphics

In smaller companies the boardroom and the conference room are the same room. In larger companies they can be separate facilities. Of the two, the boardroom is a much better environment for presentations. Boardrooms often have the latest and greatest in presentation gadgets and equipment, including built-in large-screen displays and projection systems.

Media

If you're making a presentation in one of the ultramodern boardrooms, chances are you'll be expected to make a totally professional-looking electronic presentation. Overheads and slides will be considered old-fashioned and out-of-date. Find out what kind of equipment the room has and plan your media choices accordingly.

Electronic presentations that play off your own computer and that you can control during the presentation may be your best bet. You can also bring along standalone video and audio clips if a video player is available. Really, the sky is the limit if you have a large enough budget. You will certainly have an audience that is accustomed to the latest and greatest technology in presentations.

Content And Design

Once again, it's time to focus on content and let the special effects play a supporting role. Your content must be accurate and compelling, and your presentation must be flawless. Have a professional proofreader or editor check all materials, especially text, and even look for mistakes inside stock art you use.

Double-check all the images and video you use for potential problems. You wouldn't want to use the cover of a magazine from a rival publishing house or a product from a competitor in your presentation. It's also not a good idea to have a video clip interview of someone who was laid off or fired a week before the presentation.

Work with typefaces that seem simple, yet dignified, to you. Garamond and Times Roman are good choices. Limit the amount of text per screen to a few short sentences or bullet points even if you have to use more screens or slides than you normally would. Don't be afraid to punctuate the presentation with a few well-chosen transition effects such as slides or wipes, but leave the cute audio clips out of the presentation.

Bribe the secretary with lunch or a good book if necessary, but make sure you have a few hours in the boardroom before you finalize your presentation. Use the time to practice your presentation and work with the equipment in that room. If you can get back in after you finalize the presentation, do so and practice some more. You'll sleep better the night before the big day if you do.

Instruction And Training Materials

Some companies and facilities have rooms dedicated for training activities. Many more simply set up temporary facilities in general-purpose meeting rooms and even cafeterias. In either case, there are some generalities you can start with and verify before finalizing your presentation. There will rarely be more than 30 people in the room, and seating arrangements will be somewhat flexible, but possibly uncomfortable. Lighting may be difficult to control, and you may hear noise from adjoining areas. Keep these potential problems in mind as you create your training materials.

Media

The easiest situation to cope with for these kinds of presentations is a room that is set up for training and used only for training. You can usually set up the room to suit your needs and leave your materials there between sessions. Your media choices are unlimited if the classroom is modern and has a large computer screen display on the wall. Otherwise, slides and overheads will work well.

If you want to use overhead projectors, look into a projector display that can project images directly from your computer. These nifty gadgets are not cheap, but they allow you to create full-color screens and make on-the-fly changes to your presentation. So, if someone asks what happens if you change a figure in a spreadsheet analysis, you can show him or her immediately.

Plan on handouts of all the relevant points of the presentation. Include self-tests and small quizzes in the material to help the students reinforce what they've learned in class. Strive to give them a complete summary of the presentation plus some material to take away with them. A list of resources for more detail or in-depth learning will also be appreciated.

If your budget can support it, consider a multimedia presentation for classroom use and even a take-away interactive presentation for the audience to use later. Research studies have proven that multimedia and interactivity help people learn faster and retain more than static presentations.

Content And Design

Match your content and design to the age, education, and experience level of the group. It's easy to see that the bright colors and images of Sesame Street characters aren't appropriate for adult training, but even more subtle differences can have a big impact. The audience may be more familiar with the complete works of William Shakespeare than the latest movie blockbuster, so adjust your content accordingly.

Don't be afraid to reevaluate your design choices periodically if you plan to use the same materials for several training programs. Times change and so should your material. The easiest way to set up a presentation to allow for design changes later on is to use the style commands in your word processor or page layout program. That way, to change the presentation, all you have to do is change the style definitions.

Keep a copy of your graphics in their native digital file format to make it easier to change them later. Otherwise, you may end up re-creating the images just to make a few color changes.

Moving On

There is often no one right way to handle a presentation. Each presentation situation is unique, which is part of the fun and the challenge of making presentations. The scenarios in this chapter will give you some good guidelines for surviving just about any kind of presentation, but you will gain knowledge and experience of your own as you make more presentations. Your experience and the material presented in this chapter will help you make good decisions about the options available to you.

In the next chapter, I'll conclude our study of presentation design with a few words of advice on polishing your presentation to make it as effective and professional as possible.

A Final Glance

14

Once all the pieces of your presentation are in place, it's time to take a fresh look at the finished product to ensure you reached your intermediate and overall goals.

To complete our exploration of the ways and means of creating effective presentations, let's take a brief look at the last few steps in the preparation process. After doing all the initial work described in the previous chapters, it may seem like overkill to ask you to take more time before wrapping up your presentation. Yet these final steps may be the most rewarding ones of all, allowing you to feel totally confident about your work and the end result.

From this vantage point near the end, you can look over the entire presentation and ask yourself some important questions that will help strengthen the presentation. You can ask yourself if every element in the presentation contributes to the communication of your message. If not, now is the time to correct the situation. You can also ask yourself if you have allowed design elements to elbow the contents aside and take center stage. If so, you still have time to redirect the situation so all the players are in the proper places.

Rhythm, Pace, And Depth

A presentation can be given within several minutes or can take days to complete. The longer the length of the presentation, the more you will have to work at holding the audience's attention. Varying the rhythm, pace, and depth of your presentation style is one way to keep their attention and keep them learning.

The rhythm of a manned presentation is a combination of the speed at which the audiovisual materials are presented and the speed of the presenter (including voice, speech, and gestures). In a nonmanned presentation, the audiovisual material sets the pace by itself. Regardless, your goal should be to have the material unfold at a comfortable, yet slightly rigorous pace. The audience should have to work a little to keep up, but not so much that with a few stumbles they are left hopelessly behind.

You will be able to determine your own pace once you've made a few presentations. If you're unsure how to set the pace, allow yourself about one to two screens of information for each minute of your presentation. You would speak about 30 to 50 seconds per screen.

If the presentation materials contain a lot of detail, break the detail into more screens, but talk less per screen. Look for naturally occurring breaks in the material. A 15-step process can be broken down into 5 major steps, and you could use 5 screens to explain the process. Remember to keep highly detailed material out of the main presentation and put it in handouts for the audience to study later.

Production Strategy

The best way to produce a presentation is to start at the first frame, create the second, and move in presentation order to the end. Doing it this way makes it next to impossible to skip an important screen or series of screens. You probably won't be able to produce the entire presentation in one setting, but move ahead in this order anyway—roughing in the screens you can't complete at the moment.

Spring Cover

Summer Cover

Fall

As you go, check to make sure you are presenting all the content in a logical, organized way. If you use a term or acronym on screen 7, it should be defined or introduced earlier in the presentation or on that screen. If you refer to a certain graph or diagram, make sure the audience has seen or heard about that diagram before that point. Work from the simple to the complex in the entire presentation, as well as within each section. Avoid repeating material unless you are reviewing it. When you finish, the content should stand out and the design should facilitate the delivery of the content.

Proofreading

You must proofread your presentation. Nothing is more embarrassing, and ultimately avoidable, than misspelled words or incorrect figures in a presentation. Leave yourself plenty of time to proofread and verify information in the screens and in any handouts. Running a spell checker over the text isn't enough. You can have the wrong words spelled correctly, but they are still the wrong words. Mistakes like this give your audience the impression that you couldn't be bothered to check your work.

A good tip I learned from a copy editor long ago will help you at this point. To check for spelling errors, read the copy backwards. If you read it in the normal manner, your brain can often skip over such errors. Reading it backwards keeps the mind on its mental toes.

> **backwards read you if find to easier are Mistakes**

You should check for other kinds of errors at this stage as well. Make sure all punctuation marks are used correctly. Check the legends and titles on charts and graphs for spelling errors. Check to see that the bars and slices in graphs are correctly proportioned to the data. Look carefully at all images, still and moving, for gaffes such as using a competitor's product or the image of someone who no longer works at your company.

Then have several people with experience in proofreading check over the material. If you can have those people check over your materials for other problems and errors such as those mentioned here, that's a wonderful bonus. If not, have one or two of them sit with you while you run the presentation on screen and stop you if they find anything confusing.

Back To The Drawing Board

Once you have checked the presentation and have done some proofreading, you'll probably want to make some minor changes. Take the time to fine-tune your presentation, but be wary of making major changes unless you are correcting factual errors. If you're making major design changes at the last minute, you may be giving into last-minute jitters and changing a perfectly fine design.

To help you avoid a last-minute crisis in confidence, set a time limit of a day or two to make changes. Make the factual and error-correcting changes first, then stop for a while. If you have to change your color scheme or typeface, do so only after you've done everything else first.

Parting Thoughts

Before you wrap up a presentation, take the time to review your initial purposes in creating the presentation and compare the finished product to them. If the two coincide nicely, you're in great shape. If not, you may have gotten carried away—and you should take the time to bring the presentation back into line with your communication goals.

Imagine yourself as a member of the audience seeing the presentation for the first time. Do you still think it meets your goals? Better yet, ask a few people to sit in on a dry run and ask them later what they learned.

Preflight Checklist

Here's a final preflight checklist for your presentation. If you can answer each question with a firm yes, you're in good shape and near the end of the process of creating your presentation:

- Can the viewers in the back row read everything on the screens without straining or squinting?

- Is there a good balance of content to white space on each screen?

- Are the screen changes and transitions comfortable?

- Is the color contrast appropriate to the type size?

- Do the viewers' eyes move through each screen in the right order, seeing the most important information first?

- Does the content have center stage throughout the presentation?

- Are the images integrated smoothly into the overall graphic design?

When your presentation is successful, you know it instinctively. You can also tell when the audience is interested and active if afterward people come forward wanting to know more. By taking these last-minute steps, you'll be one step closer to creating and delivering a successful presentation every time. The reward is more than additional business or a promotion; you'll also have the emotional pleasure of helping your audience understand and remember your message.

APPENDIX A: STORYBOARD SHEETS

No one tells you about storyboards in school, but they are a great tool for planning any kind of public presentation, including plays and commercials.

To plan your presentation visually, you'll need to create a storyboard sheet for each screen in the presentation. On the following pages, you'll find storyboard frames to use in this process. Photocopy the page with the frame most appropriate to your presentation. Make enough copies to give you a frame for each screen, plus a few more in case you make some mistakes. Cut the sheets so you have a single page per frame.

Next, take your pencil and make rough drawings of the contents of each screen. Use double lines or hash marks to represent type and line length. Simple boxes will do for images, but make sure to keep the proportions of the type to the boxes as they will be in the finished screen.

Aim for consistency between elements in the presentation by flipping through the roughed-in storyboards. Check, too, to see how many charts and diagrams you would like to use. You may not have time to create them all, so adjust the presentation to fit the time you have to create it.

Repeat the above process until you have your presentation roughed out to your satisfaction.

Slides

Screens And Web Sites

Transparencies

Handouts

APPENDIX B: GRID SKETCH SHEETS

To effectively design screens for your presentations, you'll need grid sheets to help you position elements. If you don't use them, you can end up with too much, or not enough, material for your presentation.

During the process of creating storyboards for each screen in your presentation, you will want to refer to the grid sheets on the following pages or create your own to help you lay out each screen. If you are having trouble sketching out the screens in an orderly fashion just by looking at the grids, you can also photocopy the grid sheets and draw on those photocopies. If you need more space to draw, enlarge the grid when you photocopy it.

You can create your own customized grid sheets with graph paper. Mark the grids on the graph paper by using a felt-tip pin and a ruler. You can photocopy those sheets if you need more than a few.

No matter which grid sheets you use, make sure to pick a few key grid lines before you start drawing, including both the horizontal and vertical center grid lines and the horizontal grid lines that mark the upper and lower boundaries for text.

On the sketch of each screen, write down all special production details for that screen, including color choices, animation sequences, three-dimensional treatments, and drop shadows. Also list each of the graphics you'll be using.

4×3 Grid

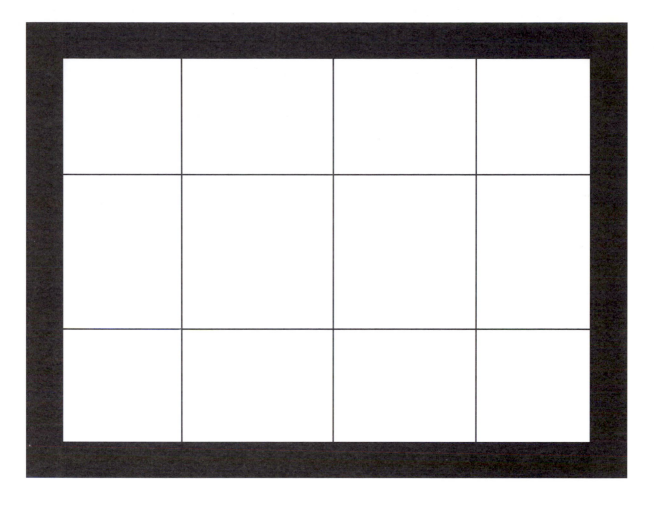

4×4 Grid

5×5 Grid

Page Grid

APPENDIX C:
CREATING
3D OBJECTS

Movies and real life come in 3D and so can presentations—or at least part of them, which gives you a neat way of adding dimension to your presentation.

We all know what is meant when something is 3D, right? If you think so, try asking three people to define the term for you and give you some examples. You'll be amazed at the variety of answers you get. To some people, the term brings to mind anything with depth, such as a shadowed object. Others think of 3D as objects that look real on a page or that you need special glasses to see in the movies. You'll find there is no clear consensus.

This lack of consensus isn't really a problem, because you're only asking to investigate a concept, you're not trying to write a definition for a new dictionary. I only mentioned the variety of ideas because as you use various image-editing and presentation software packages, you'll discover the term *3D* is used in a variety of ways and means different things in almost every program that offers 3D capability.

The Classic Concept

The classic definition of a 3D object is one that has height, width, and depth (the three dimensions). In contrast, 2D objects have only height and width. In school we all drew simple 3D boxes, such as the following one, to help us understand the concept and to amuse ourselves.

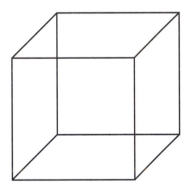

Our perception of the orientation or construction of the same object changes considerably if you change the shading on one panel of the box.

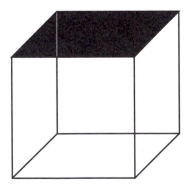 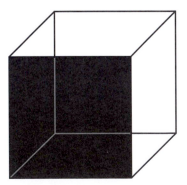

One of the boxes appears to be shaped differently from the other, even though the wireframe of the two boxes is identical. This brings up an important concept for how 3D objects can be used in presentations. The previous boxes were sketched in a computer drawing program in only a few minutes. Within five minutes, I produced two images that looked markedly different using the same basic image.

You can do the same thing to add variety and depth to your presentations by using 3D objects. Some 3D effects, such as shading, are easily done inside presentation software packages. Others, such as drawing and scaling, need to be done in drawing and image-editing software. These effects can be applied to any object, including text.

You don't need to be an artist to do any of these 3D effects. It takes only a few minutes to create 3D effects in most programs unless you are committed to doing something complicated. You can even buy clip art images of objects complete with shadows; all you do then is drop these images into your presentation.

Even though you don't need to be an artist, being imaginative will help. The following image is the same wireframe box used for the other images, but two areas have been shaded and one line removed. Now the box looks like a shelf turned to the side. That's a simple example of what a little imagination will help you accomplish.

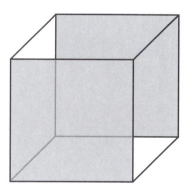

Casting Shadows

Several times in the book, I recommend adding shadows to a box or behind an image to give the object a sense of depth. Shadows, used sparingly, are a good way to give the whole screen a feeling of depth. It's easy to give almost any object a simple shadow, and there are ways to cast more realistic shadows.

An easy way to give a square or any other geometric object a shadow is to create an identical shape and fill it with a shade of gray. The fill color does not have to be solid. In the figures that follow, the second square was filled with various shades of gray.

Next, take the gray-filled shape and position it to the rear and slightly out of line with the object you want to draw attention to. Make sure only a small portion of the gray object shows. If too much gray shows, the gray box will draw too much attention to itself.

Shadowing is such an easy and popular special effect that many presentation programs have built-in tools for instantly creating shadows for objects. In the following screen, taken from Microsoft PowerPoint, a popular presentation creation program, you can see the dialog box for creating shadows.

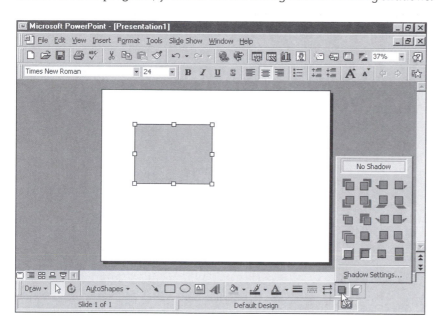

Before you go out and buy image-editing or drawing software, experiment with the 3D effects, including shading, in your presentation software. You might find everything you need to achieve the effects you're looking for. Remember, you're trying to draw attention to the content, not create a work of art.

Examples Of 3D Effects

Image-editing and drawing programs exist so you can create or change images. They therefore have a lot of special effects built into the software for you to use to these ends. Here are a few examples of the 3D special effects found in these kinds of programs. We start by showing you the 2D image of a lightbulb as the "before," followed by a few "after" images.

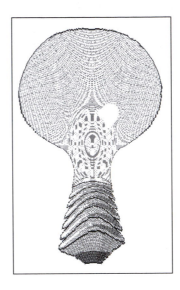

Some of these programs, including presentation software packages, allow you to apply 3D effects to type. If your software allows you to do this, experiment with the effects and find a few you like that are easy to accomplish. Remember, all the type must be legible if you want people to read it. Don't create a special effect that makes the text too hard to read. In the example below, a subtle 3D effect has been added to the plain text.

Widgets

Premade 3D

Creating custom shadow effects for complicated objects is something graphic artists do on a regular basis. It's also something they work hard at mastering before they can do it correctly and consistently. Creating shadow effects can be a time-consuming process involving the creation of a digital mask (a way of selecting only a portion of an image) using image-editing software, followed by the application of several special effects to get just the right shade at just the right angle. After all, they are working on images to make the unreal look real. You're just trying to get your presentation finished on time.

You can take advantage of all this hard work without doing it yourself by investing in a few stock image or clip art collections that have the shadows and 3D effects already in the images. These images can be a very powerful way of adding punch and originality to your presentation, so check the Resource Guide for stock image companies and investigate their 3D offerings.

Following are a few examples of images with shadows and 3D objects from Dynamic Graphics, a stock image and clip art company, to give you an idea of the kinds of images that are available.

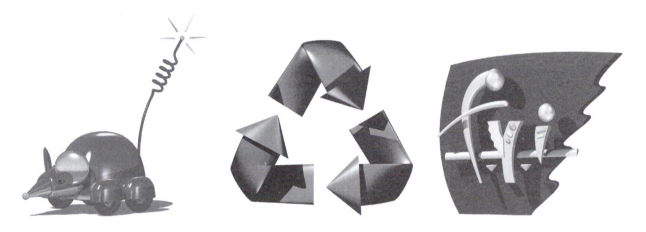

You can also purchase images of objects such as buttons and other kinds of graphics with a 3D effect. These kinds of objects look great in Web site presentations, but they can also add a new look to other kinds of presentations. Following are a few examples of these kinds of images from stock image and clip art company Little Men Studios.

GLOSSARY

A

additive color—Color produced by the combining of beams of light. Red, green, and blue (RGB) are the additive primaries; receptors in the human eye are sensitive to red, green, and blue.

alignment—Arrangement or positioning of type or graphic elements along an invisible, straight, vertical line, such as the left or right margin.

annotation—Titles, labels, and so on added to charts, graphs, diagrams, and other illustrations to identify portions of the images.

ascender—The extension or upward stroke of any of the tall lowercase letters, such as b, d, and t.

aspect ratio—The ratio of an image's width to its height. The typical aspect ratio of presentation slides is 3:2; for overhead transparencies, 4:5; for video monitors, 4:3.

B

bar graph—A single-scale graph drawn with parallel bars, used to compare quantities at a specific time or to show activity of one thing through time.

baseline—The imaginary horizontal line on which type rests. Descenders of lowercase letters fall below it, giving variety and establishing character identity (see *descender*).

bitmapped—A bitmapped image is made up of individual dots, as opposed to a vector or object-based image, where a page description language specifies lines or other discrete shapes.

blank frame—A frame in a slide presentation used as a placeholder. Useful for a pause while members of the audience ask questions and so forth.

blinds—Transition technique to draw in or erase out an image in horizontal strips, much like a mini-blind opening or closing.

boldface—A heavier or darker version of a typeface, often used to add emphasis to a word or phrase.

build sequence—A series of frames or screens in which each new frame adds or emphasizes a new point or portion of a point. A build sequence is a useful technique for pacing a presentation, for delivering detailed information, or for working from the simple to the more complex portion of a concept.

bullet list—A list whose items are preceded by small graphic symbols, often bullets, that set items apart from each other and from headings and other text.

C

CD-ROM—Acronym for compact disc read-only memory. A compact disc player can read the information stored on a compact disc, but only a CDR (compact disc recorder) can record information on blank discs. A compact disc is now the primary means of distributing software and large amounts of data.

centering—A type alignment scheme in which lines are centered over one another on a vertical axis, making left and right margins uneven. This is a formal, conservative alignment used for invitations but discouraged for presentations.

class interval—A range of points between observations in a chart or graph, particularly a histogram (see *observation; histogram*).

clip art—Previously created illustrations available for purchase or as freeware.

CMY (subtractive) color—A method of mixing pigment based on the subtractive primary colors (Cyan, Magenta, Yellow). These colors are used to print many full-color graphics. When black ink is included for printing black or gray, it is known as CMYK (Cyan, Magenta, Yellow, and Black).

color wheel—A circular chart depicting the colors of the spectrum, showing primary, secondary, and complementary relationships between colors. Used as a reference image for discussing color.

complements—Colors opposite one another on the color wheel, such as blue and orange, which, when added together, create a neutral color.

condensed type—A variation of a typeface that retains the shape of the original, but in which characters have been made narrower and taller, allowing more type to fit into a given amount of space.

critical path method (CPM) diagram—A project management diagram, often in the form of a Gantt chart, showing a succession of project activities from beginning to end (see *Gantt chart*).

D

data symbols—Points, bars, lines, and other graphics that represent values in a graph.

descender—Portion of a lowercase letter, such as g, p, and y, that drops below the baseline (see *baseline*).

deviation bar graph—A graph with bars to the left or right of the reference axis, indicating the area of standard deviation. This emphasizes differences from the expected value.

digital audio—Audio tones that are stored as digital data rather than as sound, as with analog recording methods.

display type—A typeface usually selected for style rather than readability, designed to be used in large sizes for titles or parts of a design where large type is needed.

dissolve—A transition effect between two screens in a presentation in which the first gradually fades as the second gradually appears. The two images may share the screen for a portion of time.

dissolve unit—A device used to work two or more slide projectors at once, making slide changes occur more smoothly and quickly.

divided bar graph—A complex bar graph showing more detail and elaboration. Its concept is similar to that of pie chart; however, the divided bar graph uses bars.

dot map—A map or graph on which colored dots represent data collected at discrete locations, similar to colored pushpins on a map.

double-scale graph—A graph in which two vertical scales show two values or variables, such as one scale for a product price and one for the number of products sold.

drop (flat) shadow—A shadow behind a graphic element or letter to make the image appear three-dimensional.

dry mounting—Method of mounting posters for presentation on rigid board so the posters can be displayed on an easel or in some other way.

E

em space—An amount of space equal to the space required for an uppercase M in a given type size. Used as a convenient measuring unit for a paragraph indent, dash length, or bullet width.

en space—An amount of space half the width of an em space (see *em space*).

exploded graphic—A three-dimensional representation of an object, created with perspective drawing, to detail an object's inner component parts. The object is drawn as though it were exploding and flying apart.

extended type—A variation of a typeface that retains the original design of the typeface, but in which the individual characters have been made wider and, therefore, fill up more space.

extent—The ending point of the part of a graph on which you present data, typically the upper right-hand corner.

F

fade—A transition technique for the gradual closing or opening of a frame, usually to or from black.

figure/ground—Relationship of type or other graphic element to the design, texture, color, and quality of the background on which the element is imposed.

fillet—A decorative curved corner used to join rules together to form a frame or border.

flip book—Unmounted posters of presentation materials; the posters are bound together at the side into a large book whose pages are turned by the presenter.

flip chart—Unmounted posters of presentation materials; the posters are bound together at the top into a large book whose pages are turned by the presenter.

flush-left alignment—Type aligned with the left margin, leaving a ragged-right margin.

flush-left/flush-right alignment—Type aligned with both left and right margins; also called justified alignment.

flush-right alignment—Type aligned with right margin.

font—The full alphabet, number, and symbol set in one weight and design of a typeface (see *typeface*).

frame—An individual slide or overhead transparency in a presentation; also an individual video image.

frame grabber—Software and hardware working in combination to isolate and store one individual frame from a videotape or live video signal.

frequency—The number of times an event, value, or variable occurs in a given period, as represented in a graph.

frequency distribution—The size or magnitude of an observation recorded in a graph.

G

Gantt chart—A process diagram representing activities along a time line (see *process diagram*).

graduated color—Also called ramped color, a special graphic effect that allows one color to dissolve into another with no discernible break. Some computer software allows you to specify colors and the direction of the blend.

graph window—The portion of a graph on which you present your data, with a beginning and an ending point (see *origin*; *extent*).

grid—A rectangular pattern of perpendicular intersecting lines on a graph, or simply the intersection of a graph's two axes.

H

high resolution—See *resolution*.

histogram—A type of graph that shows frequency data in two-dimensional rectangles. The width of each rectangle represents the class interval, whereas the height represents the number of occurrences (see *frequency*; *class interval*).

horizontal bar graph—A graph with only one scale, used to show relationships between people, products, regions, or other items. Observations, represented by horizontal bars, are usually ranked by size, with the largest on top.

hot button—An area of the screen shown as a button that the designer specifies as the means of accessing additional screens.

hot spot—An area in a Web-based presentation that, when clicked, takes the viewer to another part of the presentation. The hot spot is not usually shown as a button, but as another kind of image or object. When the cursor passes over a hot spot, it changes shape to indicate the existence of the hot spot.

hue—A specific color.

I

interactive media—Presentations that rely on the viewer to choose the content areas and depth of detail in a presentation, as well as to actively participate in the flow and order of information presented. These presentations allow for random access of screens to some degree. They may be created for use on CD-ROM or the World Wide Web.

italic—A slanted version of a typeface, often used to emphasize words or denote titles of publications.

J

justified alignment—Type aligned with left and right margins.

K

kerning—Adjustment of space between letters to improve the appearance and readability of text.

L

leading—Space added between lines of type to enhance readability and appearance (see *line spacing*).

legend—A caption or notation explaining symbols used in an illustration or a graph.

line graph—A graph used to illustrate trends, consisting of plotted observation points joined by curved or straight lines.

line spacing—Space between lines of type, sometimes measured in points. In most word-processing and page layout programs, you can adjust the line spacing. Also called *leading*.

links—Combined with nodes, the building blocks of many kinds of diagrams. Links show process and flow, such as chains of commands.

live area—The display area of an overhead transparency or slide; the size of the visual minus a mounting allowance.

location map—A scaled representation of a three-dimensional surface (such as a building) as it would appear if viewed from overhead.

loupe—A small magnifying glass, sometimes set in a stand, used to view detail of slides, text, or images.

low resolution—See *resolution*.

M

MIDI—Acronym for musical instrument data interface, a standard interface system for digital audio and electronic music.

multimedia presentation—A digital presentation that combines material from a variety of media sources (audio effects or tracks, digital video clips or single frames, graphics or illustrations, text, animation, and so on).

N

nodes—Items representing static entities that are linked together in a diagram to show process and flow (see *links*).

NTSC video—Video that adheres to the National Television Systems Committee standards for broadcast television and a signal compatible with many computers that lets you record graphics on videotape or output graphics to video monitors and projectors.

O

observation—An item of measurement or value represented by a plotted point on a graph.

one-point perspective—A method of drawing three-dimensional objects so that all depth vanishes to a single spot.

organic layout—Positioning type and other graphic elements without a distinct alignment plan.

organizational diagram—A chart often used by institutions and corporations to show hierarchy, titles, and responsibilities of individuals and departments.

origin—The starting point in a graph window, usually the lower left-hand corner (see *graph window*).

overhead—A sheet of clear film used to create screens for presentations to be projected.

overlay—A flap of thin, transparent plastic mounted to a piece of artwork to produce colored or screened graphics on an overhead or poster at the time of the presentation.

P

palette—A subset of the colors of the spectrum or the set of colors selected for use in a presentation.

PERT chart—A type of chart used for management planning showing the correct order of events and activities in a particular project. Nodes represent events, whereas activities requiring time are shown as lines linking the events (see *links; nodes; scale*).

pica—A typographic unit of measurement (there are 6 picas to an inch, 12 points to a pica, and 72 points to an inch).

pie graph—A single-scale, circular graph that shows proportions relative to the whole; each pie wedge represents an observation.

pigment—Coloring matter, derived primarily from metallic and organic compounds, used in inks and paints.

pixel—A tiny dot of light that, with other pixels, forms an image on a computer monitor. Resolution depends on the number of pixels the monitor is capable of displaying, usually given in pixels per inch.

point—A unit of measure for typographic elements (see *pica*).

popping—A visual effect that can occur when certain fully saturated colors that reside opposite each other on the color wheel are placed next to each other in an image or design. Also called *buzzing* or *vibrating*.

presentation graphics—High-quality slides, overhead transparencies, posters, or computer-generated images used to illustrate information in a presentation.

primary colors—Colors that can be combined in various proportions to produce another color.

process diagram—A type of diagram that shows a procedure from start to end. It may include nodes, sequences, conditional branches, relationships, functions, and changes. When many details are included in a presentation, a wise presenter will break the information up among several screens (see *nodes*).

Q

quick cut—A transition effect; the rapid displacement of one image with another without a visible transition.

R

ragged-right or *ragged-left*—See flush-left alignment; flush-right alignment.

ramped color—See *graduated color*.

range—The spread between minimum and maximum values of data as shown in a graph. The range helps establish the proper graph size and scale necessary to allow room for all values in the data set (see *scale*).

Reference values—The terms of progression from the starting point for observation counts or measures in a map or graph(see *observation*).

regression line—A line drawn in a scattergram whose slope and position on the vertical axis are calculated to represent the trend of the data set and its scatter points (see *scattergram*).

resolution—The sharpness and clarity of a printed image, usually expressed in dots per inch. High-resolution images may contain 1,200 or more dots per inch, whereas low-resolution images may have only 300 dots per inch.

RGB color—See *additive color*.

rule—In typography and graphic design, a horizontal, vertical, or diagonal line of various widths, textures, and colors. Used to border, accent, or define other page elements or graphics.

S

sans serif type—Typeface characters designed without serifs (small strokes on the ends of the main character stems).

saturation—The intensity of a given hue or color.

scale—To reduce or enlarge an image according to a fixed ratio; in an illustration, the proportion the image bears to the thing it represents; also, the measuring marks along the X- or Y-axis of a graph.

scattergram—A graph that shows how two data sets correlate. Points are plotted in reference to two scales, but the points representing each observation are not linked. The pattern alone reveals the nature and relationship of the data.

scheme—A palette of colors selected for use in a design or presentation.

screen—See *frame*.

script—A decorative typeface designed with flowing character strokes that resemble handwriting.

secondary color—A color derived from mixing two primary colors. In the typical color wheel where the primary colors are red, blue, and yellow, the secondary colors are purple, green, and orange.

serif—Small finishing stroke at the end of a letter's main character stems.

single-scale graph—A graph that uses only one unit of measure.

spectral neighbors—Colors that sit side by side on a color wheel.

statistical map—A graphic representation of activities observed by geographical site, showing the prevalence, intensity, or density of activities. Symbols on these maps often represent tangible objects.

storyboard—A visual and textual outline of your presentation showing the layout in screen sequence.

subtractive color—Color formed by the combination of pigments (see *CMY color*).

T

thematic map—A graphic representation of activities observed by geographical site. Similar to a statistical map; however, symbols in this type of map often represent nontangible objects or items.

thumbnail sketch—A rough drawing of a screen or the layout of a presentation showing space for headings, copy, and artwork. The simplest form of layout used to present or evaluate ideas for a presentation (see *storyboard*).

tick mark—Mark used to call attention to detail, to indicate value, or to serve as a division in a grid.

tiling—Creating an enlarged graphic by pasting together several letter-size laser-printed pages. Also, term used in some computer software applications to indicate the same process of putting pieces together to form a whole.

time line—A line plotted in a diagram or graph designed to show historical perspective in telling a story. A standard time line is the horizontal axis of a time-series graph, freed from the vertical axis (see *time-series graph*).

time-related graph—See *time-series graph*.

time-series graph—A graph that uses vertical lines or bars rising from the horizontal axis, with variables counted or measured as time passes.

title slide—Normally the first slide or overhead transparency in a series; a title slide usually shows the presenter or sponsor's name or a corporate logo, in addition to the title or subject of the presentation.

transition device—A technique used in electronic presentations to move from one screen to another. Transition devices include blinds, dissolves, fades, quick cuts, and wipes. Also called *transition effects*.

transparency—See *overhead*.

trend line—A line in a graph that shows a trend based on known values.

triad—A group of three primary colors, three secondary colors, or any set of three hues spaced equidistant from each other around the color wheel.

type family—A typeface grouping that includes several variations on one typeface design.

typeface—A particular type design of the letters of the alphabet, numerals, and other character symbols and punctuation marks.

typography—The selection, arrangement, and fitting of type in a design.

U

units—In graphing, the terms of measurement (such as dollars or percentage points). Units and their scaled values are indicated along the axes of the graph.

V

value—Shade or degree in which a color approaches black or white.

variable—The set of observations depicted in a graph (see *observation*). A plotted variable is a collection of points on a graph used to shape a bar, trend line, or other graphic element.

vertical bar graph—A type of time-series graph in which each observation in a series is marked by a bar rising or falling from a horizontal axis. Bar heights illustrate differences in values through time (see *observation*).

W

window—See *graph window.*

wipe—A transition effect that replaces one image with another in a set pattern. The second image seems to be pushing the first off the screen.

X

x-height—The height of a lowercase x in a typeface. The ratio of the x-height to a type's body size determines the visual impact of the lowercase letters in the typeface.

FURTHER
READING

Books

Bender, Peter Urs. *Secrets of Power Presentations*. Buffalo, New York: Firefly Books Ltd., 1995.

Fahey, Mary Jo. *Web Publisher's Design Guide for Macintosh,* 2nd ed. Scottsdale, Arizona: The Coriolis Group, 1997.

Farace, Joe. *Stock Photo Smart*. Gloucester, Massachusetts: Rockport Publishers, 1998.

Gaulke, Sue. "101 Ways to Captivate a Business Audience" (transcript). Presented at AMACOM, 1996.

Joss, Molly. *Clip Art Smart*. Gloucester, Massachusetts: Rockport Publishers, 1998.

Joss, Molly (with Lycette Nelson). *Graphic Design Tricks & Techniques*. Cincinnati, Ohio: North Light Books, 1997.

Kennedy, Grace, Ida Ramirez (contributor), and Ritch L. Sorenson. *Business and Management Communication: A Guide Book,* 3rd rev. ed. New York: Prentice Hall Press, 1996.

Kops, George, and Richard Worth (contributor). *Great Speakers Aren't Born: How to Develop Winning Presentations*. Hollywood, Florida: Lifetime Books, 1996.

Kostelnick, Charles, David D. Roberts, and Sam Dragga (editor). *Designing Visual Language: Strategies for Professional Communicators* (Allyn & Bacon Series in Technical Communication). Needham Heights, Massachusetts: Allyn & Bacon, 1997.

Krannich, Caryl Rae. *101 Secrets of Highly Effective Speakers: Controlling Fear, Commanding Attention*. San Luis Obispo, California: Impact Publishers, 1998.

Kroger, Lin. *The Complete Idiot's Guide to Successful Business Presentations*. Malibu, California: Alpha Books, 1997.

Meggs, Philip B. *A History of Graphic Design,* 3rd ed. New York: John Wiley & Sons, Inc., 1998.

Newstrom, John W. (with Edward E. Scannell). *The Big Book of Presentation Games: Wake-Em-Up Tricks, Icebreakers, & Other Fun Stuff*. New York: McGraw-Hill, 1998.

Oldach, Mark. *Creativity for Graphic Designers: A Real-World Guide to Idea Generation—From Defining Your Message to Selecting the Best Idea for Your Printed Piece*. Cincinnati, Ohio: North Light Books, 1995.

Parker, Roger C. *Looking Good In Print,* 4th ed. Scottsdale, Arizona: The Coriolis Group, 1998.

Pirouz, Raymond. *Click Here: Web Communication Design*. Indianapolis, Indiana: New Riders Publishing, 1997.

Pocket Pal: A Graphic Arts Production Handbook, 16th ed. (Pocket Pal Series). Nashville, Tennessee: International Paper, 1995.

Timm, Paul R. *How to Make Winning Presentations: 30 Action Tips for Getting Your Ideas Across with Clarity and Impact* (30-Minute Solutions Series). Franklin Lakes, New Jersey: The Career Press Inc., 1997.

Toor, Marcelle Lapow. *Graphic Design on the Desktop: A Guide for the Non-Designer,* 2nd ed. New York: John Wiley & Sons, 1998.

Weinman, Lynda (with Bruce Heavin). *Coloring Web Graphics*. Indianapolis, Indiana: New Riders Publishing, 1996.

Periodicals

Adobe Magazine
411 First Ave. S.
Seattle, WA 98104-2871
(206) 628-2321
(206) 470-7106 fax
www.adobe.com/publications/adobemag.html

Computer User
220 South Sixth St., Suite 500
Minneapolis, MN 55402-4500
(612) 339-7571
www.computeruser.com

Desktop Publishers Journal
Business Media Group
462 Boston St.
Topsfield, MA 01983
(978) 887-7900
www.dtpjournal.com

Inc. Technology
Subscriber Services
P.O. Box 54129
Boulder, CO 80322-4129
(800) 234-0999
www.inc.com

PC Computing Online
Subscriber Services
P.O. Box 58229
Boulder, CO 80322-8229
(303) 665-8930
www.pccomp.com

PC Magazine Online
One Park Ave.
New York, NY 10016-5802
(212) 503-5255
www.pcmag.com

PC World Online
Subscriber Services
P.O. Box 55029
Boulder, CO 80322-5029
(303) 604-1465
www.pcworld.com

Publish Magazine
Subscriber Services
P.O. Box 5039
Brentwood, TN 37024
(800) 656-7495
www.publish.com

Seminars And Trade Shows

1st Communications
4700 Rockside Rd., Suite 635
Independence, OH 44131
(216) 901-8000
(216) 901-8181 fax
www.1st-Communications.net

ZD Events (ZD Comdex & Forums)
300 First Ave.
Needham, MA 02194-2722
(617) 449-6600
www.zd.com

RESOURCES

This treasure trove of resources is for anyone involved in presentations. Scan through it to find companies that offer software, hardware, images, and other goods and materials you can use to make your presentations better than ever. When you see a company listed more than once, it's because that company makes software or hardware that fits into more than one category.

If you're interested in a particular category, such as presentation software, visit the Web sites of the companies listed in that category to get a general idea of what the products offer. You may also find demonstration versions of the software ready for you to download from the Web site.

If you want to spend more time surfing, look at the last section for Web sites where you can download free (or nearly free) images and fonts for your presentations. You may also be able to find free samples at the Web sites of vendors listed in the stock image, clip art, and font sections, so don't forget to look there too. Happy browsing!

Presentation Software

These companies make (usually among other products) software for creating your own presentations.

Corel Corp.
1600 Carling Ave.
Ottawa, ONT KIZ 8R7, Canada
(800) 772-6735
www.corel.com

Lotus Development Corp.
800 El Camino Real West
Mountain View, CA 94040
(415) 335-6400
(415) 960-0840 fax
www.lotus.com

MetaCreations Inc.
6303 Carpinteria Ave.
Carpinteria, CA 93013
(805) 566-6200
(805) 566-6385 fax
www.metacreations.com

Microsoft Corp.
One Microsoft Way
Redmond, WA 98052-6399
(206) 882-8080
(206) 936-7329 fax
www.microsoft.com

Software Publishing Corp.
3 Oak Rd.
Fairfield, NJ 07004
(973) 808-1992
(973) 808-2645 fax
www.spco.com

Multimedia/Animation Software

These companies make software than enables you to create multimedia titles (including presentations) and/or animate still images.

Apple Computer
One Infinite Loop
Cupertino, CA 95014
(408) 974-0173
www.apple.com

Avid Technology
Corporate Headquarters
Metropolitan Technology Park
One Park West
Tewksbury, MA 01876
(800) 949-AVID
(978) 640-1366 fax
www.avid.com

Extensis Corp.
55 S.W. Yamhill St., 4th Fl.
Portland, OR 97204
(503) 274-2020
(503) 274-0530 fax
www.extensis.com

Macromedia Inc.
600 Townsend St.
San Francisco, CA 94103
(415) 252-2000
(415) 626-0554 fax
www.macromedia.com

Paceworks
960 San Antonio Rd., Suite 221
Palo Alto, CA 94303
(415) 855-0900
(415) 493-5321 fax
www.paceworks.com

Image Creation And Editing Software

As the section title implies, these companies make software that allows you to create images in some way, such as freehand drawing or by allowing the computer to create them, as well as edit digital versions of images, such as scans or computer-generated illustrations.

Adobe Systems Inc.
345 Park Ave.
San Jose, CA 95110-2704
(408) 536-6000
(408) 537-6799 fax
www.adobe.com

Deneba Software
400 S.W. 87th Ave.
Miami, FL 33173
(305) 596-5644
(305) 273-9069 fax
www.deneba.com

Macromedia Inc.
600 Townsend St.
San Francisco, CA 94103
(415) 252-2000
(415) 626-0554 fax
www.macromedia.com

MetaCreations Inc.
6303 Carpinteria Ave.
Carpinteria, CA 93013
(805) 566-6200
(805) 566-6385 fax
www.metacreations.com

Microsoft Corp.
One Microsoft Way
Redmond, WA 98052-6399
(206) 882-8080
(206) 936-7329 fax
www.microsoft.com

Pantone Inc.
590 Commerce Blvd.
Carlstadt, NJ 07072-3098
(201) 935-5500
(201) 896-0242 fax
www.pantone.com

Strata Inc.
2 West St. George Blvd.
St. George, UT 84770
(435) 628-5218
(435) 628-9756 fax
www.strata3d.com

Image Management And Image Database Software

Images start to pile up inside your computer once you've created a few presentations, so you may want to explore the programs offered by these companies. The software enables you to keep track of images and to store them efficiently.

Canto Software
330 Townsend St., Suite 212
San Francisco, CA 94107
(415) 905-0300
(516) 328-5069 fax
www.canto.com

Extensis Corp.
55 S.W. Yamhill St., 4th Fl.
Portland, OR 97204
(503) 274-2020
(503) 274-0530 fax
www.extensis.com

G & A Imaging Ltd.
975 St. Joseph Blvd.
Hull, Quebec J82 1W8, Canada
(819) 772-7600
(819) 772-7640 fax
www.ga-imaging.com

Imation Publishing Software Corp.
1 Imation Place
Oakdale, MN 55128-3414
(888) 466-3456
(800) 537-4675 fax
www.imation.com

Computer Hardware And Peripherals

AGFA Corp.
100 Challenger Rd.
Ridgefield, NJ 07660-2199
(201) 440-0111
(201) 440-8187 fax
www.agfahome.com

Apple Computer
One Infinite Loop
Cupertino, CA 95014
(408) 974-0173
www.apple.com

CalComp
2411 W. LaPalma Ave.
Anaheim, CA 92801
(714) 821-2000
(714) 821-2832 fax
www.calcomp.com

Canon USA
One Canon Plaza
Lake Success, NY 11042
(516) 488-6700
(516) 328-5069 fax
www.usa.canon.com

Compaq Computer
P.O. Box 692000
Houston, TX 77269-2000
(281) 370-0670
(281) 374-1740 fax
www.compaq.com

Epson America
20770 Macrona Ave.
Torrance, CA 90503
(310) 782-0770
(310) 782-5220 fax
www.epson.com

Heidelberg USA
1000 Gutenberg Dr.
Kennesaw, GA 30144
(770) 419-6600
(770) 437-7388 fax
www.heidelberg.com

Hewlett-Packard
16399 W. Bernardo Dr., Suite 6042
San Diego, CA 92127
(619) 592-4522
(619) 592-8117 fax
www.hewlett-packard.com

Iomega
1821 W. 4000 S., Bldg. 3
Roy, UT 84067
(801) 778-3143
(801) 778-3450 fax
www.iomega.com

Iris Graphics
6 Crosby Dr.
Bedford, MA 01730
(617) 275-8777
(617) 275-8590 fax
www.irisgraphics.com

Mag InnoVision
20 Goodyear
Irvine, CA 92618-1813
(800) 827-3998
(949) 855-4535 fax
www.maginnovision.com

Microtek Lab
3715 Doolittle Dr.
Redondo Beach, CA 90278-1226
(310) 297-5111
(310) 297-5050 fax
www.mteklab.com

QMS Inc.
1 Magnum Pass
Mobile, AL 36618
(334) 633-4300
(334) 633-7252 fax
www.qms.com

Tektronix
26600 S.W. Parkway, M/S 63-630
P.O. Box 1000
Wilsonville, OR 97070-1000
(503) 685-3411
(503) 685-3063 fax
www.tek.com

Toshiba America
9740 Irvine Blvd.
Irvine, CA 92718
(714) 583-3181
(714) 583-3134 fax
www.toshiba.com

UMAX Technology
3561 Gateway Dr.
Fremont, CA 94538
(510) 651-8883
(510) 651-8834 fax
www.umax.com

Digital Cameras

AGFA Corp.
100 Challenger Rd.
Ridgefield, NJ 07660-2199
(201) 440-0111
(201) 440-8187 fax
www.agfahome.com

Nikon
1300 Walt Whitman Rd.
Melville, NY 11747-3064
(516) 547-4381
(516) 547-0305 fax
www.nikonusa.com

Olympus America
2 Corporate Center Dr.
Melville, NY 11747
(516) 844-5000
(516) 844-5262 fax
www.olympus.com

Panasonic
Two Panasonic Way
Secaucus, NJ 07094
(201) 348-7000
www.panasonic.com

Sony Electronics
Three Paragon Dr., Suite 205
Montvale, NJ 07645
(201) 372-2812
(201) 930-7837 fax
www.sony.com

Presentation Equipment

Boxlight Corp.
19332 Power Hill Place
Poulsbo, WA 98370
(800) 943-6516
www.boxlight.com

Epson America
20770 Macrona Ave.
Torrance, CA 90503
(310) 782-0770
(310) 782-5220 fax
www.epson.com

Focus Enhancements
142 North Rd.
Sundbury, MA 01776
(800) 699-3972
www.focusinfo.com

Hitachi America
110 Summit Ave.
Montvale, NJ 07645
(201) 573-0774
(201) 573-7660 fax
www.hitachi.com

InFocus
27700B SW Parkway Ave.
Wilsonville, OR 97070-9215
(503) 685-8885
(503) 685-8887 fax
www.infocus.com

JVC Professional Products
17811 Mitchell Ave.
Irvine, CA 92714
(800) JVC-5825
(949) 261-9690 fax
www.jvcpro.com

Lightware
9875 SW Sunshine Ct., Suite 200
Beaverton, OR 97005
(800) 445-9396
(503) 643-9756 fax
www.lightware.com

Mitsubishi Electronics America
5665 Plaza Dr.
Cypress, CA 90630
(714) 220-2500
(714) 236-6172 fax
www.mitsubishiimaging.com

NEC Technologies
1414 Massachusetts Ave.
Boxborough, MA 01719
(508) 264-8000
(508) 264-8719 fax
www.nec.com

Panasonic Industrial
Two Panasonic Way
Secaucus, NJ 07094
(201) 348-7000
www.panasonic.com

Proxima Corp.
9440 Carroll Park Dr.
San Diego, CA 92121-2298
(800) 447-7692
(619) 457-9647 fax
www.proxima.com

Sharp Electronics
Sharp Plaza
Mahwah, NJ 07430
(201) 529-9500
(201) 529-9637 fax
www.sharpelectronics.com

Smart Technologies
1177 11th Ave. S.W., Suite 600
Calgary, AB T2R 1K0, Canada
(403) 245-0333
(403) 245-0366 fax
www.smarttech.com

Sony Electronics
Three Paragon Dr., Suite 205
Montvale, NJ 07645
(201) 372-2812
(201) 930-7837
www.sony.com

Toshiba America
9740 Irvine Blvd.
Irvine, CA 92718
(714) 583-3181
(714) 583-3134 fax
www.toshiba.com

Stock Image Sources

Adobe Systems Inc.
345 Park Ave.
San Jose, CA 95110-2704
(408) 536-6000
(408) 537-6799 fax
www.adobe.com

Artbeats Software Inc.
2611 South Myrtle Rd.
Myrtle Creek, OR 97457
(541) 863-4429
(541) 863-4547 fax
www.artbeats.com

Artville
31017 N. 56th St.
Cave Creek, AZ 85331
(602) 595-8896
(602) 595-8897 fax
www.artville.com

Beachware
9419 Mt. Israel Rd.
Escondido, CA 92029
(760) 735-8945
www.beachware.com

Classic PIO Partners
87 E. Green St., Suite 309
Pasadena, CA 91105
(800) 370-2746
www.classicpartners.com

Comstock
30 Irving Place
New York, NY 10003
(212) 353-8600
(212) 353-3383 fax
www.comstock.com

Corbis
15395 SE 30th Place, Suite 300
Belluvue, WA 98007
(206) 641-4505
(206) 643-9740 fax
www.corbis.com

Corel Corporation
1600 Carling Ave.
Ottawa, ONT KIZ 8R7, Canada
(800) 772-6735
www.corel.com

Diamar Interactive Corp.
1107 First. Ave., Suite 1802
Seattle, WA 98106-0902
(206) 340-5975
(206) 340-1432 fax
www.diamar.com

Digital Stock Corp.
400 South Sierra Ave., Suite 100
Solana Beach, CA 92075-2262
(619) 794-4040
(619) 794-4041 fax
www.digitalstock.com

Digital Wisdom Inc.
300 Jeanette Dr.
Tappahannock, VA 22560-2070
(800) 800-8560
(804) 758-4512 fax
www.digiwis.com

Eclectiocollections Publications Ltd.
191 Niagara St.
Toronto, ONT M5V-1C9, Canada
(416) 703-6800
www.sonar.com/collections

Image Club
833 4th Avenue S.W., Suite 800
Calgary, AB T2P 3TB, Canada
(800) 661-9410
www.imageclub.com

Image Farm Inc.
110 Spadina Ave., Suite 309
Toronto, ONT M5V 2K4, Canada
(416) 504-4161
(416) 504-4163 fax
www.imagefarm.com

IMSI
895 Francisco Blvd. East
San Rafael, CA 94901-5506
(415) 257-3000
(415) 257-3565 fax
www.imsisoft.com

MetaCreations Inc.
6303 Carpinteria Ave.
Carpinteria, CA 93013
(805) 566-6200
(805) 566-6385 fax
www. metacreations.com

PhotoDisc
2013 Fourth Ave., Suite 200
Seattle, WA 98121
(206) 441-9355
(206) 441-9379 fax
www.photodisc.com

Photosphere Images Ltd.
380 West 1st Ave., Suite 201
Vancouver, BC V5Y 3TY, Canada
(604) 876-3206
(604) 876-1482 fax
www.photosphere.com

Rubberball Productions
44 N. Geneva Rd.
Orem, UT 84057
(801) 224-6886
(801) 224-3353 fax
www.rubberball.com

Vivid Details
8228 Sulphur Mountain Rd.
Ojai, CA 93023
(805) 646-0217
(805) 646-0021 fax
www.vividdetails.com

Weatherstock
P.O. Box 31808
Tucson, AZ 85751
(602) 751-9964
(602) 751-1185 fax
www.stormchaser.com

Clip Art Sources

A Bit Better Corp.
127 Second St., Suite 2
Los Altos, CA 94022
(415) 948-4766
(415) 917-0151 fax
www.bitbetter.com

Aridi Computer Graphics
P.O. Box 797702
Dallas, TX 75739
(800) 755-6441
(214) 404-9172 fax
www.aridi.com

Broderbund Software
500 Redwood Blvd.
Novato, CA 94947
(800) 548-1798
www.clickart.com

Cartesia Software
5 South Main St.
Box 757
Lambertville, NJ 08530
(609) 397-1611
www.map-art.com

Corel Corporation
1600 Carling Ave.
Ottawa, ONT KIZ 8R7, Canada
(800) 772-6735
www.corel.com

DS Design
1157 Executive Circle, Suite D
Cary, NC 27511
(919) 319-1770
(919) 460-5983 fax
www.dsdesign.com

Dubl-Click Software Corp.
20310 Empire Ave., Suite A102
Bend, OR 97701-9713
(541) 317-0355
(541) 317-0430 fax
www.dublclick.com

Dynamic Graphics
6000 N. Forest Park Drive
Peoria, IL 61656-3592
(309) 688-8800
(800) 488-3492 fax
www.dgusa.com

Image Club (a division of Adobe)
833 4th Ave. S.W., Suite 800
Calgary, AB T2P 3TB, Canada
(800) 661-9410
www.imageclub.com

Little Men Studio Inc.
17 Highland Ave.
Redding, CT 06896
(203) 544-8708
www.littlemenstudio.com

One Mile Up
7011 Evergreen Ct.
Annandale, VA 22003
(703) 642-1177
(703) 642-9088 fax
www.onemileup.com

Techpool Software Inc.
1463 Warrensville Center Rd.
Cleveland, OH 44121-2576
(216) 382-1234
(216) 382-1915 fax
www.techpool.com

Zedcor Inc.
3420 N. Dodge Blvd.
Tucson, AZ 85716
(800) 482-4567
(800) 482-4511 fax
www.arttoday.com

Font Sources

Adobe Systems Inc.
345 Park Ave.
San Jose, CA 95110-2704
(408) 536-6000
(408) 537-6000 fax
www.adobe.com

Bitstream
Aethenaeum House
215 First St.
Cambridge, MA 02142
(617) 497-6222
(617) 868-4732 fax
www.bitstream.com

Letraset USA
400 Eisenhower Dr.
Paramus, NJ 07653
(800) 526-9073
(206) 771-5911 fax
www.letraset.com

Monotype Typography
985 Busse Rd.
Elk Grove Village, IL 60007-2400
(847) 718-0400
(847) 718-0500 fax
www.monotype.com

Free Stuff Web Sites

Fonts

softseek.com
mediabuilder.com
www.lodelink.com/mrw/freefonts.html

Clip Art And Images

onlinebusiness.com
barrysclipart.com
free-graphics.com
mediabuddy.com
boulder.earthnet.net/~jlinhoff

Shareware And Freeware

zdnet.com

INDEX

35mm slide presentations
  for boardroom presentations, 241
  build sequences, 130–131
  color palettes, 114–115
  for courtroom presentations, 239
  for instructional and training materials, 243
  overview, 40–41, 42–43
  for peer group presentations, 230–231
  presentation environment, 41–42
  production and design, 41
  question frames, 137
  for sales presentations, 237
  for scientific and professional presentations, 235–236
  section divider frames, 125
  for traveling presentations, 238
3D graphics
  area graphs, 151, 153–155
  bar graphs, 152
  exploded diagrams, 180
3D objects, creating, 271
3D shadows, 73

A

Abbreviations, 28–29
Acronyms, 28–29
Alignment of frame elements. *See also* Organic layout.
  centered alignment, 60, 62, 225
  design guidelines, 225–226
  flush-left alignment, 59, 62
  flush-right alignment, 60, 62
  justified alignment, 60–61, 226
  overview, 58
  table entries, 134
Alternative paths in presentations
  interactive presentations, 29, 199
  question frames, 137
Ambient lighting
  electronic presentations, 36
  impact on design, 32

  35mm slide presentations, 41–42
  overhead transparency presentations, 39
Animation. *See also* Motion.
  building from still images, 194
  in graphs, 149, 151, 154, 160
  overview, 69
  use of in presentations, 18, 196–198
Area graphs, 144, 151, 153–155
Artwork. *See also* Graphics; Images.
  creating, 21
  illustrated text frames, 136–137
  locating on Web, 20
  use of in presentations, 19–22
  in Web-based presentations, 204
Aspect ratio
  35mm slides, 40
  overview, 56
Associating information using color, 106, 110
Audience considerations
  acronyms and abbreviations, 28–29
  boardroom presentations, 241
  color preferences, 102, 107
  financial reports, 240–241
  instructional and training materials, 243
  35mm slide presentations, 42
  motivations for attending, 7
  peer group presentations, 230–232
  professional presentations, 234, 236
  sales presentations, 237
  scientific presentations, 234, 236
  size of audience, 33
  tone of presentations, matching to audience, 8
  traveling presentations, 238
  Web-based presentations, 45, 232–233
Audio clips
  creating, 198
  in electronic presentations, 37
  hardware limitations, 191
  use of in presentations, 190, 193–195
Avant Garde typeface, 80

B

Backgrounds
    contrasting boxes, 67–68
    design guidelines, 221
    electronic presentations, 113
    graduated colors, 117
    graph windows, 146
    gray backgrounds, 68
    ground relationships, 70–73
    35mm slide presentations, 114–115
    multiple background colors, 112, 115
    overhead transparency presentations, 38, 113–114
    patterns, 117–118, 218
    selecting colors for, 110
    Web-based presentations, 116
Bar graphs
    clustered bar graphs, 154
    deviation bar graphs, 160
    divided bar graphs, 157
    horizontal bar graphs, 143, 158–160
    time-related vertical bar graphs, 143
    vertical bar graphs, 143, 152, 153–155
Baseline of type, 78, 95, 219–220
Black and white palette, 106, 117–118
Blank frames, 138
Boardroom presentations, 241–242
Bodoni Poster typeface, 79
Body type, 217
Bookman Demi typeface, 79
Borders, 66–67, 220
Boxes, 67–68, 220
Build sequences, 130–131
Bullet entries, 127–128
Bullet lists
    build sequences, 130–131
    bullet symbols, 92, 128–129
    detail-reveal sequences, 131
    headings, 126
    list entries, 127–128
    list subentries, 129
    numbered lists, 129
    organization of, 125, 126
    punctuating, 27, 126, 128
    summary frames, 129–130
Bullet subentries, 129

Bullet symbols, 92, 128–129
Butterfly graphs, 159–160

C

Callout lists, in pie graphs, 156
Centered alignment, 60, 62, 225
Century typeface, 88
Change, representing
    in bar graphs, 152, 153–155
    line graphs, 143, 150–151
    in presentations, 18
Charts. *See also* Graphs.
    design guidelines, 219
    Gantt charts, 175
    "org charts," 176–177
    PERT charts, 173–174
    use of in presentations, 17
Checklist for presentation design, 250
Cited quotes, typographical treatment of, 27
Clichés, 227
Clip art, 20. *See also* Artwork; Graphics.
Closing titles, 124
Clustered bar graphs, 154
Colons, 27
Color. *See also* Color palettes.
    ambient lighting, impact on colors, 32
    audience preferences, 102, 107
    color wheel, 108–109
    complementary colors, 111
    contrasting colors, 67–68, 112
    in courtroom presentations, 240
    design guidelines, 222–223, 226
    in electronic presentations, 36, 110, 113, 116
    examples of color use, 102–105
    figure-ground relationships, 70–71
    graduated color, 116–117
    in graph windows, 146
    in graphs, 149, 156
    hue, 109
    impact on legibility, 108
    matching color to content, 105
    in 35mm slide presentations, 114–115
    multiple background colors, 112, 115
    organizing content using color, 106
    in overhead transparency presentations, 37, 113–114

in peer group presentations, 231

presentation media, selecting colors for, 36, 37, 57, 105, 110, 113–116

relationships between colors, 111–112

saturation, 109

spectral neighbors, 111, 117

in tables, 133, 136

text over screened background patterns, 118

in thumbnail sketches, 108

triads, 112

type, color of, 226

unappealing combinations, 112

value, 109

in Web-based presentations, 116, 204

Color palettes. *See also* Color.

black and white palette, 106, 117–118

depth, representing, 70–71

design guidelines, 223

grayscale palettes, 117–118

overview, 102

selecting for presentations, 110–112

Columns and rows

grids, in frame design, 57–58, 59

tables, 132–136

Combination graphs, 153–155

Complementary colors, 108, 111

Component parts, representing

exploded diagrams, 179–180

graphs, 144, 149, 155–157

Computer-based presentations. *See also* Web-based presentations.

for boardroom presentations, 241

build sequences, 130–131

color palettes, 110, 113, 116

equipment considerations, 35

for financial reports, 240

for instructional and training materials, 243

overview, 34–35, 37

presentation environment, 36–37

production and design, 35–36

question frames, 137

for sales presentations, 237

for scientific and professional presentations, 234–235

section divider frames, 125

for traveling presentations, 237–238

Conceptual outlines, 15

Condensed fonts, 92

Connectivity in Web-based presentations, 205

Consistency

bullet list entries, 127–128

continuity in frame design, 63–64

distorted type, 93

use of graphic devices, 65

variety, appropriate use of, 6, 23, 64

Contact information, in Web-based presentations, 45, 210–211

Content of presentations

acronyms and abbreviations, 28–29

in boardroom presentations, 242

build sequences, 130–131

bullet list entries, 127–128

in courtroom presentations, 239–240

credibility of information, 23–25

critical points, 16, 26

detail-reveal sequences, 131

downloadable content files, 212

in financial reports, 240–241

graph data, 140–142. *See also* Graphs.

in instructional and training materials, 243

link-and-node diagrams, 166–167, 168–169. *See also* Diagrams.

matching color to content, 105

narrative information, 25–29

organizing content using color, 106

in peer group presentations, 232

proofreading, 248

punctuation, 27, 126, 128, 228

in sales presentations, 237

in scientific and professional presentations, 235–236

section divider frames, 124–125

subtitles, 26–27

summary frames, 129–130

table entries, 134

text frames, 120–121

title frames, 122

titles, 26

in traveling presentations, 238

in Web-based presentations, 204, 206–208, 212–213, 233

Continuity in frame design, 63–64. *See also* Consistency.

Contrast
  complementary colors, 111
  contrasting boxes, 67–68
  contrasting colors, 112
  in electronic presentations, 36, 113
  in graph window, 146
  graphic design element, 53
  in graphs, 149, 156
  in 35mm slide presentations, 114–115
  in overhead transparency presentations,
    113–114
  spectral neighbor colors, 111, 117
  in tables, 133, 136
  titles and subtitles, 123
Copy fitting, 98–100
Correlation between data sets, graphing, 162–163
Courtroom presentations, 238–240
Critical path method (CPM) diagrams, 174

D

Data. *See also* Numerical data; Relationships
  between data, representing.
    credibility of information, 23–25
    graph data, 140–142. *See also* Graphs.
    interpretive device, selecting, 23
Data symbols, 148–149
Decimal points in tables, 134
Demographic information, graphing, 159
Depth, representing
    opacity and transparency, 71
    perspective, 73
    shadows, 72–73
    using color, 70–71
    using monochrome palette, 71
Depth of presentations, 246–247
Design elements
    borders, 66–67, 220
    boxes, 67–68, 220
    colors, assigning to elements, 106, 110
    contrast, 53
    focus, 51–53
    graduated colors, 117
    ground relationships, 70–73
    negative space, 68–69, 220
    rules, 66

sections, identifying, 124–125
size of elements, 226–227
typographical elements, 92
Designing presentations. *See also* Audience considerations; Graphic design principles; Planning
  presentations; Relationships between data.
    blank frames, 138
    boardroom presentations, 241–242
    build sequences, 130–131
    bullet lists, 125–131
    checklist, 250
    clichés, 227
    continuity among frames, 63–64
    conveying message, 15–23
    courtroom presentations, 238–240
    credibility of information, 23–25
    depth of presentations, 246–247
    design guidelines, 216
    designing for other presenters, 10–11
    diagramming information, 166–170, 175. *See
      also* Diagrams.
    dry runs, 33–34, 191, 248, 249, 250
    environment, 32–33. *See also* Presentation
      environment.
    equipment considerations, 33–34. *See also*
      Display media.
    evaluating presentations, 2–3
    financial reports, 240–241
    graphing data, 140, 142. *See also* Graphs.
    illustrated text frames, 136–137
    instructional and training materials, 242–243
    layout of frames, 57–65, 220–221
    multimedia presentations, 190
    narrative information, 25–29
    overview, 4–6
    pace of presentations, 9, 235, 246–247
    peer group presentations, 230–232
    preliminary ideas, sketching, 53–57
    proofreading content, 248
    question frames, 137
    rhythm of presentations, 246–247
    sales presentations, 236–237
    scientific and professional presentations,
      234–236
    section divisions, 124–125
    summary frames, 129–130
    tables, 132–136

teams, working with, 9–11

text frames, relationship to live presentation, 120–121, 126, 131

time considerations, 8–9

title frames, 122–124

tone of presentations, 7–8, 22–23, 122

traveling presentations, 237–238

type and typefaces, 217–218. *See also* Typography.

Web-based presentations, 232–233

Detail-reveal sequences, 131

Deviation bar graphs, 160

Diagonals, in frame layout, 61

Diagrams

critical path method diagrams, 174

exploded diagrams, 179–180

flow of information, representing, 168–169, 169–170

Gantt charts, 175

integrating into presentations, 168

labels, 169

layout, 167, 168

links, 166–167, 170

organizational diagrams, 176–177

overview, 166

PERT charts, 173–174

process diagrams, 170–176

scale drawings, 181

time lines, 177–179

use of in presentations, 17

Differentiating information using color, 106

Dimensions, representing using shadows, 72–73

Display media. *See also individual media types.*

for boardroom presentations, 241

electronic presentations, 34–37

flip chart presentations, 46–47

handouts, 47–48

impact on color choices, 105, 110, 113–116

impact on design process, 56–57

for instructional and training materials, 243

35mm slide presentations, 40–43

multimedia presentations, 188–200

overhead transparency presentations, 37–40

overview, 33–34

for peer group presentations, 230–231

poster presentations, 46–47

potential problems, 33. *See also* Technological considerations.

for sales presentations, 236

for scientific and professional presentations, 234–235

size of type, 96

for traveling presentations, 237–238

for Web-based presentations, 43–46, 232–233

Display typefaces, 82

Distorted baselines, 219–220

Distorted type, 91–93, 219–220

Divided bar graphs, 157

Double-scale graphs, 154

Downloadable content files, 212

Dry runs, 33–34, 191, 248, 249, 250

E

Electronic presentations. *See also* Web-based presentations.

for boardroom presentations, 241

build sequences, 130–131

color palettes, 110, 113, 116

equipment considerations, 35

for financial reports, 240

for instructional and training materials, 243

overview, 34–35, 37

presentation environment, 36–37

production and design, 35–36

question frames, 137

for sales presentations, 237

for scientific and professional presentations, 234–235

section divider frames, 125

for traveling presentations, 237–238

Em spaces, 95

Email connections in Web-based presentations, 210–211

Emphasizing visual elements

borders, 66–67, 220

boxes, 67–68, 220

contrast, 53

design guidelines, 226–227

exploded pie slices, 157

focus, 51–53

in graph window, 147

ground relationships, 70–73

highlighting content using color, 106, 110

motion and animation, 18, 69

negative space, 68–69, 220

patterns, 118, 218

rules, 66

sequences, 18

En spaces, 95

Environment (presentation environment)

ambient lighting, 32, 36, 39, 41–42

boardroom presentations, 241

courtroom presentations, 239–240

electronic presentations, 36–37

flip chart presentations, 47

35mm slide presentations, 41–42

overhead transparency presentations, 39

peer group presentations, 230

poster presentations, 47

sales presentations, 236

size of audience, 32

size of room, 32

traveling presentations, 237

Web-based presentations, 44, 45, 232–233

Equipment (display equipment). *See also individual equipment types.*

for boardroom presentations, 241

electronic presentations, 34–37

flip chart presentations, 46–47

handouts, 47–48

impact on color choices, 105, 110, 113–116

impact on design process, 56–57

for instructional and training materials, 243

35mm slide presentations, 40–43

multimedia presentations, 188–200

overhead transparency presentations, 37–40

overview, 33–34

for peer group presentations, 230–231

poster presentations, 46–47

potential problems, 33. *See also* Technological considerations.

for sales presentations, 236

for scientific and professional presentations, 234–235

size of type, 96

for traveling presentations, 237–238

for Web-based presentations, 43–46, 232–233

Evaluating presentations, 2–3

Expectations for presentations

audience considerations, 7–8

being realistic, 5–6

for boardroom presentations, 242

for peer group presentations, 232

time considerations, 8–9

Exploded diagrams, 179–180

Exploded pie slices, 157

Extended fonts, 92

Extent of graph window, 145–146

F

Faces. *See* Typefaces.

Figure-ground relationships

color, 70–71

opacity and transparency, 71

perspective, 73

shadows, 72–73

Figures (numerical data). *See also* Data; Graphs.

decimal points, 134

tables, 132–136

use of in presentations, 16–17

Financial reports, 240–241

Flip chart presentations

build sequences, 130–131

overview, 46, 47

for peer group presentations, 230–231

presentation environment, 47

production and design, 46–47

for sales presentations, 237

section divider frames, 125

for traveling presentations, 238

Floor plans, 182

Flow charts, 17. *See also* Diagrams.

Flush-left alignment, 59, 62

Flush-right alignment, 60, 62

Focus, in graphic design, 51–53

Fonts. *See also* Typefaces; Typography.

Century, 88

condensed fonts, 92

extended fonts, 92

Frutiger Condensed, 90

Futura, 87, 90

Gill Sans, 89, 90

Helvetica, 81, 85–86, 90

italics, 92
kerning, 83
Optima, 81, 86, 90
overview, 83, 85
Palatino, 89, 90
Stemple Schneidler, 89, 90
Stone Sans, 89, 90
Tekton Oblique, 90
Times Roman, 87–88
type families, 84
use of in presentations, 85
Zapf Dingbats, 92
Formatting. *See* Alignment; Typography.
Forms in Web-based presentations, 210–211
Frame layout
    alignment options, 58–61
    continuity within presentation, 63–64
    design guidelines, 220
    diagrams, 168
    graphs, 146
    gridlines, 57–58
    ground relationships, 70–73
    multimedia transitions, 195–196
    nonconforming elements, 64–65
    organic layout, 61–62
    separating elements, 66–69
    units of measurement, 63
Framing. *See* Borders.
Frequency distribution graphs, 161–162
Frutiger Condensed typeface, 90
Futura typeface, 87, 90

G

Gantt charts, 175
Gill Sans typeface, 89, 90
Goals for presentations, 15, 249
Graduated color, 116–117, 146
Graph window, 145–146
Graphic design principles. *See also* Design elements.
    continuity, 63–64
    contrast, 53
    focus, 51–53
    generating ideas, 53–57
    graphic devices, 65–69
    ground relationships, 70–73

layout, 57–65
    motion, 69
    overview, 50–51
    simplicity, 73–74
Graphic devices. *See also* Design elements.
    borders, 66–67, 220
    boxes, 67–68, 220
    negative space, 68–69, 220
    rules, 66
    typographical design elements, 92
Graphic style, 22–23
Graphics
    3D graphics, 151, 153–155, 180
    ambient lighting, impact on colors, 32
    bullet symbols, 129
    creating, 21
    financial reports, 241
    illustrated text frames, 136–137
    locating on Web, 20
    in overhead transparency presentations, 38
    projection, impact on visual quality, 33
    use of in presentations, 19–22
    in Web-based presentations, 205, 212
Graphs
    area graphs, 144, 151, 153–155
    bar graphs, 143, 152, 153–155, 157, 158–160
    combination graphs, 153–155
    component parts graphs, 144, 149, 155–157
    creating, 140
    data, 140–142
    data symbols, 148–149
    design guidelines, 219
    deviation bars, 160
    graph window, 145–146
    grids, 141, 146, 163
    histograms, 161–162
    line graphs, 143–144, 150–151, 153–155
    observations, 141
    overview, 140, 142
    pie graphs, 144, 149, 155–157
    plotted variables, 141
    range of data, 141
    reference values, 147
    scales, 141, 146
    scattergrams, 162–163
    text annotations, 150

time-related graphs, 150–155
units of measurement, 141
use of in presentations, 17, 140, 142
variables, 141
window grid, 146–147
Gray backgrounds with black type, 68
Grayscale palettes, 117–118
Grid sketch sheets, 261
Grids
in frame design, 57–58, 59
in graphs, 141, 146, 163
Ground relationships
color, 70–71
opacity and transparency, 71
perspective, 73
shadows, 72–73

H

Handouts
financial reports, 240
overhead transparency presentations, 40
for peer group presentations, 231
for traveling presentations, 238
use of in presentations, 47–48
Headings in bullet lists, 126
Helvetica typeface, 81, 85–86, 90
Hierarchies of information, displaying using colors, 106
Histograms, 161–162
Horizontal bar graphs, 143, 158–160
Hue, 109

I

Icons, 235
Ideas, sketching
display media considerations, 56–57
storyboards, 55, 251
thumbnail sketches, 53–54, 108
Illustrated text frames, 136–137
Images
3D graphics, 151, 153–155, 180
ambient lighting, impact on colors, 32
bullet symbols, 129
creating, 21
financial reports, 241

illustrated text frames, 136–137
locating on Web, 20
overhead transparency presentations, 38
projection, impact on visual quality, 33
use of in presentations, 19–22
Web-based presentations, 205, 212
Impact, visual. *See also* Color.
borders, 66–67, 220
boxes, 67–68, 220
contrast, 53
design guidelines, 226–227
exploded pie slices, 157
focus, 51–53
ground relationships, 70–73
highlighting content using color, 106, 110
motion and animation, 69
negative space, 68–69, 220
patterns, 118, 218
rules, 66
Instructional materials, 242–243
Interactive presentations. *See also* Web-based presentations.
alternative paths, 29, 199
multimedia presentations, 198–199
Internet. *See* Web-based presentations.
Irregular edges, in frame layout, 61
Italics, 92

J

Justified alignment, 60–61, 226

K

Kerning, 83, 98
Kiosks, 236

L

Labels
in bar graphs, 152, 157
design guidelines, 218
in diagrams, 169
double-scale graphs, 154
in pie graphs, 156
reference values in graphs, 147
table columns and rows, 135–136
in time lines, 178

Layers
    alternative paths, 29, 199
    overhead transparency presentations, 39
Layout of frames
    alignment options, 58–61
    continuity within presentation, 63–64
    design guidelines, 220
    diagrams, 168
    graphs, 146
    gridlines, 57–58
    ground relationships, 70–73
    multimedia transitions, 195–196
    nonconforming elements, 64–65
    organic layout, 61–62
    separating elements, 66–69
    units of measurement, 63
Leading, 94, 95
Legibility of text
    color choices, 108
    display typefaces, 82
    distorted type, 91–93
    flush-right alignment, 60
    leading, 94, 95
    sans serif faces, 36
    serif faces, 79
    type size, 38
Letter spacing, 98–99
Lighting, ambient
    electronic presentations, 36
    impact on design, 32
    35mm slide presentations, 41–42
    overhead transparency presentations, 39
Line graphs, 143–144, 150–151, 153–155
Line length, 99–100
Line spacing
    between bullet entries, 127–128
    leading, 94
Link-and-node diagrams. *See* Diagrams.
Links
    in critical path method diagrams, 174
    overview, 166–167, 170
    in pert charts, 173
    in Web-based presentations, 205, 224
List entries, 127–128
Lists
    build sequences, 130–131
    bullet symbols, 128–129

    detail-reveal sequences, 131
    headings, 126
    list entries, 127–128
    list subentries, 129
    numbered lists, 129
    organization of, 125, 126
    punctuating, 27, 126, 128
    summary frames, 129–130
Locating images online, 20
Location maps, 182–184
Logarithmic scales, 178–179
Logical progression scales, 178–179

M

Magnitude, representing
    area graphs, 144, 151, 153–155
    histograms, 161–162
Mapping symbols, 183–184
Maps
    location maps, 182
    statistical maps, 183
    thematic maps, 183
Material. *See also* Content.
    credibility of information, 23–25
    determining suitability for presentations, 3
    narrative information, 25–29
Matrices. *See* Tables.
Measurement units
    frame layout, 63
    in graphs, 141
    type size in projected images, 96–97
    typographical units, 93–96
Media (display media). *See also* Technological considerations; *individual media types.*
    for boardroom presentations, 241
    electronic presentations, 34–37
    flip chart presentations, 46–47
    handouts, 47–48
    impact on color choices, 105, 110, 113–116
    impact on design process, 56–57
    for instructional and training materials, 243
    35mm slide presentations, 40–43
    multimedia presentations, 188–200
    overhead transparency presentations, 37–40
    overview, 33–34
    for peer group presentations, 230–231

poster presentations, 46–47
potential problems, 33
for sales presentations, 236
for scientific and professional presentations, 234–235
size of type, 96
for traveling presentations, 237–238
for Web-based presentations, 43–46, 232–233
Monochrome palettes, 71, 117–118
Motion. *See also* Animation.
    design guidelines, 223–224
    in diagrams, 169–170
    in Gantt charts, 175
    in graphs, 149, 151, 154
    in multimedia presentations, 189
    overview, 69
    representing flow of information in diagrams, 168–169
    use of in presentations, 18, 197–198
Multimedia presentations
    animation and pseudo-animation, 196–198
    audio clips, 190, 193–195
    design guidelines, 223–224
    design software, 191–192
    for instructional and training materials, 243
    for interactive presentations, 198–199
    materials, collecting, 192–194
    motion clips, 197–198
    overview, 188–189
    production, 194
    technological considerations, 190–191
    transition effects, 195–196
    use of in presentations, 190
    video clips, 190, 192–193, 194–195
Multiple-area graphs, 153
Multiple background colors, 112, 115

N

Narrative information
    acronyms and abbreviations, 28–29
    bullet lists, 125–131
    content in text frames, 120–121
    overview, 25–26
    punctuation, 27, 228

section divisions, 124–125
subtitles, 26–27
titles, 26
words, use of, 15–16
Negative space, 68–69, 220
Nodes (link-and-node diagrams), 166–167, 169, 170. *See also* Diagrams.
Numbered lists, 129. *See also* Bullet lists.
Numerical data. *See also* Data; Graphs.
    decimal points, 134
    tables, 132–136
    use of in presentations, 16–17

O

Objectives of presentations, 4–5, 15, 249
Observations, 141
One-point perspective, 73, 180
Online ordering, 213
Opacity, 71
Open space, 68, 220
Optima typeface, 81, 86, 90
"Org charts," 176–177
Organic layout of frames, 61
Organizational diagrams, 17, 176–177
Origin (graph window), 145–146
Outlines
    conceptual outlines, 15
    sequential outlines, 15
    storyboards, 55, 251
Overhead transparency presentations
    for boardroom presentations, 241
    build sequences, 130–131
    color palettes, 113–114
    for courtroom presentations, 239
    financial reports, 240
    for instructional and training materials, 243
    overview, 37, 39–40
    for peer group presentations, 230–231
    presentation environment, 39
    production and design, 38
    for scientific and professional presentations, 234
    section divider frames, 125
    size of type, 97
    for traveling presentations, 238

P

Pacing of presentations, 9, 235, 246–247

Paired horizontal bar graphs, 159–160

Palatino typeface, 89, 90

Parallel projection, 73, 180

Parentheses, 27

Patterns, 117–118, 218

Periods, 27

Perspective techniques

    exploded diagrams, 180

    figure-ground relationships, 72, 73

PERT charts, 173–174

Photographs

    use of in presentations, 21–22

    using as backgrounds, 221

    in Web-based presentations, 206

Picas, 92

Pie graphs, 144, 149, 155–157

Planning presentations. *See also* Designing presentations.

    checklist, 250

    conceptual outlines, 15

    designing for other presenters, 10–11

    expectations, 4, 5–6. *See also* Expectations for presentations.

    goals, 15, 249

    multimedia presentations, 190

    objectives, 4–5, 15, 249

    overview, 4

    practicing presentations, 33–34, 191, 248, 249, 250

    preliminary ideas, sketching, 53–57, 251

    sequential outlines, 15

Plotted variables, defined, 141

Point size of type, 95

Points, 92

Population pyramids, 159

Poster presentations

    for courtroom presentations, 238–240

    overview, 46, 47

    presentation environment, 47

    production and design, 46–47

Practicing presentations, 33–34, 191, 248, 249, 250

Presentation environment

    ambient lighting, 32, 36, 39, 41–42

    boardroom presentations, 241

    courtroom presentations, 239–240

    electronic presentations, 36–37

    flip chart presentations, 47

    35mm slide presentations, 41–42

    overhead transparency presentations, 39

    peer group presentations, 230

    poster presentations, 47

    sales presentations, 236

    size of audience, 32

    size of room, 32

    traveling presentations, 237

    Web-based presentations, 44, 45, 232–233

Presentations. *See* Designing presentations.

Primary colors, 108, 112

Printed material. *See* Handouts.

Process diagrams. *See also* Diagrams.

    critical path method diagrams, 174

    design guidelines, 175–176

    Gantt charts, 175

    overview, 170–173

    PERT charts, 173–174

Production

    electronic presentations, 35–36

    flip charts, 46–47

    35mm slides, 41

    multimedia presentations, 194

    overhead transparencies, 38

    overview, 247–248

    posters, 46–47

    Web-based presentations, 44

Professional presentations, 234–236

Program Evaluation Review Technique (PERT) charts, 173–174

Project schedules. *See* Process diagrams.

Projection. *See also* Overhead transparency presentations.

    of electronic presentations, 35

    impact on image quality, 33

    impact on type size, 96

Proofreading content, 248

Pseudo-animation, 196–198

Punctuation

    in bullet lists, 126, 128

    design guidelines, 228

    in text frames, 27

Q

Question frames, 137
Quotation marks, 27
Quoted citations, 27

R

Ragged right edges, 59
Ramped color, 116–117
Range of data in graphs, 141
Reference values, 147
Regression lines in scattergrams, 163
Relationships between data, representing. *See also* Data.
    in presentations, 17, 140, 142
    using diagrams, 166–170. *See also* Diagrams.
    using graphs, 140–142. *See also* Graphs.
    using tables, 132–136
Representational art, 19–22. *See also* Artwork; Graphics.
Rhythm of presentations, 246–247
Rows and columns
    grids in frame design, 57–58, 59
    tables, 132–136
Rules, 66
Running heads, 125

S

Sales presentations, 236–237
Sans serif typefaces
    Avant Garde, 80–81
    Frutiger Condensed, 90
    Futura, 87, 90
    Gill Sans, 89, 90
    Helvetica, 81, 85–86, 90
    Optima, 81, 86, 90
    overview, 80–81
    Stone Sans, 89, 90
    Tekton Oblique, 90
Saturation of colors, 109, 111, 112
Scale drawings, 181–184
Scales
    defined, 141
    double-scale graphs, 154
    histograms, 162

    logarithmic scales, 178–179
    logical progression scales, 178–179
    in paired horizontal bar graphs, 159–160
    in pie graphs, 155
    in scale drawings, 181–184
    starting point, 146
    in time lines, 178
Scattergrams, 162–163
Schedules. *See* Process diagrams.
Scientific presentations, 234–236
Script typefaces, 82
Secondary colors, 108, 112
Section dividers
    multimedia transitions, 195–196
    text frames, 124–125
Section subheads, in Web-based presentations, 206–208
Segues, 125
Self-guided presentations, 199
Separation of visual elements
    borders, 66–67, 220
    boxes, 67–68, 220
    negative space, 68–69, 220
    rules, 66
Sequences
    build sequences, 130–131
    combination graphs, 154
    detail-reveal sequences, 131
    transition effects, 133, 195–196, 197
    use of in presentations, 18
Sequential outlines, 15
Serif typefaces
    Bodoni Poster, 79
    Bookman Demi, 79
    Century, 88
    overview, 78–80
    Palatino, 89, 90
    Stemple Schneidler, 89, 90
    Times Roman, 87–88
Shadows, 72–73
Single-variable graphs, 141
Size of design elements, 226–227
Size of type
    leading, 94
    overview, 93
    in projected images, 96–97
    proportional sizing, 96–97
    terminology, 95–96

Sketching ideas
display media considerations, 56–57
storyboards, 55, 251
thumbnail sketches, 53–54, 108
Slide presentations, 35mm
for boardroom presentations, 241
build sequences, 130–131
color palettes, 114–115
for courtroom presentations, 239
for instructional and training materials, 243
overview, 40–41, 42–43
for peer group presentations, 230–231
presentation environment, 41–42
production and design, 41
question frames, 137
for sales presentations, 237
for scientific and professional presentations, 234–235
section divider frames, 125
for traveling presentations, 238
Software
multimedia design, 191–192
Web-based presentation design, 209
Sources of information, 23–25
Spaces, typographical, 77
Spacing
between bullet entries, 127–128
letter spacing, 98–99
line spacing (leading), 94
word spacing, 99
Spatial relationships
figure-ground relationships, 70–73
scale drawings, 181–184
Special characters, 77
Stacked graphs, 149
Standalone presentations
alternative paths, 29, 199
sales presentations, 237
Stemple Schneidler typeface, 89, 90
Steps in processes. *See* Process diagrams.
Stone Sans typeface, 89, 90
Storyboard sheets, 251
Storyboards, 55, 251
Subentries, bullet lists, 129
Subheads
bullet lists, 126
Web-based presentations, 206–208

Subtitles
distinguishing from titles, 123
use of in presentations, 26–27
Summary frames, 129–130
Supplementary screens
alternative paths, 29, 199
blank frames, 138
question frames, 137
Symbols
bullet symbols, 92, 128–129
data symbols, 148–149
dingbat fonts, 92
mapping symbols, 183–184

T

Tables
decimal points, 134
format, 133–134
labels, 135
overview, 132
Tabletop flip charts, 47
Teams, working with
designing for other presenters, 10–11
overview, 9–10
Technological considerations
color on computer monitors, 110, 113, 116
computer-based presentations, 35, 37
35mm slide presentations, 41, 42
multimedia presentations, 190–191, 199
overhead transparency presentations, 39
printer output, 68, 114, 117
scientific and professional presentations, 235
Web-based presentations, 44, 45, 203, 208–209, 233
Tekton Oblique typeface, 90
Text. *See also* Legibility of text; Text frames; Typefaces; Typography.
alignment options, 58–61
in electronic presentations, 36
graph annotations, 150
over screened background patterns, 118
in overhead transparency presentations, 38
proofreading content, 248
underlining text, 220
in Web-based presentations, 206–208, 212–213

Text frames. *See also* Text; Typography.
    acronyms and abbreviations, 28–29
    blank frames, 138
    bullet lists, 125–131
    charts, 17
    content guidelines, 120–121
    diagrams, 17. *See also* Diagrams.
    graphic style, 22–23
    graphs, 17. *See also* Graphs.
    illustrated text frames, 136–137
    motion, 18
    narrative information, 25–29
    numerical data, 16–17
    photographs, 21–22
    punctuation, 27, 126, 228
    question frames, 137
    relationship to live presentation, 120–121, 126, 131
    representational art, 19–21
    running heads, 125
    section divider frames, 124–125
    sequences, 18
    subtitles, 26–27
    tables, 132–136
    title frames, 122–124
    titles, 26
    video clips, 21–22
    words, 15–16
    written pages *vs.,* 120
Three-dimensional graphics
    area graphs, 151, 153–155
    bar graphs, 152
    exploded diagrams, 180
Three-dimensional objects, 271
Three-dimensional shadows, 73
Thumbnail sketches, 53–54, 108
Time, representing in diagrams, 168–169
Time considerations
    overview, 8–9
    pacing presentations, 9, 235, 246–247
    time limits, 230
Time lines, 177–179
Time-related graphs, 143, 150–155
Time-series graphs, 153–155
Times Roman typeface, 87–88
Title frames
    closing titles, 124
    content, 122, 123

    overview, 122
    subtitles, 123
    typography, 122–124
Titles, use of in presentations, 26
Tone of presentations
    matching to audience, 7–8
    setting tone in title frames, 122
    setting tone with graphic style, 22–23
Touch-screen-based presentations, 29
Tracking adjustments, 98
Training materials, 242–243
Transition effects
    multimedia presentations, 195–196
    pseudo-animation, 197
    in tables, 133
Transparency, 71
Traveling presentations, 237–238
Two-point perspective, 180
Two-tone backgrounds, 115
Two-variable graphs, 141
Type, color of, 226
Type families, 84
Type size. *See also* Legibility of text.
    leading, 94, 95
    overview, 93
    in projected images, 96–97
    spacing, 94, 98–99
    terminology, 95–96
Typefaces. *See also* Fonts; Typography.
    baseline of type, 78, 95, 219–220
    design guidelines, 217–218
    display faces, 82
    distorted type, 91–93
    em spaces, en spaces, 95
    kerning, 83, 98
    leading, 94, 95
    overview, 77–78
    point size of type, 95
    sans serif faces, 80–81
    script faces, 82
    selecting for presentations, 85
    serif faces, 78–80
    tracking adjustments, 98
    x-height of type, 95
    Zapf Dingbats, 92
Typography. *See also* Fonts; Legibility of text; Typefaces.
    for boardroom presentations, 242

copy fitting, 98–100
design elements, 92
design guidelines, 217–220
distorted type, 91–93
financial reports, 241
labels, table rows and columns, 135–136
leading, 94, 95
letter spacing, 98–99
line length, 99–100
line spacing (leading), 94, 127–128
measurement units, 93–96
picas, 92
points, 92
in projected images, 96–97
size of type, 93–97
spacing, 98–100
special characters, 77
stacked characters, 218–219
terminology, 95
title frames, 122–124
upper-case letters, 227
Web-based presentations, 207, 233
word spacing, 99

U

Underlining text, 220
Units of measurement
    frame layout, 63
    in graphs, 141
    type size in projected images, 96–97
    typographical units, 93–96
Upper-case letters, 227

V

Value of colors, 109, 112
Vanishing points, 73
Variables, defined, 141
Variety, use of in presentations, 6, 23, 64
Vertical bar graphs, 143, 152, 153–155
Video clips
    hardware limitations, 191
    use of in presentations, 21–22, 190, 193–195
Videotape presentations, 238
Visual impact. *See also* Color.

borders, 66–67, 220
boxes, 67–68, 220
contrast, 53
design guidelines, 226–227
exploded pie slices, 157
focus, 51–53
ground relationships, 70–73
highlighting content using color, 106, 110
motion and animation, 69
negative space, 68–69, 220
patterns, 118, 218
rules, 66
Volume, representing in area graphs, 151, 153–155

W

Web-based presentations
    alternative paths, 29, 199
    color palettes, 116
    contact information, 45, 210–211
    contact information, including, 210–211
    content, 204, 206–208, 212–213
    design software, 209
    downloadable content files, 212
    home pages, 203
    images, 205–206, 212
    links, 205, 224
    organization of information, 203–204
    overview, 43–44, 45–46, 202, 213–214
    presentation environment, 44, 45
    production and design, 44
    technological considerations, 203, 208–209
    testing, 211
    Web hits, 203
Web hits, 203
Window grid, 146–147
Word spacing, 99
Words, use of in presentations, 15–16

X

X-height of type, 95

Z

Zapf Dingbats typeface, 92

Colophon

From start to finish, The Coriolis Group designed *Looking Good In Presentations, Third Edition* with the creative professional in mind.

The cover was created on a Power Macintosh using QuarkXPress 3.3, Adobe Photoshop 5, Alien Skin Black Box 2 filters, and the Trajan and Futura font families. It was printed using four-color process, metallic silver ink, and spot UV coating.

The interior layout was also produced on a Power Macintosh with Adobe PageMaker 6.52, Microsoft Word 98, Adobe Photoshop 4, and Adobe Illustrator 7.0.1. The body text is Stone Informal, heads are Avenir Black, and chapter titles are Copperplate 31ab.

Looking Good In Presentations, Third Edition was printed by Courier Stoughton, Inc. of Stoughton, Mass.

LOOKING GOOD
IN
PRESENTATIONS

LOOK AT WHAT THE CORIOLIS GROUP HAS FOR THE CREATIVE PROFESSIONAL!

Creative Professionals Press offers the graphic designer, Web developer, and desktop publisher the hottest titles in the design industry today! Whether you're a professional working for a design studio, a freelance designer searching for the latest information about design tools, or a student who wants to supplement a textbook, Creative Professionals titles address your design and creative needs.

The f/x and design and In Depth series are highly interactive and project-oriented books that are designed to help the intermediate to advanced user get the most out of their design applications and achieve real mastery. These two series perfectly complement each other and assure that the Creative Professionals Press provides the creative professional with the tools that will help them accomplish their tasks quickly and with the greatest return on investment.

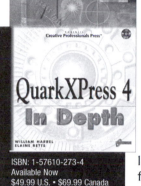

ISBN: 1-57610-273-4
Available Now
$49.99 U.S. • $69.99 Canada

CREATIVE PROFESSIONALS DEMAND IN DEPTH RESOURCES!

Creative Professionals Press' In Depth series is the expert's choice when selecting a comprehensive, reference guide. These guides focus on presenting in depth techniques to show readers how to expand their skills and master their tools. Packed with "insider" tips, techniques, and a rich, vibrant, full-color Studio, readers will definitely get up to speed on the hottest design tools, or latest revisions, available! The In Depth series is the ideal complement to the f/x and design series.

CREATIVE PROFESSIONALS CREATE WITH F/X AND DESIGN!

The f/x and design series appeals to the intermediate to advanced user who seeks a companion guide to a specific design application or niche topic. With the designer in mind, f/x and design books focus on creating impressive special effects and presenting unique design approaches. Numerous step-by-step projects, a full-color Studio, special tips and techniques, and insight from graphics professionals make these books the ideal creative professional's practical "show and tell" guide. Creative professionals need thorough knowledge of today's design tools to compete in tomorrow's market—f/x and design books can take you there!

ISBN: 1-57610-300-5
Available Now
$49.99 U.S. • $73.99 Canada

ISBN: 1-56604-856-7
Available Now
$29.99 U.S. • $41.99 Canada

CREATIVE PROFESSIONALS ARE LOOKING GOOD!

The Looking Good series is used by a wide variety of creative professionals, such as desktop publishers and graphics designers. These books act as comprehensive reference guides that are non-vendor- or software-specific; provide advice, tips, and trade secrets from major studios and artists; and provide hands-on exercises. The "Do It In Color" section includes a bonus project in full color and makes our Looking Good series the indispensable creative guide!

CORIOLIS
Creative Professionals Press™

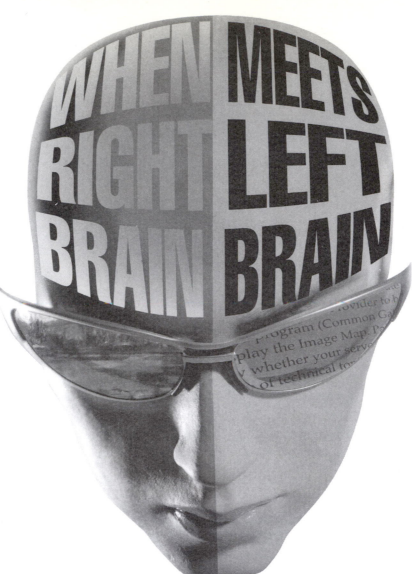

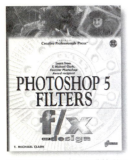
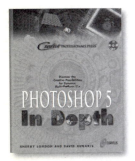
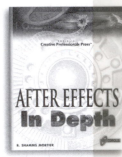

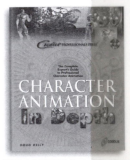